D1711676

JOHN COSIN

A Collection of Private Devotions

EDITED BY

P. G. STANWOOD

THE UNIVERSITY OF BRITISH COLUMBIA
VANCOUVER

WITH THE ASSISTANCE OF

DANIEL O'CONNOR

ST. STEPHEN'S COLLEGE, DELHI

OXFORD
AT THE CLARENDON PRESS
1967

Oxford University Press, Ely House, London W. 1
GLASGOW NEW YORK TORONTO MELBOURNE WELLINGTON
CAPE TOWN SALISBURY IBADAN NAIROBI LUSAKA ADDIS ABABA
BOMBAY CALCUTTA MADRAS KARACHI LAHORE DACCA
KUALA LUMPUR HONG KONG TOKYO

PRINTED IN GREAT BRITAIN

PREFACE

THE chief purpose of this volume is to provide a reliable text of John Cosin's *A Collection of Private Devotions* in the form in which he first presented it to the world in 1627, noting such modifications as were made to the text during his lifetime. In addition, the Introduction aims to place the *Devotions* in its setting in Cosin's life and times and in the history of Christian devotion, while the Commentary points to Cosin's sources and to comparable items in other devotional books, as well as to the influence of the *Devotions* on revisions of the Book of Common Prayer.

Only recently, attention has been drawn to Cosin's liturgical work with the publication of G. J. Cuming's admirable edition of *The Durham Book*. With some trepidation, the editors have approached the task of providing in this edition a definitive text of the only extended work of either liturgical or private devotion to be completed by Cosin alone. Although widely known and much admired by liturgical scholars as well as by literary students and historians of the seventeenth century, Cosin's *Devotions* has not appeared in any satisfactory modern edition. The early editions are excessively rare, and the various nineteenth-century editions which are still fairly easy to find are all unreliable; even the edition in the Library of Anglo-Catholic Theology, whose editor clearly took some pains with his work, besides having a modernized spelling, is in other respects inaccurate as a text, and is, in any case, not based throughout on the first edition. With the methods of modern scholarship and publishing the present editors, therefore, hope to restore Cosin's *Devotions* to its just place among important English texts of the seventeenth century.

A word of explanation about the form of editorial collaboration: the editors discovered that they shared an interest in

John Cosin and his work while the one was engaged in research on seventeenth-century history at Peterhouse, and the other was preparing a Master's thesis on the *Devotions* at Durham. Within weeks of their agreeing to work together, however, they found themselves moving in opposite directions, the one to the New World, the other to the Orient. In these circumstances the close collaboration at first envisaged has proved difficult, and the original plan of a joint edition unworkable. The editors have consequently discovered themselves to be senior and junior partners in the project, the former entirely responsible for the preparation of the text and variants, and sharing with the latter the composition of the Introduction and the Commentary. In addition, the principal editor has seen the entire work through the press, and he accepts ultimate responsibility for this edition.

The editors are most grateful for much friendly advice and assistance given to them. They both wish to thank Dr. A. I. Doyle, Keeper of Rare Books in the University Library at Durham, for his readiness in answering many questions; the late L. W. Hanson, Keeper of Printed Books in the Bodleian Library, and Dr. H. Boone Porter, Jr., Professor of Liturgics at the General Theological Seminary in New York, for permission to use information from their published studies of the *Devotions*. The assistant editor wishes to acknowledge particularly the help of a number of persons, with regard to various points of detail: the late Dean Milner-White of York; Dr. A. C. Bouquet of Trinity College, Cambridge; Professor H. E. W. Turner and Canon A. H. Couratin of Durham; the Reverend E. G. Midgley of St. Edmund Hall, Oxford. The senior editor wishes to express his special thanks to the Master and Fellows of Peterhouse, Cambridge, for permission to reproduce the portrait of John Cosin in the College Hall, and also for the unfailing hospitality of their Senior Common Room during several long visits, and particularly to Mr. E. J. Kenney, Fellow of Peterhouse and Perne Librarian, for many favours; to the Frank L. Weil Institute, the Tufts University Faculty Research Fund, and the University of British Columbia for their financial support; to various libraries—the Bodleian for providing microfilm copies of the first and second editions, and Jesus College, Oxford, for the opportunity of examining the fourth edition, the British Museum (and North Room), the Cambridge University Library (especially the most helpful staff of the Anderson Room), the Widener and Houghton Libraries of Harvard University, and the Henry E. Huntington Library; to Dr. J. S. Macauley of the University of Kansas, whose conversation with the editor and Cambridge dissertation on Richard Mountague have given him ideas and information about the period; to Professor Bernard McCabe of Tufts University for reading and improving the Introduction; to the Reverend Thomas J. Talley of Nashotah House for his help with the Ember Collects; to Mrs. G. C. Allen, who prepared the Index; finally, deep thanks to Dorothy Stanwood for her indispensable help in preparing the manuscript and reading proofs. Both editors gratefully acknowledge the expert guidance and advice of the Clarendon Press who have made all their work worth doing.

P. G. S.
D. O'C.

Durham,
St. James's Day 1967

CONTENTS

LIST OF PLATES

INTRODUCTION

I

JOHN COSIN was born in Norwich on 30 November 1595,[1] of a wealthy father, probably a merchant, and a mother who came of a landed family. Educated at the Grammar School at Norwich, Cosin was selected at the age of fifteen to fill one of the scholarships reserved for the school at Gonville and Caius College, Cambridge, then under the Mastership of William Branthwaite.[2] He took his B.A. in 1614 and M.A. in 1617; his D.D. was conferred in 1630. Little is known of Cosin's life while at Caius, either as an undergraduate, or, from 1620 to 1624, as a Junior Fellow. He evidently showed remarkable ability, since in 1616 he attracted the attention of two eminent churchmen: both Lancelot Andrewes, then Bishop of Ely, and John Overall, Bishop of Lichfield, offered him a position as episcopal librarian and secretary. On the advice of his tutor, Cosin decided in favour of Overall, remaining in his service until May 1619, when Overall died at Norwich, to which see he had only a few months previously been translated. This short period probably marked the beginning of Cosin's association with the 'Arminians', that party of the Church most vigorously opposed to the Puritans. Whatever influence Overall had, there can be no doubt of Cosin's lasting fondness for his memory, for years later, in 1669, he erected a handsome memorial to him in the Cathedral Church of Norwich.

After an interval of four years at Caius, during which time he was Rhetoric Praelector (1620–1) and University Preacher (1622), Cosin was called by Bishop Neile of Durham to be one of his domestic chaplains. He received immediate preferment to the Mastership of Greatham Hospital, a position he soon resigned in favour of a prebendal stall at Durham and the Rectory of Elwick. In 1625, his second year at Durham, he was made Archdeacon of the East Riding, and finally in 1626 Rector of Brancepeth, a living which he seems to have particularly enjoyed and often occupied. Cosin must have spent much time, however, with Bishop Neile at Durham House in London, which had become a centre for discussion of theology and the current problems of the Church. They were often joined there by many of the most important churchmen of the day, such as William Laud, Francis White, Richard Mountague, and John Buckeridge. Cosin's early biographer, Thomas Smith, wrote concerning the year 1626:

> *Londini* in aedibus D. *Neli*, *Dunelmensis* Episcopi, tanquam in Collegio & sacro consessu, venerabiles viri, D.D.D. *Laudus*, Episcopus *Bathoniensis* & *Wellensis*, *Whitus*, mox Episcopus *Carleolensis*, *Richardus Montacutus*, aliique pietate, doctrina, & flagranti Ecclesiae *Anglicanae* contra tum Pontificiorum, tum Puritanorum insidias & impetus tuendae zelo insignes, de rebus ad Ecclesiam & religionem spectantibus consultaturi, convenire soliti erant: quorum colloquiis *Cosinus*, licet annis & dignitate longe inferior, praesens aderat.[3]

These meetings of Church leaders at Durham House may have provided inspiration for one of the most important controversial books of the time, *Appello Caesarem* (1625), by Richard Mountague, Canon of Windsor and later Bishop of Chichester. Mountague knew Cosin at Durham House and, though by many years the older man, came especially to trust in his judgement. He submitted his book to Cosin, instructing him to alter it in any way that he saw fit. *Appello Caesarem* sets out a part of the Arminian position—that the Church of Rome is a true Church though in error—and it naturally brought down a storm of abuse from the Puritans in the House of Commons as soon as it appeared, for it substantiated all too well their worst fears of the leadership of the Church. Mountague had already written polemical works—especially,

A Gagg for the new Gospell? No: A New Gagg for an Old Goose (1624)—so the Puritans now regarded him with extreme disfavour. Another response to Mountague's books was a conference at York House, in London, at which arguments for and against his theology were heard, with Cosin acting as secretary and also speaking in his defence.[4]

Cosin defended Mountague (and had perhaps even written some of the *Appello*) because he believed the Anglican tradition was best expressed as a way of finding the mean between the 'excesses' of Geneva and Rome, while yet retaining Catholicity, with 'Antiquity [as] the best Expositer of Faith'. From the first, then, Cosin declared himself the friend of those who understood the English Church to be a sound branch of the Catholic Church, purged of the corruptions of Rome on the one side, and of Calvinism on the other. Like Hooker, he appealed to the authority of the early Church, the Fathers and the first general councils, in order to vindicate the Church of the *via media*, Catholic and reformed, a Church 'which ever held firm (and we are able to make it good) in a continued line of succession from former known bishops, and so from this very mission of the Apostles'.[5] This is a theme that runs through Cosin's thought, and we see it well expressed in one of his early sermons spoken at the consecration of the Bishop of Carlisle, Dr. Francis White, a friend and regular visitor at Durham House. The text was from John 20. 21, 22: 'As My Father sent Me, even so send I you':

We demand . . . How was Christ sent? And He was sent for two ends. The first, to be the Redeemer of our souls, and to reconcile God unto men, which He did by His death; the second, to be the Bishop of our souls, and to reconcile men unto God, which He did by leaving us a Gospel, His life and doctrine, in a Church behind Him. In the first sense the Apostles were not sent, they were to be no redeemers nor mediators neither. For it cost more to redeem men's souls, and both they and their successors must let that *sicut* alone for ever. And yet there is a *sicut similitudinis* in it for all that, though there be no *sicut aequalitatis*, there is some likeness in their sendings this way. He, sent by His Father to be a Mediator for mankind, and to reconcile the world by His death and sacrifice upon the cross. They, sent by Him, to mediate and to pray for the people, to be ministers of the reconciliation, as St. Paul speaks, and in a manner, to be sacrificers too, representers at the Altar here, and appliers of the Sacrifice once made for all; without which last act, the first will do us no good.[6]

At the same time, Cosin would probably have agreed with Mountague's assertion, 'I professe my selfe none of those furious ones in point of difference now-a-dayes, whose profession and resolution is, That the farther in any thing from communion with the Church of *Rome*, the neerer unto GOD and Truth . . . the Church of *Rome* is a *true*, though not a *sound* Church of CHRIST, as well since, as before the Councell of *Trent*; a part of the Catholick, though not the Catholick Church . . .'.[7] Since Cosin had been identifying himself from the outset of his career with these principles and the party that most keenly espoused them, he was himself destined to become the butt of considerable Puritan abuse.

The appearance of Cosin's *Devotions* in the first part of 1627 aroused immediate opposition, for the disagreements between Charles and the High Churchmen, on the one hand, and the Puritans, sustained by the majority of the House of Commons, on the other, were growing increasingly acute and bitter. The hard words over Mountague, whom the King had advanced to a Bishopric, surely had not been forgotten, nor had Cosin's connexion with him. To the Puritans the *Devotions* seemed one more effort to advance 'Popery', with Cosin a champion of the Arminian position. In 1628 William Prynne and Henry Burton wrote fierce pamphlets about it, apparently to attract the attention of the Parliament then sitting. In the same year Cosin upset one Peter Smart, a fellow Prebend at Durham, who on 27 July preached in the Cathedral an extraordinarily abusive sermon, directed principally against him: *The Vanitie & Downe-fall of Superstitious Popish Ceremonies*. . . . Cosin, in keeping with the High Churchmen's desire to enrich the liturgy by splendid ceremonial, had supported the reform of services at Durham Cathedral—though it is likely that the services had been 'reformed' even before his arrival: he may have extended only what was already begun. Smart's attack reflects numerous Puritan dislikes: there is a passing, slighting reference to the *Devotions* in the preface to the printed version of the sermon, but the sermon itself is concerned with such things as music in the Church, the wearing of copes, the placing of the altar in the east end with the font at the west entrance, bowing to the altar, the use of candles. It was, of course, the theological implications of these things that troubled the Puritans. Thus, Smart says, 'Now indeed the originall cause of most of our superstitious Ceremonies, is that Popish opinion, that Christs Church hath yet Priests Sacrifices and Altars: when as indeed Christ was sent of God to be the last priest, which should offer the last sacrifice upon the last Altar, that ever the world should have.'[8] Because Cosin could not agree, he had no peace.

The next Parliament saw in Cosin a sinister figure. The King had followed his general pardon for Mountague, Cosin, Sibthorpe, and Mainwaring—all of whom had outspokenly offended the Puritans—with a proclamation issued on 17 January 1629, calling in Mountague's book, an action meant to put an end to discussion of it. Soon after the opening of this Parliament a petition of 4 February was preferred against Cosin, 'with articles annexed thereunto, tending to the introduction of Popish doctrine and Popish ceremonies [at Durham]'.[9] Cosin was also ordered to answer to the Commons on 23 February. On the 24th the famous 'Head and Articles Agreed upon by the House' was put forward, and in it Cosin was particularly named. Religion, it was declared, struggled sadly in a troubled state, for not only did books supporting Arminianism flourish, but also services were being established full of Popish imitation. Cosin must obviously fall on both points, with appropriate condemnation. It was recommended that the books of Mountague and Cosin, including the *Devotions*, described as his 'Horary', be burned, and 'that such as have been authors or abettors of those Popish and Arminian innovations in doctrine may be condignly punished'.[10] Only the Royal intervention, adjourning and then dissolving Parliament, saved Cosin from the implementation of these proposals. The 'Eleven Years' Tyranny' which followed gave him a respite from the attacks of the Puritans, but they renewed them in 1640. Peter Smart laid a set of charges against him, and although his responsibility for the *Devotions* was not discussed again, his other offences confirmed the Puritans in that opposition to him which finally forced him into years of voluntary exile.[11]

In 1634 Bishop White, lately translated from Carlisle to Ely, doubtless remembering his earlier association with Cosin and his approval of his views, preferred him from the nominations of the Fellows to the vacant Mastership of Peterhouse, Cambridge. At the same time, Cosin retained his Durham appointments—although his patron, Neile, had been elected to Winchester (1627) and to the Archbishopric of York (1631) —and his post as a chaplain-in-ordinary to the King, which he had been given in 1627. When he came to Peterhouse, Cosin set out to enforce the High Church attitudes he discovered there. The College was already known for the High Churchmanship of the two previous Masters, Leonard Mawe and Matthew Wren. Mawe and Wren were both known to the Court and had enjoyed preferment: they had both accompanied the Prince to Spain on behalf of the ill-fated marriage settlement with the Infanta, and Wren had left Peterhouse for the Bishopric of Hereford.

In Tudor and Stuart times, Crown and Church constantly

interfered with the Universities. Both Masters and Fellows were frequently intruded by Royal proclamation, 'local statutes notwithstanding'; appointment to College office was a common way of rewarding a favourite, or someone with suitable views. James had thus intruded Matthew Wren into the Mastership. Although Cosin's appointment to the Mastership appears to have followed the usual, legal custom, he was nevertheless enjoying the benefits of faithful service to the established order. As Master of Peterhouse he could be securely counted on to promote the doctrine and welfare of the Church and King in the University—an obviously important area of influence.

At Peterhouse Cosin applied his love of ceremony and his devotion to 'the ordered past'. He enriched the Chapel, begun under Wren, with lavish decorations, introducing an elaborate ritual, which included incense, and possibly, if Prynne's subsequent allegation is correct, the use of the canonical hours from his *Devotions*. He further enforced an exacting discipline on the scholars, requiring fines, for example, for absence from prayers.[12] In generally Puritan Cambridge, Peterhouse was pre-eminently Loyalist. It was first among the Colleges to forward its silver to the Royal Mint in July 1642,[13] while Cosin, as principal in all its affairs, early fell victim to the new Parliament. He had been Vice-Chancellor of the University in 1639–40, and, since the end of 1640, Dean of Peterborough, an office to which the King preferred him.[14] As Vice-Chancellor, Cosin instituted into the University Church of Great St. Mary's 'innovations' which recalled his activities at Peterhouse and the ceremonies Smart had criticized at Durham.

Such continuing practices could not be tolerated by the Commons; they sent for Cosin on 21 November 1640 as a 'Delinquent'. In the following year, on 11 March, he was impeached, being held unfit to hold any office. It is not certain just when he left Cambridge—he could not have remained long in safety—but he had certainly set off well before the visitation by the Earl of Manchester in March 1644 with his order from the Long Parliament to 'regulate the Universities'.[15]

Before leaving England, Cosin perhaps spent some time with friends, in hiding to avoid Parliamentary arrest. We next know of him in Paris, but not until 1645. There he passed the long period until the Restoration as Chaplain to the little group of Anglican Royalists, preaching encouragement to them, conducting English services at Faubourg St. Germain in the old Laudian way with ceremony and dignity, and writing defences of the English Church and her doctrines—of these there were the *Regni Angliae Religio Catholica* (1652) and *History of Popish Transubstantiation* (1655). He was in difficult circumstances, living on gifts from friends and a small pension from the French Government, but all the while under Queen Henrietta Maria's cold neglect. Yet Cosin remained strong within the English Church, 'the Atlas of the Protestant Religion', proving his faith to be based on more than political or economic expediency.[16] He enjoyed small comfort for his loyalty now, nor, when fortunes were so low, could he have looked forward to any ease later.

At the Restoration, Cosin returned to his Mastership at Peterhouse, while as Dean of Peterborough he resumed services there; soon, however, in October 1660, he was elected to the see of Durham, being consecrated on 2 December. At Durham, until his death on 15 January 1672, he proved an energetic Bishop, improving and enriching the diocese with lavish building and gifts; he attended as well to the details of diocesan business with watchful interest. Because Cosin was one of the chief survivors of the Laudian régime, he exercised also an important role at the Savoy Conference, and at the Convocation for revising the Book of Common Prayer—not since Cranmer had a single man exercised so much influence on the English liturgy.[17]

It has been said that Cosin returned from his exile less of a High Churchman than he had been in his younger days,[18] but there is little evidence for this. If the *Devotions* gives us a reliable picture, then Cosin's position in 1627 was in fact a good deal more moderate than the clamour of his Puritan opponents would lead us to expect, while a consideration of his work for the revision of the Book of Common Prayer leads to the conclusion that in 1661 he wanted to go on from where he had left off twenty years before.[19] Varied and long as Cosin's life was, it reveals a consistency of doctrine and purpose.

His early love for the Church of the *via media* finds comparable expression in his later years; his last will reveals him, as we should expect, as firm and unequivocal with respect to Rome as he had always been:

I am now, and have ever been from my youth, altogether free and averse from the corruptions and impertinent new-fangled or papistical (so commonly called) superstitions and doctrines, and new superadditions to the ancient and primitive religion and Faith of the most commended, so orthodox, and Catholic Church, long since introduced, contrary to the Holy Scripture, and the rules and customs of the ancient Fathers.[20]

Equally, his last will reveals his continuing distaste for

the separatists, the anabaptists, and their followers, (alas) too too many, but also the new independents and presbyterians of our country, a kind of men hurried away with the spirit of malice, disobedience, and sedition, who by a disloyal attempt (the like whereof was never heard since the world began) have of late committed so many great and execrable crimes, to the contempt and despite of religion and the Christian Faith.[21]

His contacts with the continental reformed Churches during his exile left him, if sympathetic, firmly persuaded of their inferiority to the Church of England, which he saw as, of all the reformed Churches, 'both for doctrine and discipline, the most eminent, and the most pure, the most agreeable to Scripture and antiquity of all others'.[22] He could, as in his last will, rise above the divisive issues of the day and state:

I take it to be my duty, and of all my brethren, especially the Bishops and Ministers of the Church of God, to do our utmost endeavours, according to the measure of grace which is given to every one of us, that at last an end may be put to the differences of religion, or at least that they may be lessened, and that we may 'follow peace with all men, and holiness'.[23]

Yet here also his lifelong love for the English Church finds expression as he confesses himself 'most addicted to the symbols, synods, and confessions of the Church of England, or rather the Catholic Church'.[24]

With an abiding sense of the majesty and holiness of God, Cosin loved liturgical order and beauty in religion, and devoted much of his life and ability to the advancement of these ideals; to this end he offered the splendid chapel at Auckland Castle—the residence of the Bishops of Durham—where he caused his tomb to be inscribed: 'In non morituram memoriam Joannis Cosini, Episcopi Dunelmensis . . . .'

II

The *Devotions* is properly described as a Primer, and belongs, therefore, to an old tradition of Christian devotion, while the provision it makes for the observance of the canonical hours of prayer associates it with an even older and more universal tradition.[25]

The observance of the canonical hours can be traced back to the time of the early Fathers, Clement of Alexandria, Origen, Tertullian, and Cyprian, when it was a matter of purely private devotion. By the sixth century in the West, however, as the *Regula* of St. Bernard implies, the daily offices at the canonical hours had become public services, for the lay people and secular clergy as well as the ascetics. Bernard's elaboration of the existing Roman scheme provides for a daily recitation of Matins and Lauds, Prime, Terce, Sext, None, Vespers, and Compline. Such a scheme of public observances constituted the Divine Office, which, in various forms, was to be used throughout the West for many centuries.

The individual offices said at the hours followed a general pattern, with an invocation, Psalms preceded or followed by a hymn, antiphons, one or more lessons, responsories, and prayers. Such offices would vary according to the liturgical season as well as the time of day. In the course of time, however, the Breviary, the book in which the various divisions of the Divine Office were collected, became so complicated, with its continually varying texts, that in England in the Middle Ages its use had become restricted almost exclusively to the clergy. Lay observance of the canonical hours of the Divine Office had so much declined by the late fourteenth century that Langland might refer in *Piers Plowman* to 'the lawe of holy churche':

And up-on sonedays to cesse · godes seruyce to huyre,
Boþe matyns and messe · and, after mete, in churches
To huyre here evesong · every man ouhte.
('C' Text, ed. Skeat, x. 227–9.)

In place of the Divine Office, popular devotion in the Middle Ages found expression in the prayers of the Primer. The origin of the Primer lies in a series of devotions supplementary to the Divine Office, devised as early as the ninth century by the piety of individuals in the Carolingian monasteries. These devotions were gradually and voluntarily adopted in the course of two or three centuries by the secular clergy in many parts of the Western Church, so that by the fourteenth century they had come to be regarded as obligatory, and almost a part of the public daily office itself. They included six basic divisions: offices of the dead, and of the Blessed Virgin

Mary (the latter known as the Little Office), three groups of Psalms (penitential, gradual, and the commendations), and the Litany. The *Ancrene Riwle*, an anonymous early thirteenth-century work, gives interesting testimony to the growing importance of these supplementary devotions: the author bases the devotional scheme for his three anchoresses entirely on these devotions while making no provision for the use of the Divine Office itself.

Such devotions formed the basis of the book known as the Primer (apparently from the Latin word *primarium*, for prime) which we first find towards the end of the thirteenth century. The central feature of the early Primers is the Little Office, an invariable form which modified the seven hours of the Divine Office by the frequent use of the Ave Maria, with a choice of other material—canticles, hymns, little chapters—appropriate to the Blessed Virgin (hence the name by which the medieval Primer was most often known, *Horae Beatissimae Virginis Mariae*). The Primer thus continued to provide for the observance of the canonical hours of prayer; frequently, however, a certain amount of other matter came to be included along with the Little Office and the other basic parts, such as an almanac or table to find the date of Easter, a calendar of saints' days, the Paternoster, the Creed, and the Ten Commandments, with brief expositions, one or more edifying treatises, any number of approved special prayers and graces, a form for the confession of sins. Invariably, however, the hours of the Blessed Virgin, and usually some of the other basic constituents, recur in all the Primers of the period. The Primer, in Latin or English or both, could therefore be used to follow at least some of the services recited in Latin in the Church, if not the Divine Office itself. In fact, however, it was probably more often regarded and used as a book of private devotion. Whichever way it was used, the Primer established itself as the prayer book of the English lay people in the Middle Ages, becoming the most widely known book among all classes of people. It was the book upon which oaths were sworn, as one of the *Paston Letters*, of 1460, indicates: 'My Maister Fastolf, . . . by his othe made on his Primer ther, grauntted and promitted to me . . .' (ed. Gairdner, I. 539).

During the upheavals of the sixteenth century, the Primer enjoyed an extensive popularity: more than 180 editions appeared during the crucial years from 1525 to 1560, most of them in English (although after 1549, when the Book of Common Prayer first appeared, they can have been useful only for private devotion). Several of these were officially authorized, by Henry VIII, Edward VI, Mary, and Elizabeth, who clearly intended to use them to help establish and protect current theological positions. They reveal the shifting theological emphases of the Reformation. By the time we come to the Elizabethan Primers, for example, the Little Office could in no sense be described as 'of the Blessed Virgin Mary'. Elizabeth put forth her first Primer in 1559, and it appeared in a Latin version, the *Orarium*, in the following year; it is this 1560 Primer that Cosin notes on his title-page and obviously used as a model. The *Orarium* provides for the observance of the seven canonical hours, drawing material from the Breviary and the Prayer Book as well as from the Little Office of the earlier Primers, and includes two other basic features of the Primer, the Penitential Psalms and the Litany. Cosin's second acknowledged source is the Primer authorized by Elizabeth in 1564, *Preces Privatae*, which appeared again in 1568 and, with revisions and additions, in 1573. Here no midday hours appear at all, but only matins and vespers. Both of these Elizabethan Primers include, like many of their predecessors, a large amount of that extra devotional material which made the Primer a means of touching a wide variety of personal and daily requirements.

The growing ascendancy of the Book of Common Prayer during this period, with the accompanying development of private devotions of a more informal, non-liturgical type, helps to explain the virtual disappearance of the Primer after 1564, the few to appear being based on the *Preces Privatae* and the other official Elizabethan Primers. Cosin's *Devotions* represents a Caroline revival, the classical Anglican version of the Primer and of the canonical hours of prayer.

Cosin's book must have seemed curious to the well-intentioned and literate layman of the time, brought up to approve a less traditional style of devotion. Nothing like it, apart from various unreformed Primers for the use of recusants, had been published in England for almost fifty years. The new type of Elizabethan prayer book, such as Thomas Becon's *The Flower of Godly Prayers* (1551) and *The Pomaunder of Prayer* (1558), John Bradford's *Private Prayers and Meditations* (1559) and *Godly Meditations upon the Lordes Prayer* (1562), and John Day's *A Booke of Christian Prayers* (1578), had stirred the popular spirit. These writers offered their wisdom to meet ordinary, everyday needs. Becon, for example, in *The Flower of Godly Prayers*, provides prayers which are like little homilies: 'A Prayer against the temptations of the Devil, the World, and the Flesh', 'A Prayer against Whoredom', 'A Prayer against Slandering and Backbiting'. Bradford's *Godly Meditations* relates practical life to the familiar Christian material, the Lord's Prayer and the Commandments, and gives instruction in Christian life, as in 'A Meditation for the exercise of true mortification'. Often prayers are provided, as in many of the Primers, to see one through the day; thus Day's *Booke* has 'A Prayer to be said at our first waking', 'A Prayer at our uprising', 'A Prayer at the putting on of our clothes', and so on, to 'A Prayer when we be ready to sleep'.

The considerable popularity of this type of book accounts to some extent for the failure of the *Devotions* to win such acclaim as one might expect from an age that took new religious books so eagerly to heart. Sought after and admired in a comparatively small circle, it never won anything like the popularity of a contemporary devotional work, Lewis Bayly's *The Practice of Piety*, which first appeared in 1612, reached its eleventh edition by 1619, and was destined for a fifty-eighth by 1734. Bayly's book (which Bunyan called his favourite) appealed in a different way from Cosin's; Bayly looked back to the popular Tudor books with their prayers fitting many occasions, their meditations on the Faith and directives for pious living, while also providing direction and instruction in prayer but not regular prayers at the traditional intervals. Cosin's *Devotions*, standing in the ancient tradition of the Primer, was a very different matter. In a small way it does recall the interests of these newer devotional manuals, with their ample provision of occasional prayers: two at least of Cosin's 'Prayers and Thanksgivings for Sundry Purposes' derive from Becon's *Pomaunder of Prayer*, and a few other prayers are similar in type; yet the *Devotions* remains essentially and unmistakably a Primer, a somewhat isolated phenomenon in relation to the popular devotional literature of the time.

The *Devotions* is not, however, fully understood when we have seen its important place in the history of the Primer and its tenuous relationship to popular contemporary devotional literature. It needs to be seen also against the background of Laudian churchmanship which Cosin supported. In describing the character of Laudian devotion, one must recognize a dominant and a minor attitude, a more and a less representative form, though both forms may occur together, in varying proportions, within the same work. In its less representative form, Laudian devotion looked towards contemporary Rome, showing an interest in recusant publications such as *A Christian Directorie* (1582) by the Jesuit Robert Persons, and in the translations of continental Roman Catholic writers such as St. Francis de Sales, St. Teresa, and Luis de Granada. This interest generally involved no doctrinal infidelity, and borrowings from Roman Catholic sources were in the spirit of Hooker's distinction:

> Where Rome keepeth that which is auncienter and better; others whome we much more affect leaving it for newer, and changing it for worse, we had rather follow the perfections of them whome we like not, then in defects resemble them whome we love. (*Lawes*, v. 28.)

Sometimes, however, doctrines which the Church of England had repudiated at her Reformation were either asserted or implied, as in, to cite perhaps the most extravagant example, Anthony Stafford's *The Femall Glory: or, The Life, and Death of our Blessed Lady, the holy Virgin Mary, Gods owne immaculate Mother* . . . (1635).[26]

In its more characteristic forms, however, Laudian devotion paid little attention to contemporary Rome. Deriving to a large extent from Hooker, with Andrewes and Overall as something like the 'fathers' of the movement, the more typical Laudian churchmanship sought to express, in worship and prayer and liturgy, that essentially reformed Catholicism which many increasingly recognized as the distinctive development of the English Church, and which made it for them, in the words of Cosin's later friend, Sancroft, 'the most glorious Church upon earth'. A frequently wide and profound acquaintance with the early Fathers, an intense sacramentalism, and a firm stress on the liturgical life as provided for in the Book of Common Prayer marked the ethos of this more typical Laudian devotion. Within this ethos Andrewes and Donne preached their sermons, the former framed his *Preces Privatae* (1648), George Herbert wrote *The Temple* (1633) and his manual for *A Priest to the Temple* (1652), Nicholas Ferrar evolved the community at Little Gidding, and Laud sought to establish 'decency and an orderly settlement of the external worship of God in the Church'.[27]

Among these men there were of course those whose devotional life was not unaffected by contemporary Roman Catholicism, but always the doctrinal norm was that of the Church of England as they understood it, and the liturgical background that provided by the Book of Common Prayer. While celibacy finds a renewed esteem in Andrewes's praise in his *Preces Privatae* for 'the beauty of virgins', while his deep sacramentalism shows itself in reference to 'the power of the thrice holy keys and the mysteries in Thy Church', and while his highest aspiration is 'in the holy and catholic Church to have my own calling, and holiness, and portion, and a fellowship of her sacred rites, [and] prayers', there is nevertheless no doubt—the position he took in the controversy with Bellarmine can leave us in no doubt—that such Catholic devotion was for Andrewes part of a full and loyal membership in the Church of England. Likewise with the community at Little Gidding: part of the household's rule possibly derived from that of the Oratories of St. Philip Neri, Nicholas Ferrar could translate a moral treatise by the Belgian Jesuit, Lessius, as well as the 'Divine Considerations' of the Spaniard, Valdez, and the sisters bind a copy of the *Introduction to the Devout Life* of St. Francis de Sales, yet the whole life of the community was conducted in such a manner as was 'agreable to the Doctrine of the Church of England'.[28] Even Laud, who felt able to give official approval to Stafford's floridly Mariolatrous book, was proud to assert that he had lived and should be willing to die 'in the faith of Christ, . . . as it is professed in the present Church of England'.[29] He appealed constantly to the English articles and canons, to the Prayer Book and the Bible, and he went about his improvements to the conduct and setting of public worship with the moderate conviction that, with regard to externals,

too many overburden the service of God, and too few leave it naked. And scarce anything hath hurt religion more in these broken times than an opinion in too many men, that because Rome hath thrust some unnecessary and many superstitious ceremonies upon the Church, therefore the Reformation must have none at all; not considering therewhile, that ceremonies are the hedge that fence the substance of religion from all the indignities which profaneness and sacrilege too commonly put upon it. And a great weakness it is, not to see the strength which ceremonies,—things weak enough in themselves, God knows,—add even to religion itself. . . .[30]

With much about it that is redolent of older ways, then, the more typical Laudian devotion is yet unequivocally Protestant and shares many of the insights and attitudes of the Reformation.

Within this setting Cosin's *Devotions* is best understood. He does not hesitate to quote some of the later Catholic theologians, to borrow and adapt from the Sarum liturgical texts, to make use of a little recusant book of prayers, *A Manual of Prayers newly gathered out of many . . . authours . . .* (1583); but his work is, from a doctrinal point of view, firmly in the tradition of the Book of Common Prayer. Cosin emphasizes those features of Christian spirituality most strongly reminiscent of the Catholic ethos, and yet he was convinced that his was a position of complete, even especial, loyalty to the Church of England.

One finds in the *Devotions* many of the most characteristic attitudes of the seventeenth-century High Churchmen. Cosin reveals a wide and sympathetic knowledge of the teaching and practice of the primitive Church 'before Popery'. Besides adducing the testimony of Scripture on many points, he refers with great frequency to the early Fathers and Councils, and to 'the ancient Discipline and religious custome of the Church'. He also draws upon the formularies of the reformed Church of England, and implies throughout that the Church of England is a true and sound branch of '*Christs Catholicke Church*'. At the same time we get hints of his understanding of the Reformation in England as a wise and moderate one, and of his disapproval of the unseemliness of Puritan worship and of the corruptions of the Church of Rome. Essentially for Cosin, as for most of the sixteenth-century reformers, and for Hooker, Andrewes, and Laud, the English Church's choice of the middle way is a positive option for primitive and Catholic Christianity.

Cosin shares with his Laudian contemporaries, moreover, a deep reverence for the sacraments, because 'they have Gods marke upon them, being set apart and dedicated to the service of his most Holy and fearefull Name'. He is careful to distinguish between the two 'principall, and truly so called', and the other five which have 'not the like nature'—the Puritan jibe, whereby he was 'Cossens, the 7 sacramentary man', was typically unfair.[31] The frequent references to Baptism show that Cosin's attitude is strongly objective: he speaks of it as 'the first regeneration'. In the Holy Eucharist he understands Christ's most blessed Passion and Sacrifice to be 'represented before' God. Cosin also lays great stress upon the liturgy and upon the details of the liturgical year. His 'Precepts of the Church', for example, imply a corporate, organic notion of life in the Church, a life centred upon the liturgy.[32] In various places he makes it clear that the *Devotions* is to be regarded not as a substitute for, but as a complement to, common prayer; and, in fact, one of the most impressive features of his book is the way in which what it provides interlocks with the Book of Common Prayer.

There are many less prominent features which identify Cosin's *Devotions* as typically Laudian. Among these should be noticed the emphasis on worship and adoration, the 'heavenly duty . . . of . . . *Daily* & Christian *Devotions* to Almighty God', in which we have 'a perpetuall *Communion* with the *Saints* triumphant'; the recommendation that such worship should be 'with the lowly reverence, even of our Bodies also'; the encouragement to auricular or sacramental confession, 'especially before the receiving of Christs blessed Sacrament'; the belief in the Real Presence in the Eucharist (the communicant is advised to say 'Amen' after the words of administration); the evident attraction of the 1549 Prayer Book; the strongly 'affirmative' character of the prayers. Cosin also shows his close kinship with the Laudians in his citation of the Visitation Articles of Andrewes and Overall, the prefatory refutation of 'the common conceit of most Recusant Papists', the attack upon the Sabbatarianism of the Puritans, who on the Lord's Day, 'under a pretence of serving God more strictly than others (especially for hearing and meditating of Sermons), doe by their Fasts, and certaine Judaizing observations, condemne the joyfull Festivitie of this High & Holy day', the attitude of reverence to the King, to 'his sacred power, and his Soveraigne Authoritie over us'. In all of these ways, and in many others, Cosin's *Devotions* belongs essentially in the Laudian setting.

Cosin also reveals many personal qualities in the Devotions. The stress upon the Passion, its 'extreme sorrow and anguish', but the much greater emphasis upon the goodness and bounty of God and the joyful potentialities of life, 'the blessings of Heaven above, and the blessings of the earth beneath', indicate something of the character of his faith—a faith reminiscent, in this respect, of his near contemporary, Thomas Traherne. The evidence of his knowledge of the Patristic writings demonstrates his considerable learning. The care with which he quotes so many authorities, and, in controversial matters, specifically Anglican ones, points to the importance to him of orthodoxy. His literary ability is also marked in both prayers and prefaces. An analysis of his prayers reveals a variety of structure, rhythm, and language similar to that of the prayers of the Book of Common Prayer, while the frequent scriptural allusions give an additional richness. From the delicate beauty of the brief prayer 'At the washing of our hands', or the Ember prayers 'For the health of our Bodies' and 'In the time of Advent', to the long and splendid 'Prayer and Thanksgiving for the Whole Estate of Christs Catholic Church', Cosin manifests notable skill as a composer and reviser of prayers. His many introductory and explanatory passages—something of an innovation in the Primer—form a distinguished series of lucid expositions on a number of topics, in a prose at once concise, dignified, and pleasing. Many of the earlier Primers were untidily put together, often containing matter of little relevance to normal devotional requirements; but the *Devotions*, with its few rubrical directions precise and useful, its neatness of arrangement and comparative economy of content, is an encouragement to an ordered and unburdened devotional life, and reveals an orderly and practical mind in its compiler.

Finally, we may discover in the relationship of the *Devotions* to the Book of Common Prayer, to one aspect of which—that of its complementary quality—we have already briefly referred, its most distinctive contribution to devotional literature and to the development of Anglican liturgy. Cosin was not alone of his times in commending the hours of prayer. For example, Andrewes does this in his *Preces Privatae* and Jeremy Taylor in *A Collection of Offices, Or Forms of Prayer in Cases Ordinary and Extraordinary* (1658), while Laud's *Summarie of Devotions* (1667) gives several prayers at the hours for each day of the week. Cosin's is the fullest Anglican version of the hours in Caroline times, but this is not its only distinction. Cosin's particular achievement lies in providing a series of private devotions which are linked to the medieval offices and are alternative (in certain circumstances prescribed in the Preface) to the public prayers of the Church which derive from the same medieval sources. Cosin frequently looked back beyond the Prayer Book of 1549: the offices for matins and vespers in the *Devotions*, for example, are close to those in the Book of Common Prayer because Cosin and Cranmer drew upon common sources, the Primer and the Breviary. The *Devotions* thus provides an integral and homogeneous *private* complement to the *common* prayer of the Church. That Cosin's compilation should have had a creative influence upon subsequent revision of the Book of Common Prayer is a natural consequence of its unique character.

III

There are two contemporary descriptions of the occasion of Cosin's coming to compile the *Devotions*. John Evelyn, in an entry in his *Diary* dated 1 October 1651, records a story he says he heard from Cosin himself:

> . . . at the first coming over of the *Queene* into *England* she, & her *French* Ladys, were often up-braiding our Religion, that had neither appointed, nor set forth, any *Houres* of Prayer, or *Breviaries*, which Ladies & Courtie[r]s (that have much spare time) might edifie by, & be in devotion, as they had: Our Protestant Ladys scandaliz'd it seemes at this, moved the matter to the *King*, whereupon his Majestie, presently call'd *Bishop White* to him, and asked his thoughts of it, & whither there might not be found some formes of Prayer, proper on such occasions, collected out of some already approved formes? that so the Court-Ladys &c. (who spend much time in trifling) might at least appeare as devout, and be so too, as the new-come-over *French* Ladys, who tooke occasion to reproch our want of zeale, & Religion: Upon which the *Bish*[*o*]*p* told his Majestie that it might be don easily, & was very necessary: Whereupon the K. commanded him to employ some Person of the *Cleargy* to compile such a Work, & presently the *Bishop* naming *Dr. Cosin*: & the King injoynes him to charge the Doctor in his name to set about it immediately: which *Mr. Deane* told me he did, & 3 monethes after bringing the book to the *King*, he commanded the *Bishop* of *London* to reade it over, & make his report: which was so well liked; that (contrary to former customs [by Chaplan]) he would needes give it a warrant [& Imprimatur] under his owne hand. . . .[33]

The second report occurs in Peter Heylyn's biography of Laud:

> [There] came out a Book entituled, *A Collection of Private Devotions, or the Hours of Prayer*, composed by *Cozens* one of the *Prebends* of *Durham*, at the Request, and for the Satisfaction, as

it was then generally believed, of the Countess of *Denbigh*, the only Sister of the Duke, and then supposed to be unsetled in the Religion here established, if not warping from it.[34]

A wave of fashionable 'conversions' to Rome was taking place at the Court early in the reign of Charles I. They were, for the most part, sponsored by Endymion Porter's wife, Olivia, and were almost invariably feminine. The Countess of Denbigh was one of the ladies of the Court—she was the first lady of the bedchamber to Henrietta Maria—and she may well have been 'warping from' the 'Religion established' at this time, for she was notoriously unstable in her ecclesiastical allegiance, and did in fact become a Roman Catholic later in life. Probably the Countess was one of the 'Protestant ladys' who, according to Evelyn, complained to the King. It seems that Charles and his advisers hoped that a book of devotion such as that envisaged might help to sustain some of the ladies in their loyalty to the Church of England.

Evelyn's and Heylyn's accounts, of course, complement each other, but neither of them supports Prynne's later assertion that Cosin had already prepared his collection of devotions quite independently '*for his owne private use*', nor is there any other evidence for Prynne's statement.[35] Cosin's interests certainly lay in this direction, and he would naturally have felt moved to do such a work, his own interest coinciding with the Royal pleasure. Most likely Cosin began his work on the *Devotions* in November or December 1626; working in considerable haste, he had the book licensed on 22 February 1627, and entered in the Stationers' Register on 1 March 1627, to Robert Young.[36]

Although the *Devotions* did not bear the name of the compiler—Cosin's name does not appear until the ninth edition of 1676, the first edition after his death—there was evidently no secret about his part in it.[37] For the group with whom Cosin was associated it was 'a Jewel of great Price and value'[38] but to the Puritans it was, in Peter Smart's words, a 'base begotten bratt . . . that painted fardle'.[39] The Puritan reaction, which was especially noisy and outspoken, seems to have affected the second edition of 1627. Cosin altered several controversial points and included a piece entitled 'The Printer to the Reader' in which he explained that the troublesome points were due to 'the Printers haste, or the Correctors oversight', but that these had now been emended. Still later, in September of the same year, 'Observations upon Dr. Cosin's Book . . .'[40] were delivered by Sir Francis Nethersole to the Secretary of State, Lord Conway, who passed them on to the King. This concern demonstrates the effectiveness of Puritan criticism—the authorities were at least sensitive to it.

The full force of the Puritan attack is best evident in the two pamphlets by Prynne and Burton, published between March and June 1628, presumably with the hope of eliciting support from the new Parliament. Prynne, who was to become one of the principal pamphleteers in the Puritan cause, wrote *A Briefe Survay and Censure of Mr Cozens His Couzening Devotions. Proving both the forme and matter of Mr Cozens his Booke of Private Devotions, or the Houres of Prayer, lately published, to be meerely Popish. . . .* Burton, who was already deeply involved as a pamphleteer for the Puritans, produced *A Tryall of Private Devotions, or a Diall for the Houres of Prayer*.[41] Prynne's pamphlet is a good example of his work, extremely laborious, without a trace of humour, loaded with learned but often irrelevant notes citing Cosin's 'Popish' sources; Burton's is notable for its naïve, racy, and often rather scurrilous style. The gravamen of the Puritan objection to the *Devotions* becomes clear in these two works. Both complain first of all of the title-page, which, with its 'I H S' motif, is 'Jesuitical'. There are many other offensive points in Cosin's book: the use of the canonical hours; the inclusion of prayers for the dead; references to the ministry of angels; an apparently unsatisfactory distinction made between the two dominical sacraments and the five 'somtimes called' sacraments; the

Engraved title-page of the first edition (1627)

use of words like 'devotion' or 'Catholic', and besides these, many extremely trivial and doctrinally indifferent points.[42]

Prynne and Burton are hardly representative Puritans, for the former was an extreme eccentric by any standards, and the latter was embittered by his dismissal from a Court appointment; but in their attitude towards the *Devotions* they are typical of the Puritans of that time, Puritans, that is, in religion and Church policy, who felt that the Reformation in England had not gone far enough and who wished for further reform of the Church from within. The *Devotions*, with its highly traditional appearance, and in its origins associated with the Court of Charles I, naturally aroused suspicion among such men. They already regarded the Court as virtually Papist because of the presence of Henrietta Maria and her entourage and the papal agents, and feared the great influence at Court of 'Laud's faction'. There were grounds, it at least seemed, for fearing an English Counter-Reformation. Looking neither closely nor fairly at the *Devotions*, some saw in it confirmatory evidence of such an 'Apostacie from Christ to antichrist', and could charge Cosin (and his friend Mountague) with 'Mountebanke Arminianisme and Cozening Poperie'. Prynne and Burton illustrate well the radical attitude of the religious Puritans. To Burton, trying to put things into some sort of perspective, the King's Primer of 1545 appeared 'in the dawning of the Gospell in England', while the Elizabethan Primers were further measures in the process of reformation, but showing 'a tender regard . . . of the weaknesse of the time', the last of them, the 1573 edition, being 'yet more exact . . . as the more distant still from the Horarium' (the 1560 edition). Cosin's Primer, on the other hand, appearing unexpectedly and subversively in 'our aged and noontide seasons of the Gospell', was no less than a step on the way *back* to Popery, the provision for the observance of the canonical hours importing nothing else 'but a necessitie of bringing in Monkerie and so of erecting cells again'. To

Prynne the danger implicit in the publication of the *Devotions* was equally real, for he saw it as a threat to the State. He thereby reminds us of how Puritanism in religion and Church policy almost inevitably merged with political Puritanism: 'Our State Enemies, are no other but our Church Enemies; our State greivances, are but the fruites and issues of our Church annoyances' (sig. A4^{r}). However ill-founded the fears of Prynne and Burton and of many men more reasonable than they, it is easy to understand how, at a time of growing mistrust, when the tensions which finally found expression in the Civil War were mounting, a book like the *Devotions* should arouse such hostility.

In spite of the vigour of the Puritan attack upon the *Devotions* and its compiler, the book achieved an immediate popularity in a much wider circle than that offered by the ladies of the Court. The first edition was a small one, perhaps between 150 and 250, but the second and third editions of later 1627 were both much larger, estimates giving 1,000 and 1,500.[43] Interest persisted in the *Devotions*, with five more editions appearing in Cosin's lifetime. After the twelfth edition of 1719, there followed a long period during which acquaintance with the book was evidently very slight, until 1838, when a further edition was published. This renewed interest is to be attributed to the Tractarians' early intention of continuing and reviving the churchmanship of the Caroline divines; to this aspect of the Anglican revival in the nineteenth century we may attribute the publication of a further four editions up to that of 1867, the seventeenth and last edition before this present one.

There are other evidences of the persistent appeal of the *Devotions*. Cosin's version of the canonical hours was used by at least one of the early English Sisterhoods of the nineteenth century, the Church of England Sisterhood of Mercy of Devonport and Plymouth, while in Bishop Wilberforce's experiment of a retreat at Cuddesdon in 1860 it was again used.[44] There have been borrowings from the *Devotions*, from the seventeenth century to our own time, in other books of private devotion; and the revisions of the Book of Common Prayer, both in 1662, and, in various Churches of the Anglican Communion, in this century, have been influenced by Cosin's compilation.[45]

This new edition of *A Collection of Private Devotions* makes once more easily accessible an extended compilation by one of the greatest liturgists of the English Church. The long series of editions through which it has gone, its continued devotional use, and its influence upon other works of devotion and upon the various revisions of the Book of Common Prayer, are a testimony to its persisting appeal. It is a work of considerable interest in several other respects. It stands firmly within an ancient tradition of devotional literature, and is yet in many ways a fresh and individual contribution to that tradition. Its material, as written and revised by Cosin, has for the most part an intrinsic excellence, and much of it could still be used with profit today. It has, too, its own historical interest: the situation in the Court of Charles I which occasioned its compilation, and the character of the Puritan reaction to its publication, provide useful illustrations of the tensions and controversies of the times. It is a fruit of that distinctive English spirituality, Catholic and reformed, of which the Book of Common Prayer is the corporate, liturgical expression, and it provides, in particular, a wide-ranging illustration of the nature of Laudian or Caroline churchmanship and devotion, so exact an illustration, in fact, that we might describe it as the typical Laudian text. Essentially of its time, Cosin's *Devotions* nevertheless remains a fine witness to

that true *Devotion*, wherwith God is more delighted, and a good soule more inflamed and comforted, than with all the busie subtilties of the world. In which sense S. AUSTIN was wont to say, that *The pious and devout, though unlearned, went to heaven, whiles other men, trusting to their learning, disputed it quite away.*

IV

THE TEXT

This edition follows the first one of 1627 in the Bodleian Library, with only a few minor changes. Where the printer has abbreviated a word, such as wch or wth, in order to crowd a line, we have spelled it out. We have not retained the cursive ſ, or i for j, or v for u. We have silently corrected obvious printer's errors, such as transposed letters. But we have often preferred to give what seemed an error in the text along with an appropriate note about it. The original pagination has not been retained, though the format of the original has generally been preserved. We have made every effort to give a faithful version of the *Devotions* as Cosin first saw it through the press.

We have collated the first eight editions, all that appeared in Cosin's lifetime, and drawn attention to important printer's variations within an edition, as noted below. We have recorded in the textual notes all variants of any significance. By 'significant' is understood verbal change regardless of change in meaning, but not punctuation and spelling differences unless they alter meaning. Printer's errors are generally passed over except where they are interesting and help to characterize the text, as with the sixth edition.

The texts used for this collation, referred to in the notes by the number of the edition, are as follows:

1627 (*1*). Bodleian Library.
1627 (*2*). Bodleian Library.
1627 (*3*). British Museum.
1635 (*4*). Jesus College, Oxford.
1638 (*5*). British Museum.
1655 (*6*). Peterhouse, Cambridge.
1664 (*7*). British Museum.
1672 (*8*). Houghton Library, Harvard University.

The changes of the second and third editions were generally retained through the next three, the sixth edition being unique especially in its great number of errors; possibly this edition is so faulty because Cosin could not have supervised it, although we cannot be sure how close he was to the printing of any edition after the third. Nevertheless, Cosin would seem to have authorized the Restoration editions which revise Calendar and Collects in accordance with the 1662 version of the Book of Common Prayer while otherwise mainly restoring the text of the first edition, even to including some of its errors. All earlier editions of the *Devotions* follow the collects of the 1604 version of the Prayer Book. 'The Printer to the Reader', which appeared in *2*, *3*, and *6*, is reprinted here from the second edition.

Other editions of the *Devotions* appeared in 1676, 1681, 1693, 1719, 1838, 1843, 1845, and 1867. This last is evidently a new edition of the 'Devotional Portion of the Practical Christian's Library', a series published between 1840 and 1850; but we have not been able to see a copy of the earlier edition. All of these editions, apart from the one published in 'The Library of Anglo-Catholic Theology' (1845) as volume II of Cosin's *Works*, were informally printed as small devotional manuals (usually in duodecimo), without special care or accuracy. The 1845 edition attempted to be scholarly by giving notes and textual apparatus, but the commentary is incomplete and often in error, and the editor included only a few textual variants; moreover, though he mainly used the first edition, he modernized the spelling and also produced a corrupt text. The present edition, therefore, is the first one to give not only the original text but all the variations of the editions in which Cosin could have taken any personal interest, as well as a fuller commentary than has appeared hitherto.

The first three editions of the *Devotions* offer special bibliographic interest for the indications they provide of the problems of both author and printer. Because of the fierce Puritan response, Cosin took advantage of the second edition to alter many offensive phrases, but he had also made some changes within the first edition itself. As well as these editions with their variant sheets, there is also a reissue of the second edition. A description of the first edition follows:

12° (engraved t.-p.+) A^{12} B^{12} (±B11) C^{12} D^{12} (±D12 [= X12]) E–V^{12} X^{12} (±X5–X12 [= D12]).
251 leaves. pp. [72] [1–2] 3–288[2] [1–2] 3–129 [13] = 502.

The cancels can be identified by the following readings:

	Cancellandum	Cancellans
$B11^r$	Omits the Communion of Saints in the Creed.	Includes it.
$D12^r$	Has top portion of border 172 & has imprint.	Neither border nor imprint.
$X5^r$	Includes 'the succour of all holy Angels, and the suffrages of all the chosen of God'.	Omits this.

Page 62 is mispaginated 60; p. 63, 61; 66, 64; 67, 65; 70, 68; 71, 69; 209, 109; 212, 112; 221, 121; 241, 341; ²116, 118; ²117, 119; ²120, 122. X10, 11 are blank.
S.T.C. 5817.

The Bodleian copy has cancellans B11, cancellandum D12 and X12. X5 is a cancellandum leaf from another copy substituted for the original cancellandum.[46]

Thus we may notice that $X5^r$, The Blessing (p. 295), includes in our edition the offensive references to 'the succour of all holy Angels, and the suffrages of all the chosen of God', but that some copies of the first edition (such as that in the Folger Library) omit them. Since the second edition also contains several significant cancels to which reference is made in the notes, they should be identified as follows:

	Cancellandum	Cancellans
$A7^r$	God / & the Holy Ghost	God, / the Holy Ghost
$C5^r$	The dueties	The Dueties
$C6^r$	The dueties	The Dueties

H4^{r}	thine / elect Children	My / children
Q5^{v}	may by the ministry of / thy Holy Angels be brought up	may bee received / into thy Heavenly Tabernacle

The Bodleian copy has all the cancellanda and the cancellans leaves A7 C6 Q5. The last variant (p. 230) is another of the points most 'offensive' to the Puritan commentators; a third, which involves no variant sheets, occurs in the final prayer for the dead (p. 281)—the objectionable phrase 'receive this dead body' appeared again only in the seventh edition.

NOTES

1. The *D.N.B.* gives 1594, evidently an error. Cosin, in a letter to his secretary Miles Stapleton, of 2 January 1671/2, remarks that he is '76 yeares at St. Andrews day last past'. The letter is one of several, all to Stapleton, in the Peterhouse Library.

Cosin's various writings, chiefly theological, were collected in the nineteenth century in 'The Library of Anglo-Catholic Theology' as *The Works of . . . John Cosin* (5 vols., Oxford: John Henry Parker, 1843–55. Vol. II contains the *Devotions*). Much of his correspondence, 'illustrative of his life and times', was published for the Surtees Society under the editorship of George Ornsby (2 vols., Durham, 1869–72). Both collections, but particularly the latter, contain biographical notices based especially on the seventeenth-century 'life' by Cosin's domestic chaplain and preacher at his funeral, Isaac Basire, *The Dead Man's Real Speech* (London, 1673); and also on Thomas Smith's *Vita . . . Joannis Cosini*, included in his *Vitae Quorundam Eruditissimorum et Illustrium Virorum* (London, 1707). There are of course many contemporary notices of Cosin, especially by his opponents such as William Prynne, in *Canterburies Doome* (1646), but also by Thomas Fuller in *The Church History* (1655), where he finds Cosin at fault, and in *The History of the Worthies of England* (1662), where he craves pardon of Cosin for his earlier 'attack' and prays for his long life. The Durham antiquarian Robert Surtees mentions Cosin in his *History of Durham* (1843) and the long notice of him in the *D.N.B.* is by J. H. Overton. But the most recent biographical study, and the only one that attempts fullness, is *A Life of John Cosin* by P. H. Osmond (London: A. R. Mowbray, 1913), an unimaginative history which mainly summarizes Cosin's published *Works* and *Correspondence*. More recently, G. J. Cuming has prefaced his edition of *The Durham Book* (London, 1961) with a description of Cosin's importance to the liturgical conferences at the Restoration. R. S. Bosher's masterful study, *The Making of the Restoration Settlement* (London, 1951), contains much illuminating discussion of Cosin's situation, with the other Laudians, during the Paris exile. Cf. chapter II, 'Anglicans in Exile'. H. Boone Porter, Jr., contributed a valuable discussion of the *Devotions* to *Theology*, LVI (February 1953), 54–58: 'Cosin's Hours of Prayer: A Liturgical Review'. L. W. Hanson's bibliographical study of the first three editions is indispensable: 'John Cosin's *Collection of Private Devotions*, 1627', in *The Library*,

XIII (December 1958), 282–7. For a good description of Cosin's ecclesiological achievements, one might see Nikolaus Pevsner's *County Durham* in the Penguin Series of 'The Buildings of England' (1953), especially pp. 31–33.

2. He was 'admitted to the scholars' table, March 25, 1610'. His tutor was John Browne, a Fellow of the College. Cf. *Biographical History of Gonville and Caius College*, compiled by John Venn (Cambridge, 1897), I. 207.

3. Smith, *Vita*, p. 4.

4. Cf. 'The Sum and Substance of the Conferences Lately Had at York House concerning Mr. Mountague's Books...', in Cosin's *Works*, II. 17–81.

5. Cosin, *Works*, I. 93.

6. Ibid., I. 94, Sermon VI: 'Dominica Prima Adventus, Decembris 3, 1616 . . . in Durham House Chapel, in London.' White had taken part in the first two 'conferences' with Fisher in 1622—Laud met Fisher in the celebrated third and last.

For a discussion of Cosin's sermons, cf. P. G. Stanwood, 'John Cosin as Homilist', *Anglican Theological Review*, XLVII (July 1965), 276–89.

7. *Appello Caesarem*, pp. 112–13.

8. Smart, *Popish Ceremonies*, p. 6.

9. Cf. *Commons Debates for 1629*, ed. W. Notestein and F. H. Relf ('University of Minnesota Studies in the Social Sciences, 10'), Minneapolis, 1921, p. 36.

10. Ibid., p. 100.

11. Smart's Petition dated 'Novemb. 3. 1640' was read in the House only a week later.

12. Exactly what the ritual at Peterhouse consisted of is not clear; one must rely on reports given often second hand and then by those most opposed to Cosin's practices. Prynne alleges that Cosin had introduced the observance of the canonical hours into Peterhouse, based evidently upon his *Devotions*, 'as was attested upon Oath by Mr. *Le Greese* and others' (*Canterburies Doome*, p. 208). Prynne, in an earlier passage (p. 74), styles this observer 'Master *Nicholas le Greise* (late Student in Cambridge)', but he is otherwise unidentified.

Most of what is known about the Peterhouse Chapel in Cosin's time is described by R. Willis and J. W. Clark, *The Architectural History of the University of Cambridge* (4 vols., Cambridge, 1886), vol. I, part I, 'Peterhouse', chap. VI, 'History of the Chapel', pp. 45–46, and by Herbert Butterfield, the present Master, in the *Victoria County History of Cambridge and the Isle of Ely* (1959), III: 'The City and University of Cambridge', 334–40, especially p. 337. Mr. Allan Pritchard has recently noticed among the Harleian manuscripts a more detailed—though Puritan—description of Cosin's Cambridge. He discusses Harley MS. 7019 (in the British Museum) in *T.L.S.* 2 July 1964: 'Puritan Charges Against Crashaw and Beaumont'. T. A. Walker, the late Peterhouse historian, relates a few of the details of College life during Cosin's Mastership in *Peterhouse* (Cambridge, 1935), p. 56.

The overwhelming sympathy of Peterhouse lay with the Royalists, but the College did lodge some notable Puritans of whom the best known was John Hutchinson (1615–64), the 'Regicide'. His *Life*, written by his widow and first published in 1806, describes his five years at Peterhouse from which 'he came away . . . untainted with those [Arminian] principles or practises' taught by his tutor and by Wren and Cosin. Cf. *Memoirs of the Life of Colonel Hutchinson . . . Written by His Widow Lucy* (3rd ed., London, 1810), I. 78.

13. Cosin's signature appears on a College order, now in the Treasury, dated 2 July 1642, for sending plate to the King. On the forwarding of the plate, cf. J. B. Mullinger, *The University of Cambridge . . .* (1911), III. 231–7, 267–8.

14. Cosin was instituted Dean of Peterborough on 7 November 1640. Laud had written to Thomas Morton, Bishop of Durham, on 18 July 1639: 'I have received your letters of July the 3rd, by the hands of Dr. Cosin; and I heartily thank your Lordship for them. For the Doctor, I do very well know his deserts are great, and his means not so. But his Majesty hath a very good opinion of him; and that will, I doubt not, in good time mend his fortunes.' (*The Works of William Laud*, in 'The Library of Anglo-Catholic Theology', Oxford, 1847–62, VI. 567.) Among the charges against Laud which Prynne notices in *Canterburies Doome* there is his habit of promoting 'popish' and 'superstitious' men, including Cosin (p. 532). But Laud defends himself before this particular accusation (p. 356): 'I presented four of his Majesties Chaplaines in ordinary to his Majestie for the Deanery of Peterborough: His Majesty pitched upon Doctor Cosin in regard his meanes lying in the Bishoprick of Durham was in the Scots hands, and nothing left to

maintain him, his wife and children, but a poor Headship worth 40 l. per annum; And out of the same consideration, and no other, did I put his name with his Majesty.' (Cf. Laud, *Works*, IV. 293–4.)

15. The iconoclast William Dowsing made his famous visit to Peterhouse on 21 December 1643, but he makes no mention of Cosin. It is very likely that Cosin had already left by then.

16. 'Whilest he remained in *France*, he was the *Atlas* of the *Protestant Religion*, supporting the same with his Piety and Learning, confirming the wavering therein, yea dayly adding *Proselytes* . . . thereunto.' Cf. Fuller, *The Worthies of England*, p. 295. Cosin in fact seems to have felt more sympathetic to the Reformed Churches as his exile drew on; at least the French Protestants showed more friendliness than the Roman Catholics. In a letter to Richard Watson, dated 19 June 1646, and first printed in 1684 as 'The Right Reverend Doctor John Cosin . . . His Opinion . . . for Communicating rather with Geneva than Rome', Cosin says (p. 3): 'It is far less safe to joyn with these men [i.e. the Roman Catholics], that alter the *Credenda*, the *Vitals* of Religion, than with those that meddle only with the *Agenda* and *Rules* of Religion, if they meddle no farther. . . .' The letter is republished in Cosin's *Works*, IV. 385–6. Cosin's only son caused his father some sadness by leaving the Church of England for Rome in 1652. He became a Jesuit Priest while in residence at the English College in Rome, and in 1659 he was sent as a missionary to England.

17. Cf. Cuming, p. xv: '. . . with [Matthew] Wren, the most copious contributor to the Prayer Book since Archbishop Cranmer'.

18. The suggestion is made by Osmond, pp. 320 ff., who gives a certain amount of rather flimsy evidence in support of this view, and by Cuming, p. xv, who does not attempt to substantiate it.

19. This is Cuming's estimate in *The English Prayer Book 1549–1662*, ed. A. M. Ramsey, *et al.* (London, 1963), p. 110.

20. Cosin, *Works*, IV. 527. This is Basire's translation of Cosin's *Ultimum Testamentum* which he published in *The Dead Man's Real Speech.*

21. Ibid.

22. Ibid. V. 526 ('On Confirmation').

23. Ibid. IV. 527.

24. Cosin, *Works*, IV. 526–7.

25. The following discussion is indebted to several authorities: E. Bishop, *Liturgica Historica* (Oxford, 1918); C. C. Butterworth, *The English Primers, 1529–1545* (Philadelphia, 1953); E. Hoskins, *Horae Beatae Mariae Virginis . . .* (London, 1901); E. C. Ratcliff, 'The Choir Offices', in *Liturgy and Worship*, ed. W. K. Lowther Clarke (London, 1932); H. C. White, *The Tudor Books of Private Devotion* (Madison, Wisc., 1951), especially chapters III and IV; C. Wordsworth and H. Littlehales, *The Old Service Books of the English Church* (London, 1904).

26. Stafford gives a florid description of the Virgin's life: her prudence, her beauty are evoked; her Conception, her Purification, her Assumption are imaginatively detailed. In the preface 'To the Masculine Reader', however, he declared: '. . . if I have swerved in any the least point from the tenents received in the English Church, I shall bee most ready to acknowledge my selfe a true Penitent' (sig. C3[r]). Stafford's enraptured *Life* apparently found many friends, for he received the official approval of the Primate and of Bishop Juxon.

27. Laud, 'Epistle Dedicatory' to *Conference with Fisher*, *Works*, II. xvi.

28. B. Blackstone, ed., *The Ferrar Papers* (Cambridge, 1938), p. 55.

29. Laud, *Conference with Fisher*, *Works*, II. 373.

30. Ibid., 'Epistle Dedicatory' to *Conference with Fisher*, II. xvi–xvii.

31. *Acts of the High Commission Court within the Diocese of Durham* (Surtees Society, 1857), XXXIV. 200. Cosin's careful distinction is in marked contrast with the way in which Robert Shelford, an old alumnus of Peterhouse, in his *Five Pious and Learned Discourses* (Cambridge, 1635), makes an undifferentiated seven of them: 'Which way soever you turn you, here you shall finde the saying of our Saviour fulfilled, *Thus it becometh us to fulfill all righteousnesse.* Desire you new life? here is Baptisme to give it. Are you gone from it? here is the Baptisme of tears and penance to restore it. Want you weapons for the spirituall warre? here is the Catechisme, and Confirmation. Need you food for the new life? here is the bread and wine of Christs body and bloud. Want you supply of vertuous young souldiers? here is Matrimonie and Christian education. Need you leaders and governours?h ere are Christs Ministers. Want you provision for the journey to the high Jerusalem? here is the *viaticum* of the heavenly Manna expressed in the Communion of the sick' (p. 35). The contrast of this with Cosin's entry on 'The

Sacraments of the Church' points to the difference between what we have called the less and the more representative forms of Laudian devotion.

32. For some illuminating observations on Cosin's 'Precepts', cf. Martin Thornton, *English Spirituality* (London, 1963), pp. 263–4.

33. Cf. *The Diary of John Evelyn*, ed. E. S. de Beer (Oxford: The Clarendon Press, 1955), III. 45–46. There is a second version, in all essentials like this one, but dated wrongly (12 October) and apparently written long after the actual occurrence. Cf. Appendix A, pp. 634–6.

34. Cf. *Cyprianus Anglicus* (London, 1668), p. 173. Jeremy Collier follows Heylyn in his *An Ecclesiastical History of Great Britain* (London, 1714), II. 714.

35. C. J. Stranks, *Anglican Devotion* (London, 1961), p. 67, makes the same suggestion, but without reference to Prynne. Cf. Prynne, *A Briefe Survay and Censure of M*[r] *Cozens His Couzening Devotions* (1628), p. 26.

36. There are a number of indications that Cosin did his work in some haste. He told Evelyn that it was done in three months; Prynne says in *A Briefe Survay* (p. 92) that 'the Printer had his written Coppy but by peecemeale, sheete by sheete, and not compleate together'. Prynne also hints at irregularities in the licensing of the *Devotions*, as does Burton in *A Tryall of Private Devotions* (1628). For further suggestion that the *Devotions* was written in haste, cf. the Commentary on the Calendar (pp. 323–4) which quotes Richard Mountague's correspondence with Cosin.

37. It was first attributed to Cosin in a news-letter to Joseph Mead dated 16 May 1627. Cf. T. Birch, *Court and Times of Charles I* (London, 1848), I. 227, quoted in Cosin's *Correspondence*, I. 126.

38. Cf. Heylyn, p. 174.

39. Cf. 'Articles . . . to be exhibited by his Majestie's Heigh Commissioners, against Mr. John Cosin . . .', in Cosin's *Correspondence*, I. 195.

40. Ibid. I. 125–6. 'Observations upon Dr. Cosin's Book, Entitled The Hours of Prayers', S.P.D. [LXXVIII. 19]—Charles I. 1627: Sept. 13.

41. Heylyn, loc. cit., describes Prynne's attack in some detail but says nothing specifically about Burton, of whose work 'there was but little

notice taken', although Smart gives equal credit to the two pamphleteers. He says: 'This pedler's pack, going under the name of John Cosin, hath been layd open to the vew of the world by many, but chiefly by 2 very excellent writers, Mr. Burton and Mr. Prinn, who have so wel discovered the hidden cosenage of the false wares, cunningly couched togeather in that painted fardle, that now theare is little danger that any but very ideotts should be deceived therwith' (cf. Cosin, *Correspondence*, I. 195). Cosin himself seems to have regarded them as equally troublesome, referring to them in a letter to Laud as 'these two barking libellers' (*Correspondence*, I. 139).

42. Cosin's answers to many of these charges can be seen in a paper entitled 'The Objections which some have been pleased to make against a Booke intituled the Houres of Praier: with briefe Answeres thereunto', included in the *Correspondence*, I. 127–36. It is endorsed in Cosin's hand, 'For ye R^{t}. R^{d}. and my honorable good Lord, The Lord Bishop of Durham', and marked, among the State Papers Domestic [LXV. 72], 1627 [May?]; but this date must be in error since Cosin evidently takes account of the pamphlets of Prynne and Burton which appeared between March and June of 1628. It is therefore likely that Cosin sent this paper not to Bishop Neile, as Ornsby (the editor of the *Correspondence*) assumes, but to Bishop Mountain who had licensed the *Devotions*. Mountain was nominated Bishop of Durham, in succession to Neile, on 15 February 1628, although he was further nominated to York on 4 June 1628, probably before the Durham appointment was confirmed.

43. Cf. L. W. Hanson, 'John Cosin's *Collection of Private Devotions*, 1627', *The Library*, XIII (December 1958), 284. In a letter to Cosin, dated 2 July [1627], Mountague writes: 'We did in the country talk strangly of your booke before it was commen. But now, for ought I heare, *σεσίγηται*. What they say att London *οὐκ ἔχω φράσαι*, only this, you left order I should have 3, and I could scarce gett one. . . .' Cf. Cosin, *Correspondence*, I. 124.

44. The *Devotions* may well have been used at Peterhouse (cf. n. 12), and at Little Gidding, though there is little evidence for justifying either suggestion. A scurrilous anonymous pamphlet, *The Arminian Nunnery* (1641), suggests, though not with much conviction, that the *Devotions* may have been used by the Community at Little Gidding for their night offices: 'They have promiscuous private Prayers all the night long by nightly turnes, just like as the English *Nunnes* at Saint

Omers and other Popish places: which private Prayers are (as it seemes) taken out of *John Cozens* his *Cozening* Devotions, (as they are rightly discovered to be by Orthodox men) and extracted out of divers Popish *Prayer-Bookes*' (sig. B2^{r}). The author may, however, have been merely embellishing his account with appropriately lurid speculations, since his pamphlet is known to have been based on a letter written by one Edward Lenton in 1634, describing a recent visit to Little Gidding, in which he makes no reference to the *Devotions*. Cf. A. Maycock, *Chronicles of Little Gidding* (London, 1954), p. 41.

45. Borrowings from the *Devotions* in the 1662 Prayer Book, most of them by way of *The Durham Book*, are given below in the Commentary; they are described, but with a few slight inaccuracies, in F. E. Brightman's *The English Rite* (London, 1915).

An examination of *The Durham Book* indicates that, in fact, Cosin intended a good deal more from the *Devotions* to pass into the Prayer Book at the Restoration than he was in the end able to persuade the revisers to accept. The *Durham Book* proposals which derive from the *Devotions* follow. Page references refer first to the number of each *Durham Book* proposal, followed in some cases by a number in round brackets indicating the stage of drafting—these following Cuming's numbering—and, in square brackets, the page number of the equivalent items in this text.

A Table of the moveable feasts. RULES to know wn the moveable Feasts & holy Dayes begin. 36 (iii, vi); 37, 38 [35]

A Table of ye vigils, fasts, & dayes of Abstinence to be observed in the yeere. 40, 51, 53 [36–37, 305]

times in ye year, wherein Marriages are not usually solemnized. 41 (ii); 53 (vi) [37, 305–6]

Calendar: restoration of the Conversion of S. Paul, and S. Barnabas, to red-letter status. 43 [20, 25]

Calendar: to 'John Evang.' is added 'ante port. Lat.', and to 'S. Peter Apost.' is added '& St. Paul'. 43 [24, 25]

Morning Prayer: the addition of 1 John 1. 9 to the penitential sentences. 62 [235]

Morning Prayer: the canticle headings are expanded to 'this Hymne of S. Ambrose (Te Deum laudamus)' and 'Benedictus (the Song of Zachary)'. 80 (i); 82 (i, iii) [92, 99]

Morning Prayer: the alteration of 'Ponce Pilate' to 'Pontius Pilate'. 85 [100]

Morning and Evening Prayer: alteration of rubric before the three collects, to 'Then shall be said the Collect of the day . . . And these two Collects folowing' 88 (i); 101 (ii) [102]

Morning Prayer. The Second Collect for Peace: O God, Which art the Authour . . . 89 [102]

Morning Prayer: The prayer, 'Almighty God, who hast promised to heare ye petitions . . .', as a conclusion to the Prayers after the third Collect. 92 (ii) [294]

Evening Prayer: the canticle headings are expanded to 'Magnificat (ye Song of the blessed Virgin Mary)' and 'Nunc Dimittis (ye Song of Simeon)'. 97 (ii); 99 [148, 153]

Litany: the addition of 'after Morning prayer' to the introductory rubric. 108 (i) [171]

Litany: the alteration of the opening of 'A Prayer for the Prince, and other the Kings children' to 'Almighty God, the fountaine of all goodnes'. 122 [252]

Litany: various phrases in the altered 'Prayer for the Clergie, & their charge', 'Almighty . . . God, who didst powre out upon thy Apostles the great & merveilous Gifts of thy H. Spirit, & from whom all spirituall graces & gifts doe proceed, send downe upon our Bishops, the Pastors of thy Church, & all others . . .'. 123 (i) [116, 261, 263]

Prayers & Thanksgivings upon severall occasions: the first of the two Embertide prayers. 131 (i) [261]

Collects, Epistles, and Gospels: the headings 'The NATIVITIE of our LORD' and 'Thursday before Easter commonly called Mandie Thursday'. 147 (i); 168 [31, 197]

Collects, Epistles, and Gospels: the ending of the Collect for Easter Even. 172 [201, and see Appendix, 309]

Collects, Epistles, and Gospels: the Collect for the Rogation Days. 181 (i) [260]

Holy Communion: the heading of the prayer for the Church, 'Let us offer up our prayers & praises for the good estate of Christs Catholick Church', and in this prayer various phrases, 'thy holy Name . . . & the Lights of the World in their severall Generations; most humbly beseeching thee, that we may have grace to follow ye example of'. 221 (ii); 224 [284–5]

Holy Communion: the heading, 'The Prayer of Consecration'. 239 (ii); 241 [228]

Holy Communion: the form of the words of administration when 'the Priest that celebrateth, first receive the holy Communion'. 251 (i) [232]

Holy Communion: the rubric at the communion, 'And here each person receiving shall say, [Amen.]' 253 [232]

Holy Communion: two of the sentences to be sung during the Communion, Rom. 11. 33 and Ps. 103. 1–5. 259 (i) [233]

Holy Communion: Prayer of Oblation, various phrases, 'commanded . . . most blessed Passion and Sacrifice . . . into Heaven . . . now represented before'. 263, 264 [230]

Catechism: the phrase, 'To honour & worship him with ye outward reverence of my body'. 345 (i) [43]

Ordinal: the hymn, 'Veni Creator', 'as tis corrected'. 428 [111]

46. An untraced copy in the hands of Messrs. Robinson of Newcastle in 1845 was used for the text printed in Cosin's *Works*. This copy lacked B11 and X1. D12 was the cancellans, as was X5. Cf. Hanson, p. 286, whom we have followed for all these bibliographic details.

SIGLA

1	1627	Bodleian Library
2	1627	Bodleian Library
3	1627	British Museum
4	1635	Jesus College, Oxford
5	1638	British Museum
6	1655	Peterhouse, Cambridge
7	1664	British Museum
8	1672	Houghton Library, Harvard University

A
COLLECTION
OF
PRIVATE
DEVOTIONS:
IN
THE PRACTISE OF
THE ANCIENT
CHVRCH,
CALLED
THE HOVRES
OF PRAYER.

As they were after this maner published by Authoritie of Q. ELIZ. 1560.

TAKEN
Out of the Holy Scriptures, the Ancient Fathers, and the diuine Seruice of our own Church.

LONDON,
Printed by R. YOVNG. 1627.

Printed title-page of the first edition

TEXT

826614 B

THE APPROBATION.

FEBR. 22. 1626.

I Have read over this Booke, which for the encrease of private Devotions I do think may wel be printed, and therefore doe give Licence for the same.

GEO: LONDON.

ENGRAVED TITLE-PAGE (PLATE II). *As shown* *1 2 3*: *new, but similar engraving* A / Collection / of / Private devotions, / in / the practice of / the Ancient / Church. / called / the Houres / of Prayer / *4 6*: *om.* *5 7*: *a new design with Royal Arms, with date* Anno 1664 *8*

PRINTED TITLE-PAGE (PLATE III). Prayer: Praiers *6* were after: were much after *2 3 4 5 6*

THE APPROBATION. *om.* *7 8* *I do think*: *I think* *2 3 4 5 6*

THE PRINTER
to the READER.

GENTLE READER,

As it oftentimes falleth out in many Occurrences and Actions, that things are distasted before they are well knowne; and that (through false reports, and mistakings in them, that either judge before they see, or out of disaffection make sinister construction of that which deserveth better understanding) good intentions are wrested, and truth impeached: So hath it befalne this handfull of Collections for private Devotions; which was compiled out of sundrie warranted bookes, for the private use of an Honourable well disposed friend, without any meaning to make the same publike to the World; though (to save the labour and trouble of writing copies, to bee sparingly communicated to some few friends) a certaine number of them, by leave and warrant of the Ordinary, *were printed at the charge of the partie, for whose only use the same was collected. It hath therfore seemed good to* AUTHORITY, *to give leave to the reprinting therof, and permitting the same to be sold, to such as please to buy it, only for private use, as in former times way hath been given to the printing of privat prayer-books. Whereby it is presumed, all well disposed Christians may receive satisfaction, that there is not in it such cause of dislike, as it seemeth hath been rumored. And for the avoiding of all mistakings hereafter, care is had to amend such escapes, as either by the Printers hast, or the Correctors oversight were committed. Only the Collector hereof, & others that were therewith acquainted*

THE PRINTER TO THE READER. *Not in* 1: *placed after* '*The Blessing*' 2: *after* '*The Approbation*', *as here* 3: *after* '*Of the Calendar*' 6: *om.* 4 5 7 8. *The present text follows* 2

before the printing of the booke (who are as ready to engage their credits, and lives, in defence of the Faith of the present Church of England, by Law established, and in opposition of Poperie, and Romish superstition, as any others) doe with griefe observe the malevolency of some dispositions of these times; with whom a slip, or misprision of a word, or two, as liable to a faire, and charitable understanding, as otherwise, doth not only lose the thankes due for all the good conteined in the Worke: but also purchase to the Author a reprochfull imputation of way making to Popish Devotion, and apish imitation of Romish superstition. And howsoever he may be requited for his paines herein, he shall never depart from his good intention of wishing that the Reader may at all times, and for all occasions be assisted with divine grace, obtained by continuall prayer. And as for the misdeeming censures and detractions of any, he feareth them not, but rather hopeth that his prayers to God for them will bee more beneficiall to them, than any their censures, or detractions can be prejudiciall to him: Who doth in this and in all things else humbly submit himselfe to the judgement of the Church of England, whereof he is a member, and, though inferiour unto most, yet a faithfull Minister.

3 *others*: *other* 6

THE TABLE.

THE TABLE. *Only 7 gives this position; other editions prefer the last leaves of the text*

FINIS.

THE PREFACE.

TOUCHING PRAYER, AND THE FORMES OF PRAYER:

The Fountaine and Wellspring from which they all proceed, being that perfect Forme of Prayer *which Christ taught his Disciples.*

FOr the good & welfare of our soules, there is not in Christian Religion any thing of like continuall use and force throughout every Houre of our lives, as is the ghostly Exercise of *Prayer* and *Devotion.*

An Exercise it was, which the holy Apostles had often observed their Lord & Master to use, *Ever and anon to be still at his* PRAYERS; in the [a]*Morning* before day, in the [b]*Evening* before night, and otherwhiles to goe out, and spend the [c]*whole Night* in Prayer: that had it not been a matter of some principall dignitie and importance, had there not beene some excellent benefites to be got by it, doubtlesse Hee would never have prayed so often, & so much as he did.

a Marc. 1. 35.
b Mat. 14. 23.
c Luc. 6. 12.

And therefore they desired of Him to be taught a *Forme of Prayer*, as S. JOHN the *Baptist* had also taught

11–12 *Devotion.* / An Exercise it was, which: *Devotion.* / Which *7 8*
12–13 had often observed: observing *7 8*
13 Master to use: Master frequently to use *7 8*
13–14 *Ever and anon* . . . PRAYERS: *om. 7 8*
14 a Marc. 1. 35.: a Marc. 1. 25. *6*
15 goe out, and: *om. 7 8*
16 Prayer: that: Prayer. And *4 5 6*
16–20 Prayer: that . . . did.: Praier, accounted it their duty also to be followers of his example and practice, as being a matter of high importance, and great benefit thereby to be obtained. *7 8*
21 And therefore they: The Apostles therefore[d] *2 3 4 5 6*
21–22 desired . . . *Prayer*,: addressed themselves to Him, desiring Him to teach them how to pray, *7 8*

his Disciples; and a *Forme* Christ taught them, so absolute & so [d]perfect, as never was the like made before; which, from him who made it then, was ever afterwards called THE LORDS PRAYER.

d Luc. 11. 2. Mat. 6. 9.

A *Prayer*, whereby we have not only Christ's own *Name* to countenance our sutes, (*in whose name if wee aske any thing, we shal have it*, saith the [e]Gospell,) but Christ's owne *Words* also, who himselfe is our [f]Advocate, and being best acquainted with the Lawes and Phrases of his Father's Court, hath drawne up such a Bill for us, both for matter and forme, as shall make our supplications acceptable & prevalent with Almightie God. And though men should speake with Angels tongues, yet words so pleasing to the eares of God, as those which the Sonne of God did compose, cannot possibly be uttered; nor anie Prayers so well framed, as those that are made by his Patterne.

e Joh. 16. 23.
f 1. Joh. 2. 1.

It is for this cause called by the Fathers [h]*The Prayer of All Prayers*, and the *Rule* or *Square* whereby all our Petitions are to bee formed; having likewise beene thus used in all ages of the Church, not only as a common part of her Praiers and Service, but as the chiefe & fundamentall part of them, the Ground whereupon she builds,

h S. AUG. *Serm.* 2. *post Pent.* TERT. *de* Orat. *c.* 9. *Legitima Oratio*, The Prayer that is a Law to all other Prayers.

1 Disciples; . . . them,: Disciples. For which end and purpose, our Saviour taught and [d]prescribed them a *Form of Praier*, *7 8*
2 [d]perfect,: perfect, *2 3 4 5 6 7*
3 afterwards: afterward *7 8*
5–6 Christ's own *Name*: Christ's *Name* *7 8*
7 *we shal* . . . [e]Gospell,): as we ought to doe, he hath assured us in his Holy [e]Gospel that *we shall obtain it*;) *7 8*
8 *Words*: *word* *7 8*
10–12 hath drawne up . . . prevalent with: hath both for matter and form drawn up such supplications for us as will be most available and prevalent *7 8*
11 supplications: supplication *6*
13 Angels: Angels' *6*
14 as: than *7 8*
15–16 nor . . . so: nor can any Praiers be so *7 8*
17 his: this *6*: his blessed *7 8*

the Patterne wherby she frames, and the Complement wherewith she perfects all the rest of her heavenly Devotions, framing them all, as this is framed, with much efficacie, though not with any superfluitie of words.

Thus we begin at this day all our Church-Services with the *Lords Prayer*, and lay it as a foundation whereon to build the rest of our Petitions that follow, sometimes continuing (as after the *Creed*) and somtimes perfecting (as after the *blessed Sacrament*) our most holy devotions with it; thereby supplying with the fulness of that one, whatsoever may be defective in all our other prayers. *Præmissâ legitimâ Oratione* (saith TERTUL.) *quasi fundamento accidentium &c.* [This is the Law wee goe by, the ground-work & the Guide of all those holy Praiers that Christians use to make.]

A part of which ancient Pietie are THESE DAILY DEVOTIONS AND PRAYERS that hereafter follow; PRAYERS which after the same maner and DIVISION OF *HOURES as heere they are, having heretofore been published among us by HIGH AND SACRED AUTHORITY, are now also renewed, and more fully set forth againe, as for many other, so chiefly for these foure Reasons.

**Horarium Regiâ authoritate editum, &c.* 1. The Horarie set forth with the Queenes Authority 1560 and renewed 1573. Imp. with priviledge at LOND. by WILLIAM SEERS.

1. The first is to continue & preserve the authority of the ancient *Lawes*, and old godly *Canons* of the Church, which were made and set forth for this purpose, that men before they set themselves to pray, might know what to say, & avoid, as neer as might be, all extemporall effusions of irkesome & indigested Prayers, which they use to make, that herein are subject to no

2 heavenly: *om. 6*

12 (saith TERTUL.): (saith *TERT.)+*in margin *Ubi supra. 2 3 4 5*: (saith *TERT. *Ubi supra. quasi* etc. *6*

18 which after: which for the most part, after *2 3 4 5 6*

good order or forme of words, but pray both what, & how, & when they list. CAROL. MAG. IN LEGIB. *Orationes, quæ ab Ecclesiâ probatæ non sunt, rejiciantur.* (i.) [Let no Praiers be used but those which are allowed by the Church. MICR. *de eccles. obser. cap.* 5.] CONC. CARTHAG. 3. can. 23. *Quascunque sibi preces aliquis describit, non eis utatur, nisi prius eas cum instructioribus contulerit.* (i.) [What Prayers soever any man hath framed for himselfe, let him first acquaint those that are wise and learned with them, before hee presumeth to use them.]

And the reason is given in the 12. *Canon* of the MILEVITAN COUNCEL, which was also repeated in the 70. *Canon* of the COUNCEL of AFRICK, *Ne forte aliquid contra fidem, vel per ignorantiam vel per minus studium sit compositum.* (i) [Lest eyther thorough ignorance or thorough lesse care than is fit, any thing bee said which is not consonant to the faith of Christs Church.]

And that men may not thinke, these Rules are to be applyed to *Publicke Prayers* only, and not to *Private*; let them weigh those words in the COUNCELL of CARTHAGE, [*Quascunque Sibi preces, &c. The Prayers which a man makes for Himself &c.*] And let them consider, that when Christ had bidden us enter into our chamber and pray *privately*, presently hee sets us a *form* to pray by even there in secret, *Matth. 6. 7. 9.* By which passages, those Prayers are chiefly allowed and recommended unto us, (for all sudden and godly ejaculations are not to bee condemned) which with good advise and meditation are

2–3 list. . . . *Orationes,*: list. Therefore among the Ecclesiastical Laws made in the time of *Carolus Magnus* we find this to be one; *Orationes,* *7 8*

5 *cap.* 5.: *cap.* 4. *8*

22 *makes*: *maketh* *2 3 4 5 6*

25 *Matth. 6. 7. 9.*: S. *Matth.* 6. 6, 9. *7 8*

27 us, (for . . . are not: us (wee say *chiefly*; for all kind of ejaculatory or sudden, devoute, and holy Prayers are not *2 3 4 5 6*

framed before hand by Them that best know what belong thereunto. That so through this meanes the worthiest part of our Christian duetie to God-ward might suffer no such scandal & disgrace, as otherwhiles it is forced to do; & that when we speak to, or call upon the awfull Majesty of Almighty God, wee might be sure to speake in the grave & pious language of Christs CHURCH, which hath evermore beene guided by the Spirit of God & the holy Ghost; & not to lose our selves with confusion in any sudden, abrupt, or rude dictates, which are framed by Private Spirits, and Ghosts of our owne. In regard wherof, our very *Priests & Deacons* themselves are for their *private* & daily *Prayers* *enjoyned to say the *Morning* & the *Evening Devotions* of the CHURCH; and when at any time they pray or bidde the *Prayers* before their *Sermons*, there is a *set forme* of words [p]prescribed for them to use, that they also might know, it is not so lawfull for them to pray of their own heads, or suddenly to say what they please themselves.

2. The Second is to let the world understand that they who give it out, & accuse us here in ENGLAND to have set up a **New Church*, and a *New Faith*, to have abandoned *All the Ancient Formes of Piety and Devotion*, to have taken away all the *Religious Exercises and Prayers of our Forefathers*, to have despised *all the old Ceremonies*, & cast behinde us the *Blessed Sacraments of Christs Catholicke Church*: that these men doe little else but betray

**Preface before the Com. Booke* in fine. *All Priests and Deacons shall be bound daily to say the Matins and the Evensong, either openly or privately*, as it was of old ordained in the Councel at VENICE under LEO the first, *can.* 14. & in the Councel of MENTZ, *can.* 57. p *Injunctions*, cap. ult. *and* can. 55. *in the Booke of Canons and Constitutions ecclesiasticall.*

*SANDERS de schism. Angl. CALVIN. TURCIS. BRIST. Demon. CERTAIN ARTIC. or Forcible Reas. *Art.* 1. and the common conceit of most *Recusant Papists.*

2 belong: belongs *7 8*

7 language: languages *6*

9 God & the: God, the *2 3 4 5 6* *The variant in 2 is the cancellans, the cancellandum, identical with 1, being also included* (*A7*[r])

12 wherof,: of *6*

14 *Devotions*: *Devotion 6*

15 pray or bidde: pray or (as we say) bid *2 3 4*: pray, or (as we say) bid *5*: pray (as we) bid *6*

16 *Prayers*: *Praier 6*

16 *om.* their: *2 3 4 5 6*

their owne infirmities, and have more violence and wil, than reason or judgment for what they say; the common Accusations, which, out of the abundance of those partiall affections, that transport them the wrong way, they are pleased to bring so frequently against us, being but the bare Reports of such people as either doe not, or will not understand us, what we are.

3. The Third is, That they who are this way already religiously given, and whom earnest lets & impediments do often hinder from being partakers of the *Publicke*, might have here a Daily & Devoute order of *Private Prayer*, wherein to exercise themselves, & to spend *some houres* of the day at least, (as the olde godly Christians were wont to doe) in Gods holy worship & service; not imploying themselves so much to *talke* & dispute, as to *practise* religion, & to *live* like Christians; the continuall & curious disquisition of manie unnecessarie Questions among us, being nothing else but either the new seeds, or the olde fruits of malice, & by consequence the enemie of godlinesse, & the abatement of that true *Devotion*, wherwith God is more delighted, and a good soule more inflamed and comforted, than with all the busie subtilties of the world. In which sense S. AUSTIN was wont to say, that **The pious and devout, though unlearned, went to heaven, whiles other men, trusting to their learning, disputed it quite away.*

*S. AUG. *Veniunt indocti & rapiunt cœlum: & nos cum doctrinis nostris detrudimur ad infernum.*

4. The last is, That those who perhaps are but coldly this way yet affected, might by others example be stirred up to the like heavenly duty of performing their *Daily* & Christian *Devotions* to Almighty God, as being

2 reason: *reason + *in margin* *As may also appeare by the publick Liturgie & other divine offices of our Church, agreeable to them which the Ancients used. *2 3 4 5 6*

17 disquisition: disquisitions *7 8*

a work of all others the most acceptable to his divine Majestie.

In so doing, wee shall all give evident testimony to the world, *whose Servants we are*, and wherein our *chiefest delight* doth consist; wee shall enjoy a perpetuall *Communion* with the *Saints* triumphant, as well as militant, & we shal have just cause to conceive, That so much of our Life is *celestial* & *divine*, as we spend in this holy Exercise of *Prayer* and *Devotion.*

4 *chiefest*: *chief 6*
6 with: of *5*

THE CALENDAR,

WITH

THE FESTIVALLS

AND

FASTING DAYES

of the CHURCH.

And the memories of such holy men and Martyrs as are therein Registred.

Of the CALENDAR,
and the speciall use thereof in the Church of God.

THE CALENDAR *of the Church is as full of benefite as delight, unto such as are given to the due studie and contemplation thereof. For besides the admirable order and disposition of Times, which are necessary for the better transacting of all Ecclesiasticall and Secular affaires, it hath in it a very beautifull distinction of the Dayes and Seasons, whereof* [a]some are chosen out and sanctified, and others are put among the dayes of the weeke to number.

But the chiefe use of it in the Church (*saith S.* [b]AUSTIN) *is to preserve a solemne memory, and to continue in their due time, sometimes a* weekly *and sometimes an* annual commemoration *of those excellent and high Benefits, which* GOD *both by* [c]Himself, *his* [d]Son, *and his* [e]*blessed* Spirit, *one undivided* [f]Trinitie *hath bestowed upon mankind, for the founding and propagating of that Christian Faith & Religion, which we now professe.*

And this Faith of ours being no other than the very same, wherein the holy [g]Angels are *set to succour us, and which the glorious company of the* [h]Apostles, *the noble Armie of* [i]Martyrs, *and the goodly fellowship of other Gods* [k]Saints & *Servants, men famous in their generations before us, have some maintayned with the* sanctity *of their* lives, *and some sealed with the* innocencie *of their deaths; it is for this cause that the names of these holy and heavenly* Saints *are still preserved*

a Ecclus. 33. 7.
b S. Aug. *de Civit. Dei, l. 16. c. 4.*
c All the *Sundayes* of the yeere, &c.
d The *Feasts* of our Saviours *Nativity, Passion, Resurrection, Ascension &c.*
e Pentecost.
f Trinitie Sunday.
g S. Mich. *and* All Angels.
h *The* 12. Apostles *dayes.*
i S. Stephen *and others.*
k *The* Fathers a d primitive n Christians.

5–6 *due studie and contemplation*: *serious studie and due contemplation 2 3 4 5 6*
14 *time*: *season 2 3 4 5 6*
20 *And this Faith of ours . . . same*: *And forasmuch as this* Faith *of ours is no other than it was of old, even the verie same 2 3 4 5 6*
24 All Angels.: All Angels *day. 2 3 4 5 6*

in the CALENDAR *of the Church, there to remaine upon* Record *&* Register *(as of* [l]*old time they did) where they might also stand as sacred memorials of Gods mercy towards us, as* [m]*forcible witnesses of his Ancient Truth, as confirmations of the Faith which wee now professe to bee the same that theirs then was, as Provocations to the piety which they then practised, and as everlasting Records, to shew* whose blessed servants *they were on earth, that are now like the* Angels of God *in heaven.*

l Tertul. *de Cor. mil.* S. Cypr. *Ep.* 37 Pont. Diac. *in vit.* Cyp.

m Euseb. *Hist. eccl. l.* 4. *c.* 15. S. Basil *in Ascet. c.* 40.

Howbeit, forasmuch as in processe of time the multitude of Men *and* Women, *reputed* Holy, *in this kinde, became so exceeding numerous, that* all *the* dayes *of the* yeare *would not have beene sufficient for a severall* commemoration *of them; it was the great wisedome and moderation of those religious grave* Prelates, *by whom God (of his especiall blessing to our Church above others) did reforme such things, as were many wayes amisse here among us, to chuse* [n]One solemne day *alone, wherein to magnifie God for the generality of* All his Saints *together; and to retain some few* selected daies *in every* Month *for the special memory of* others, *both* holy Persons *and* holy Actions, *which they observed not* our people *alone, but the* universal Church *of Christ also, to be most affected unto, & best acquainted withall: hereby avoyding onely the burthen and the unnecessarie number of* Festivall dayes; *not disallowing the multitude of Gods true* Martyrs *and* Saints, *whose Memorials wee are to solemnize howsoever in the* generall Festival *of* ALL SAINTS DAY, *as by the* Proper Lessons, *the* Collect, Epistle, *and* Gospell *then appointed in our publike* Liturgie, *doth most evidently appeare.*

n All-Saints day.

5 *theirs*: *om.* 6
9 *forasmuch as*: *forasmuch also as* 2 3 4 5 6
14 *by whom*: *whom by* 6
14 *especiall*: *special* 6
14 *to*: *unto* 2 3 4 5 6
16 *here*: *om.* 6
19 holy: *om.* 5

JANUARY HATH XXXI. DAYES.

Num. of dayes.				The Festivals and Saints dayes &c.	Yeere of our Lord
Calends		A	1	Circumcision of our LORD.	1
Non.	4	b	2		
Non.	3	c	3		
Pr. Non.		d	4		
Nones		e	5		
Id.	8	f	6	Epiphanie of our LORD.	1
Id.	7	g	7		
Id.	6	A	8	LUCIAN a Priest of *Antioch* and	307
Id.	5	b	9	a Martyr.	
Id.	4	c	10		
Id.	3	d	11		
Pr. Id.		e	12		
Ides		f	13	HILARY, the Bishop of *Poitiers*	337
Ca. 19 *Fe.*		g	14	in *France*.	
Cal.	18	A	15		
Cal.	17	b	16		
Cal.	16	c	17		
Cal.	15	d	18	PRISCA, a Rom. Virg. & Mar.	45
Cal.	14	e	19		
Cal.	13	f	20	FABIAN, B. of *Rome* & Mart.	251
Cal.	12	g	21	AGNES, Rom. Virg. & Mart.	304
Cal.	11	A	22	VINCENT, a Deacon of *Spaine*	301
Cal.	10	b	23	and Martyr.	
Cal.	9	c	24		
Cal.	8	d	25	Conversion of S. PAUL.	37
Cal.	7	e	26		
Cal.	6	f	27		
Cal.	5	g	28		
Cal.	4	A	29		
Cal.	3	b	30		
Pr. Cal.		c	31		

2–3 { The Festivals and: The Festivals of *2 6*
The Festivals and Saints dayes &c.: The Festivals and Fasting daies, with the names of the Saints, &c. *4 5 6 variants which are repeated for each month in these three editions*

33 *after* 30 *add* King CHARLES Mart. 1648 *7 8*

FEBRUARY HATH XXVIII. DAYES.

And when it is Bissext. or Leape-yeare
it hath XXIX. dayes.

Numb. of dayes.				The Festivals and Saints dayes &c.	Yeere of our Lord
Calends		d	1	*Fast.*	
Non.	4	e	2	Purific. of MARY the Virg.	1
Non.	3	f	3	BLASE an *Armenian* Bishop and	286
Pr. Non.		g	4	Martyr.	
Nones		A	5	AGATHE, a Virgin in *Sicily* and	253
Id.	8	b	6	Martyr.	
Id.	7	c	7		
Id.	6	d	8		
Id.	5	e	9		
Id.	4	f	10		
Id.	3	g	11		
Pr. Id.		A	12		
Ides		b	13		
Cl. 16 *Ma*		c	14	VALENTINE, a Priest of *Rome*	45
Cal.	15	d	15	and Martyr.	
Cal.	14	e	16		
Cal.	13	f	17		
Cal.	12	g	18		
Cal.	11	A	19		
Cal.	10	b	20		
Cal.	9	c	21		
Cal.	8	d	22		
Cal.	7	e	23	*Fast.*	
Cal.	6	f	24	MATTHIAS Apost. & Mar.	66
Cal.	5	g	25		
Cal.	4	A	26		
Cal.	3	b	27		
Pr. Cal.		c	28		

2 Bissext.: Bissextile *5 6*
7 of MARY the Virg.: of MARY the B. Virg. *2 3 6 7 8*: of the B. Virg. *4 5*
8 BLASE . . . Martyr.: *om. entirely 7 8*
19 a Priest of *Rome*: Bishop *7 8*

MARCH HATH XXXI. DAYES.

Numb. of dayes.				The Festivals and Saints dayes &c.	Yeere of our Lord
Calends		d	1	DAVID Bish. of S. *Davids.*	584
Non.	6	e	2	CEDDE, or CHAD, Bishop of	672
Non.	5	f	3	*Lichfield.*	
Non.	4	g	4		
Non.	3	A	5		
Pr. Non.		b	6		
Nones		c	7	PERPETUA, a Virg. & Mart.	254
Id.	8	d	8	often mentioned by TERTUL-	
Id.	7	e	9	LIAN and S. AUGUST.	
Id.	6	f	10		
Id.	5	g	11	*Equinoctiall.*	
Id.	4	A	12	S. GREGORY the Great, B. of	604
Id.	3	b	13	*Rome.*	
Prid. Id.		c	14		
Ides		d	15		
Cl. 17 *Ap.*		e	16		
Cal.	16	f	17		
Cal.	15	g	18	EDWARD the King of the *West-*	978
Cal.	14	A	19	*Saxon.*	
Cal.	13	b	20		
Cal.	12	c	21	S. BENEDICT, the famous Abbot	542
Cal.	11	d	22	in *Italy.*	
Cal.	10	e	23		
Cal.	9	f	24	*Fast.*	
Cal.	8	g	25	The Annunciation of the Virgin	0
Cal.	7	A	26	MARY.	
Cal.	6	b	27	The day of K. CHARLES his	1625
Cal.	5	c	28	Inauguration.	
Cal.	4	d	29		
Cal.	3	e	30		
Pr. Cal.		f	31		

4 Bish. of S. *Davids.*: Arch-B. of *Menevia. 7 8*
16 *Rome.*: *Rome* and Confessor. *7 8*
21–22 *West-Saxon*: *West-Saxons all editions*
28–29 of the Virgin MARY.: of the B. Virgin MARY. *2 3 4 5 6*: of MARY. *7 8*
30–31 The day of K. CHARLES his Inauguration. 1625: *om. 7 8*

APRILL HATH XXX. DAYES.

Numb. of dayes.				The Festivals and Saints dayes, &c.	Yeere of our Lord
Calends		g	1		
Non.	4	A	2		
Non.	3	b	3	RICHARD, Bish. of *Chichester.*	1253
Pr. Non.		c	4	S. AMBROSE, Bish. of *Millan.*	397
Nones		d	5		
Id.	8	e	6		
Id.	7	f	7		
Id.	6	g	8		
Id.	5	A	9		
Id.	4	b	10		
Id.	3	c	11		
Pr. Id.		d	12		
Ides		e	13		
Cl. 18 *Ma*		f	14		
Cal.	17	g	15		
Cal.	16	A	16		
Cal.	15	b	17		
Cal.	14	c	18		
Cal.	13	d	19	ALPHEGE, Archb. of *Canterbury.*	1006
Cal.	12	e	20		
Cal.	11	f	21		
Cal.	10	g	22		
Cal.	9	A	23	S. GEORGE, the famous Mart.	286
Cal.	8	b	24	und. DIOCLETIAN.	
Cal.	7	c	25	S. MARK, Evang. & Martyr.	63
Cal.	6	d	26		
Cal.	5	e	27		
Cal.	4	f	28		
Cal.	3	g	29		
Pri. Cal.		A	30		

MAY HATH XXXI. DAYES.

Numb. of dayes.			The Festivals and Saints dayes &c.	Yeere of our Lord
Calends	b	1	S. PHIL. & JAC. Ap. & Mar.	53 & 63
Non. 6	c	2		
Non. 5	d	3	*Invention of the* CROSSE.	326
Non. 4	e	4		
Non. 3	f	5		
Pr. Non.	g	6	S. JOHN Evang. *Port Latin.*	98
Nones	A	7		
Id. 8	b	8		
Id. 7	c	9		
Id. 6	d	10		
Id. 5	e	11		
Id. 4	f	12		
Id. 3	g	13		
Pr. Id.	A	14		
Ides	b	15		
Cl. 17 *Jun*	c	16		
Cal. 16	d	17		
Cal. 15	e	18		
Cal. 14	f	19	DUNSTANE, Archb. of *Cant.*	988
Cal. 13	g	20		
Cal. 12	A	21		
Cal. 11	b	22		
Cal. 10	c	23		
Cal. 9	d	24		
Cal. 8	e	25		
Cal. 7	f	26	AUST. the first Arch. of *Cant.*	608
Cal. 6	g	27		
Cal. 5	A	28		
Cal. 4	b	29		
Cal. 3	c	30		
Pr. Cal.	d	31		

9 S. JOHN Evang. *Port Latin.*: S. JOHN Evang. boyled in a Caldron of hot oyle before *Port Latin*, in *Rome*. *2 3 4 5 6*: S. JOHN Evang. ante Port Latin. *7 8*

30 *after* 27 *add* Ven. BEDE, Presbyter. 735 *7 8*

32 *after* 29 *add* CHARLES II. Nativity 1630 *7 8*

33 *after* 30 *add* and Return. 1660 *7 8*

JUNE HATH XXX. DAYES.

Numb. of dayes.				The Festivals and Saints dayes &c.	Yeere of our Lord
Calends		e	1	NICHOMEDE a Priest of *Rome*	41
Non.	4	f	2	and Martyr.	
Non.	3	g	3		
Pr. Non.		A	4		
Nones		b	5	BONIFACE, an Englishman,	752
Id.	8	c	6	Bishop of *Mentz* and Martyr.	
Id.	7	d	7		
Id.	6	e	8		
Id.	5	f	9		
Id.	4	g	10		
Id.	3	A	11	S. BARNABE Apost. & Mart.	50
Prid. Id.		b	12		
Ides		c	13	*Solstice.*	
Cal.	18 *Jul*	d	14		
Cal.	17	e	15		
Cal.	16	f	16		
Cal.	15	g	17		
Cal.	14	A	18		
Cal.	13	b	19		
Cal.	12	c	20	Translation of S. EDWARD	990
Cal.	11	d	21	King of the *West-Saxons*.	
Cal.	10	e	22		
Cal.	9	f	23	*Fast.*	
Cal	8	g	24	Nativity of S. JOHN BAPT.	0
Cal.	7	A	25		
Cal.	6	b	26		
Cal.	5	c	27		
Cal.	4	d	28	*Fast.*	
Cal.	3	e	29	S. PETER, Apost. & Martyr,	68
Pr. Cal.		f	30	with S. PAUL.	

16 *Solstice*: Summer *Solstice* *2 3 4 5 6*
20 *after* 17 *add* S. ALBAN Martyr. 286 *7 8*

July hath XXXI. Dayes.

Numb. of dayes.				The Festivals and Saints dayes, &c.	Yeere of our Lord
Calends		g	1	Visitation of MARY. *Luc.* 1.	0
Non.	6	A	2		
Non.	5	b	3	Translation of S. MARTIN the	446
Non.	4	c	4	Bishop of *Towers* in *France*.	
Non.	3	d	5		
Pr. Non.		e	6		
Nones		f	7		
Id.	8	g	8		
Id.	7	A	9		
Id.	6	b	10		
Id.	5	c	11		
Id.	4	d	12		
Id.	3	e	13		
Pr. Id.		f	14		
Ides		g	15	S. SWITHUNE Bish. of *Winchester*.	862
Cl. 17 *Au*		A	16		
Cal.	16	b	17		
Cal.	15	c	18		
Cal.	14	d	19		
Cal.	13	e	20	S. MARGARET, Virgin and	243
Cal.	12	f	21	Martyr at *Antioch*.	
Cal.	11	g	22	S. MARY MAGDALEN, *Luc.* 7.	84
Cal.	10	A	23	*Luc.* 8. *Joh.* 20.	
Cal.	9	b	24	*Fast.*	
Cal.	8	c	25	S. JAMES Apost. & Martyr.	42
Cal.	7	d	26	S. ANNE, mother to the Virgin	1
Cal.	6	e	27	MARY.	
Cal.	5	f	28		
Cal.	4	g	29		
Cal.	3	A	30		
Pr. Cal.		b	31		

4 Visitation of MARY.: Visitation of the B. Virgin MARY, *7 8*
7 *France.*: *France*, and Confessor. *7 8*
18 *Winchester.*: *Winchester* transl. *7 8*
29 the Virgin: the Blessed Virg. *4 5 6*

August hath XXXI. Dayes.

Numb. of dayes.				The Festivals and Saints dayes &c.	Yeere of our Lord
Calends		c	1	*Lammas* day.	43
Non.	4	d	2		
Non.	3	e	3		
Pr. Non.		f	4		
Nones		g	5		
Id.	8	A	6	Transfig. of our Lord. *Lu.* 9	33
Id.	7	b	7	Name of Jesus. *Mat.* 1. *Phi.* 2	1
Id.	6	c	8		
Id.	5	d	9		
Id.	4	e	10	S. Laurence, Archdeacon of	259
Id.	3	f	11	*Rome* and Martyr.	
Pr. Id.		g	12		
Ides		A	13		
Cl. 19 *Sep*		b	14		
Cal.	18	c	15		
Cal.	17	d	16		
Cal.	16	e	17		
Cal.	15	f	18		
Cal.	14	g	19		
Cal.	13	A	20		
Cal.	12	b	21		
Cal.	11	c	22		
Cal.	10	d	23	*Fast.*	
Cal.	9	e	24	S. Barthol. Apost. & Mart.	73
Cal.	8	f	25		
Cal.	7	g	26		
Cal.	6	A	27		
Cal.	5	b	28	S. Augustin Bish. of *Hippo.*	432
Cal.	4	c	29	Beheading of S. John Baptist.	31
Cal.	3	d	30	*Matth.* 14.	
Pr. Cal.		e	31		

SEPTEMBER HATH XXX. DAYES.

Numb. of dayes.				The Festivals and Saints dayes &c.	Yeere of our Lord
Calends		f	1	S. GILES, Abbot of *Marborn* in	750
Non.	4	g	2	*France.*	
Non.	3	A	3		
Pr. Non.		b	4		
Nones		c	5		
Id.	8	d	6		
Id.	7	e	7	ENURCHUS, B. of *Orleans* in *France.*	374
Id.	6	f	8	Nativitie of MARY.	14 before Christ
Id.	5	g	9		
Id.	4	A	10		
Id.	3	b	11		
Prid. Id.		c	12		
Ides		d	13		
Cal.	18 *Oc*	e	14	HOLY CROSSE day.	614
Cal.	17	f	15	*Equinoctiall.*	
Cal.	16	g	16		
Cal.	15	A	17	S. LAMBERT, Bishop of *Liege*	700
Cal.	14	b	18	and Martyr.	
Cal.	13	c	19		
Cal.	12	d	20	*Fast.*	
Cal.	11	e	21	S. MATTHEW Apost. Evang.	90
Cal.	10	f	22	and Martyr.	
Cal.	9	g	23		
Cal.	8	A	24		
Cal.	7	b	25		
Cal.	6	c	26	S. CYPRIAN, B. of *Carthage* and	288
Cal.	5	d	27	Martyr.	
Cal.	4	e	28		
Cal.	3	f	29	S. MICHAEL and all Angels.	0
Pr. Cal.		g	30	S. JEROM the famous *Priest.*	420

5 *France.*: *France*, Confessor *7 8*
29 S. Cyprian, B.: S. Cyprian, A.B. *7 8*
33 S. JEROM the famous *Priest.*: S. JEROM, *Priest*, C. & D. *7 8*

October hath XXXI. Dayes.

Numb. of dayes.				The Festivals and Saints dayes, &c.	Yeere of our Lord
Calends		A	1	REMIGIUS Bish. of *Rhemes*.	544
Non.	6	b	2		
Non.	5	c	3		
Non.	4	d	4		
Non.	3	e	5		
Pr. Non.		f	6	S. FAITH, Virg. of *Agenne* in	290
Nones		g	7	*France* and Martyr.	
Id.	8	A	8		
Id.	7	b	9	S. DENIS, the *Areopagite*, *Act.* 17.	99
Id.	6	c	10	B. of *Paris* & Mart.	
Id.	5	d	11		
Id.	4	e	12		
Id.	3	f	13	S. EDWARD the Confessor, King	1163
Pr. Id.		g	14	of *England* Transl.	
Ides		A	15		
Cl. 17 *No.*		b	16		
Cal.	16	c	17	S. AUDRY or ETHELDRED, first	680
Cal.	15	d	18	foundresse of *Ely* Abby.	
Cal.	14	e	19		
Cal.	13	f	20		
Cal.	12	g	21		
Cal.	11	A	22		
Cal.	10	b	23		
Cal.	9	c	24		
Cal.	8	d	25	CRISPINE, a *Romane* and Mart.	285
Cal.	7	e	26	at *Soyssons* in *France*.	
Cal.	6	f	27	*Fast.*	
Cal.	5	g	28	S. SIMON and JUDE Apost. and	64
Cal.	4	A	29	Martyrs.	
Cal.	3	b	30		
Pr. Cal.		c	31	*Fast.*	

20 S. AUDRY or ETHELDRED: S. ETHELDRED *2 3 4 5 6*
21 Abby.: Abby, Virg. *7 8*
21 *after* 18 *all editions add* S. LUKE Evang.

NOVEMBER HATH XXX. DAYES.

Num. of dayes.				The Festivals and Saints dayes &c.		Yeere o our Lord
Calends		d	1	ALL SAINTS day.	*inst.*	613
Non.	4	e	2			
Non.	3	f	3			
Pr. Non.		g	4			
Nones		A	5	Powder Treason day.		1605
Id.	8	b	6	LEONARD Confessor, a disciple		546
Id.	7	c	7	of REMIGIUS in *France.*		
Id.	6	d	8			
Id.	5	e	9			
Id.	4	f	10			
Id.	3	g	11	S. MARTIN, Bishop of *Towers* in		397
Pr. Id.		A	12	*France.*		
Ides		b	13	BRICE, Successor to S. MARTIN.		421
Cl. 18 *De.*		c	14			
Cal.	17	d	15	S. MACHUTE a Brittain, and B.		500
Cal.	16	e	16	of *Sainctes* in *France.*		
Cal.	15	f	17	S. HUGH Bish. of *Lincolne.*		1200
Cal.	14	g	18			
Cal.	13	A	19			
Cal.	12	b	20	S. EDMUND, K. & Mart. of		870
Cal.	11	c	21	whom S. *Edm. Bury* is named.		
Cal.	10	d	22	S. CECILY Virg. and Mart.		125
Cal.	9	e	23	S. CLEMENT, 1; B. of *Rome* and		92
Cal.	8	f	24	Martyr.		
Cal.	7	g	25	S. CATHERINE, Virgin and		305
Cal.	6	A	26	Martyr of *Alexandria* in		
Cal.	5	b	27	*Egypt.*		
Cal.	4	c	28			
Cal.	3	d	29	*Fast.*		
Pr. Cal.		e	30	S. ANDREW Apost. & Mar.		62

15 *France.*: *France,* Confess. *7 8*
18 S. MACHUTE: MACHUTUS, *7 8*
29 of: at *2 3*

December hath xxxi. Dayes.

Numb. of dayes.				The Festivals and Saints dayes &c.	Yeere of our Lord
Calends		f	1		
Non.	4	g	2		
Non.	3	A	3		
Pr. Non.		b	4		
Nones		c	5		
Id.	8	d	6	S. NICHOLAS, Bish. of *Myra* in	342
Id.	7	e	7	*Lycia.*	
Id.	6	f	8	Concept. of MARY.	1466
Id.	5	g	9		
Id.	4	A	10		
Id.	3	b	11		
Prid. Id.		c	12	*Winter Solstice.*	
Ides		d	13	S. LUCIE Virg. and Mart. at	305
Cl. 19 *Jan*		e	14	*Siracusa* in *Sicilie.*	
Cal.	18	f	15		
Cal.	17	g	16	O SAPIENTIA, an *Antiphona* an-	
Cal.	16	A	17	ciently sung in the Church	
Cal.	15	b	18	(for the honour of Christs	
Cal.	14	c	19	*Advent*) from this day til	
Cal.	13	d	20	*Christmas* Eve.	
Cal.	12	e	21	S. THOMAS, Apost. & Mart.	35
Cal.	11	f	22		
Cal.	10	g	23		
Cal.	9	A	24	*Fast.*	
Cal.	8	b	25	The Nativitie of our LORD.	1
Cal.	7	c	26	S. STEPHEN the first Mart.	34
Cal.	6	d	27	S. JOHN Evang. and Apost.	101
Cal.	5	e	28	INNOCENTS day.	1
Cal.	4	f	29		
Cal.	3	g	30		
Pr. Cal.		A	31	SILVESTER Bish. of *Rome.*	335

11 Concept. of MARY.: Concept. of B. V. MARY *7 8*
19–20 anciently: heretofore *2 3 4 5 6*
23 *after* 20 *add* Fast. *2 3 5 6*

A TABLE OF THE MOVEABLE FEASTS

WHICH HAVE NO FIXED PLACE IN THE *Calendar*, as the rest there mentioned have, but vary every yeere from one day of the *Moneth* to another, according to the position of *Easter*, and the Changes of the *Moone*,

WHEREUPON THAT day doth depend.

A TABLE OF THE MOVEABLE FEASTS, ETC. *The version of this section (pp. 33–37) printed in 7 8 differs considerably from that of the other editions. It is set out in the Appendix (pp. 299–306), its variants being ignored here. In 4 and 5 the Table runs from 1631 to 1660.*

A Table of the moveable Feasts.

The yeer of our L.	Septuages. Sunday.	Easter day.	Ascension day.	Whitsun-day.	Advent Sunday.
1626	Febr. 5	Apr. 9	May 18	May 28	Decem. 3
1627	Jan. 21	Mar. 25	3	13	2
1628	Feb. 10	Apr. 13	22	June 1	Nov. 30
1629	Febr. 1	Apr. 5	14	May 24	29
1630	Jan. 24	Mar. 28	6	16	28
1631	Febr. 6	Apr. 10	19	29	27
1632	Jan. 29	Apr. 1	10	20	Decem. 2
1633	Feb. 17	Apr. 21	30	June 9	1
1634	Febr. 2	Apr. 6	15	May 25	Nov. 30
1635	Feb. 25	Mar. 29	7	17	29
1636	Feb. 14	Apr. 17	26	June 5	27
1637	Feb. 5	Apr. 9	18	May 28	Dec. 3
1638	Jan. 21	Mar. 25	3	13	2
1639	Feb. 10	Apr. 13	23	June 2	1
1640	Feb. 2	Apr. 5	14	May 24	Nov. 29
1641	Feb. 21	Apr. 25	June 3	June 13	28

4 our: the *2 3 6*

RULES TO KNOW WHEN THE MOVEABLE FEASTS AND HOLYDAIES BEGIN.

EASTER DAY (on which the rest depend) is alwaies the first Sunday after the Full Moone, which beginneth next the Equinoctiall of the Spring in *March*.

Septuagesima		9	
Sexagesima	*Sun-*	8	weekes
Quinquagesima	*day* is	7	before
Quadragesima		6	EASTER.

Rogation Sund.		5. weeks	
Ascension day.	is	40. days	after
Whitsunday		7. weeks	EASTER
Trinity Sunday		8. weeks	

ADVENT SUNDAY is alwayes the neerest Sunday (whether before or after) to the Fast of S. *Andrew*, or that Sunday which falleth upon any day from the 27. of *November*, to the 3. of *December* inclusively.

16 Fast: Feast *2 3 4 5 6*

THE FASTING DAIES OF THE CHURCH,

Or

Dayes of speciall Abstinance and Devotion.

THe fortie dayes of LENT.

2 The *Ember* weekes at the foure Seasons, being the

Wednesday, Friday, and Saturday } after {
the first Sunday in *Lent.*
the Feast of *Pentecost.*
Holy Crosse. Septemb. 14.
S. Lucies day. Decemb. 13.

3. The three *Rogation daies*, which be the *Munday*, *Tuesday*, and *Wednesday* before *Holy Thursday*, or the *Ascension* of our Lord.

4. The Evens, or Vigills before {
The Nativity of *Christ.*
The Purification } of the bles-
The Anuntiation } sed *Virgin.*
The Nativity of S. *John Baptist.*
S. *Matthias*
S. *Peter.*
S. *James.*
S. *Bartholomew*
S. *Matthew* } day.
S. *Simon* & *Jude*
S. *Andrew*
S. *Thomas*, and
All Saints day

27 *All Saints day*: *All Saints* 2 3 4 5 6

5. It hath been also an ancient religious custome to fast *All the Fridayes* of the yeere, except those that fall within the Twelve dayes of *Christmas*.

The Times wherein Marriages *are not solemnized.*

From	*Advent* Sunday,	untill	8. dayes after the *Epiphany*.
	Septuag. Sunday,		8. dayes after *Easter*.
	Rogation Sunday,		*Trinitie* Sunday.

Some of these being Times of solemne Fasting and Abstinence; some of Holy Festivity and Joy; both fit to be spent in such sacred Exercises, without other Avocations.

5 *not solemnized*: *not usually solemnized 2 3 4 5 6*
14–15 other Avocations: other unnecessary Avocations *2 3 4 5 6*

THE SUMME OF THE CATHOLIKE FAITH,

CALLED

THE APOSTLES *CREED*:

Divided into Twelve Articles.

I Beleeve in God the Father Almightie, Maker of Heaven and Earth.

2 And in Jesus Christ his only Son our Lord.

3 Who was conceived by the Holy Ghost, borne of the Virgin Mary.

4 He suffered under Pontius Pilate, was crucified, dead and buried.

5 He descended into Hell: the third day he rose again from the dead.

6 Hee ascended into Heaven, and sitteth on the right hand of God the Father Almightie.

7 From thence hee shall come to judge the quicke and the dead.

8 I beleeve in the Holy Ghost.

9 The Holy Catholike Church. The Communion of Saints.

10 The forgivenesse of sinnes.

11 The Resurrection of the body.

12 And the Life everlasting. *Amen.*

☞ *By this* Faith, *(into which, and none but which, all Christians are baptized,) we learne to beleeve:*

1 *In God the Father, who hath made us, and all the world.*

27 1 *In God the Father* . . .: *opposite, in margin* Catechis. in the B of Com Prayer. *2 3 4 5 6*

2 *In God the sonne, who hath redeemed us and all mankinde.*

3 *In God the Holy Ghost, who doth sanctifie us, and all the chosen people of God.*

THE LORDS PRAYER

DIVIDED INTO SEVEN PETITIONS.

The Preface.

Our Father which art in Heaven. Matt. 6.

The Petitions.

HAllowed be thy Name.

2 Thy Kingdome come.

3 Thy will be done in Earth, as it is in Heaven.

4 Give us this day our daily bread.

5 And forgive us our trespasses, as we forgive them that trespasse against us.

6 And leade us not into temptation.

7 But deliver us from evill.

The Doxologie.

For thine is the Kingdome, the power, and the glory, for ever. *Amen.*

☞ *This* Prayer *is the foundation whereupon, and the Patterne whereby all our other Prayers must be framed. In it we desire* **God our heavenly Father, who is the Giver of all Goodnesse, to send his grace unto us, and all others; that we* *The Preface.

7 Matt. 6.: Matth. 6. 6. 9. *8*
20 *This* Prayer . . .: *opposite, in margin* Catechis. in the B. of Com Prayer. *2 3 6*
21 *Patterne*: aPatterne +
at foot of page aCatechis. in the Booke of Common Prayer. *4 5*

1\. Petition. *may* [1]*worship him,* [2]*serve him, and* [3]*obey him, as wee ought to*
2\. 3. 4 *doe. And wee pray unto God, that he would* [4]*send us all things,*
which be needfull both for our soules and bodies; that hee would
5 *bee* [5]*mercifull unto us, and forgive us our sinnes; that it would*
6 *please him to* [6]*save and defend us in all our temptations, and*
7 [7]*preserve us from all dangers both ghostly and bodily. And*
The Conclusion. *forasmuch as we trust he will doe all this of his mercy and goodnesse, through our Lord Jesus Christ, therfore we say,* Amen, So be it.

THE TEN COMMANDEMENTS.

The First Table.

I.

Exod. 20. God spake these words, and said, I am the Lord thy God, Thou shalt have none other Gods but me.

II.

Thou shalt not make to thy self any graven image, nor the likenesse of any thing that is in heaven above, or in the earth beneath, or in the water under the earth. Thou shalt not bow downe to them, nor worship them: for I the Lord thy God am a jealous God, and visit the sinnes of the fathers upon the children, unto the third and fourth generation of them that hate mee, and shew mercy unto thousands in them that love me, and keepe my Commandements.

2 *God Him 2 3 4 5 6*
14 *Exod. 20.: om. 3 4 5*

III.

Thou shalt not take the Name of the Lord thy God in vaine: for the Lord will not hold him guiltlesse that taketh his Name in vaine.

IV.

Remember that thou keepe holy the Sabbath day. Sixe dayes shalt thou labour, and doe all that thou hast to doe: but the seventh day is the Sabbath of the Lord thy God. In it thou shalt doe no manner of work, thou and thy son, and thy daughter, thy man-servant, and thy maid-servant, thy cattell and the stranger that is within thy gates. For in sixe dayes the Lord made heaven and earth, the sea and all that in them is, and rested the seventh day. Wherefore the Lord blessed the seventh day, and hallowed it.

THE SECOND TABLE.

V.

Honour thy father and thy mother, that thy daies may be long in the land which the Lord thy God giveth thee.

VI.

Thou shalt doe no murther.

VII.

Thou shalt not commit adultery.

VIII.

Thou shalt not steale.

IX.

Thou shalt not beare false witnesse against thy neighbour.

X.

Thou shalt not covet thy neighbours house, thou shalt not covet thy neighbours wife, nor his servant, nor his maid, nor his oxe, nor his asse, nor any thing that is his.

THE DUTIES INJOYNED, AND THE SINS FORBIDDEN IN THE TEN COMMANDEMENTS.

☞ *Which may serve for a direction to know, or to make knowne our manifold offences against God and man.*

The duties of the first Commandement.

1. *Thou shalt have no other Gods, &c.*

TO acknowledge the eternal Deity of the onely true God.

2 To worship him with all inward devotion of our soules.

3 To love, honour, and obey him for his owne sake.

4 To feare and call upon him, to trust and beleeve in him, and none but him, all the dayes of our life, without giving any share of his honour to Angels, or Saints, or any other Creature.

Offenders against the first Commandement.

THey that by their evill disposition endeavour to perswade themselves that there is no God.

2 They of whom God is altogether unapprehended, and who passe away their time as if there were no God

at all, without any desire or care to know him as a rewarder of the good, and a punisher of the evill doers.

3 They that imagine, or wickedly fancy and worship any more gods than one.

4 They that preferre, or love any thing whatsoever before the service and will of God.

5 They that by despaire distrust him, or by boldnesse presume upon him.

6 They that beleeve him not, and are unstable or doubtfull in the truth of that Faith which he hath revealed.

7 They that tempt Him to shew his power without cause, and are not content with the ordinary wayes and meanes that he hath ordained for all things.

8 They that use inchantments, witchcrafts, sorceries, superstitious observation of dayes, prediction of fortunes, invocation of spirits, and other wicked inventions of the devill.

The duties of the second Commandement.

2. *Thou shalt not make to thy self, &c.*

TO apprehend God as an infinite and incomprehensible Essence, without any forme or shape of our owne fancying or framing, whereby to make a representation of him.

2 To honor and worship him with the lowly reverence, even of our Bodies also.

3 This to be religiously done unto him, and unto none but him; to his divine Essence, and not to the Images that men may vainely frame of him.

4 more gods: *mo Gods 3*

17 *after* invocation of spirits, *add* or any other creatures; which be all the wicked *2 3 4 5 6*

4 This also to be done purely, without any such outward and solemne worship to be given either to the person, or to the Image of Saint, or Angell, or any other creature whatsoever.

Offenders of the second Commandement.

THey that fancie to themselves any likenesse of the Deity, or frame and make any Image, either of God the Blessed Trinitie, or of God the Father, who never appeared to the world in a visible shape.

2 They that make any other Images, or the likenesse of any thing whatsoever (be it of Christ, and his Crosse, or be it of his blessed Angels,) with an intent to fall down and worship them.

3 They that are worshippers of idols, or representments of false gods.

4 They that are worshippers of Saints Images, and out of a false opinion of demeriting the protection of the blessed Virgin, or any other Saint of God, do give a religious adoration to those usuall representments which be made of them.

5 They also that are no due worshippers of God himselfe, that fall not lowly downe before his presence, religiously to adore him aswell with their bodies as their soules.

6 They that rudely refuse, or carelesly neglect to kneele, bow, and prostrate themselves, to uncover their heads; or to stand with seemely awe and reverence before the presence of his Majestie; as at all times of his service, so chiefly at the times, and in the places of his publike worship.

17 demeriting: promeriting *2 3 4 5 6*

7 They that regard not the threatnings of his vengeance upon them that transferre his honour to any other, nor the promises of his mercies upon them that duly worship him.

The duties of the third Commandement.

3. *Thou shalt not take the Name of, &c.*

TO honour the most holy and reverend Name of God.

2 To speake of it with religious awe and feare, and that in matters serious and weightie onely.

3 To use both it, and all things that are consecrated unto it, having his Name and stampe upon them, with all due regard.

Offenders against the third Commandement.

THey that account no more of the Great Name of God, than of another common thing.

2 They that use vaine and customarie swearing.

3 They that in matters serious sweare falsly, and perjure themselves.

4 They that abuse the Name of God, or any of his creatures, to cursing and bitter execrations.

5 They that make rash oathes, and sudden inconsiderate vowes for things unlikely, unlawfull, or impossible to be performed.

6 They that breake their holy, solemne, and deliberate vowes.

22–23 sudden inconsiderate vowes: sudden inconsiderate, or light *vowes* *2 3 4 5 6*

23 unlawfull, or: unlawfull, unprofitable, hurtfull, or *2 3 4 5 6*

25 their: any *2 3 4 5 6*

25 solemne, and: solemne, lawfull, and *2 3 4 5 6*

7 They that murmure against God, or blaspheme his Name.

8 They that make curious and wanton questions concerning the Nature, the Actions, and the secret Decrees of God, not contenting themselves with that which hee hath revealed in his Word.

9 They that contemne his Saints, that prophane his Temples, that slight his Sacraments, that regard not his service, that use and speake of these, as of common things, whereas they have Gods marke upon them, being set apart and dedicated to the service of his most Holy and fearefull Name.

The duties of the fourth Commandement.

4. *Remember that thou keepest holy, &c.*

AS men, to keepe holy one day of seven.

2 As Christians, to keepe that day of the seven, which because Christ hath instituted, it is called, The Lords day, and his Church hath ever observed.

3 Upon this Day to give God a solemne and a publike worship in the Congregation of his Saints.

4 To rest from unnecessarie servile labours, and the common affaires of the world.

5 To give almes of what we have, and to shew forth our charity in works of mercy and devotion, as we are able to performe them unto others.

4 Actions: Action *6*

17–18 which . . . observed.: *Sig. C5*[r] *appears twice in 2 as cancellandum and cancellans, the principal variants occurring in this passage*: [*a*] which (because Christ hath instituted it) is called, *The Lords day*; and his Church hath ever so observed it. [*b*] which because Christ arose on it, is called The Lords day: & his Church, according to Apostolical institution, hath ever observed it. *Later editions revise*: which (because Christ arose on it) is called, *The Lords day*; and his Church hath ever so observed it. *3*: *follow 2*[*b*]: *4 5 6*

Offenders against the fourth Commandement.

THey that put no difference betweene this solemne Festivall, and the common dayes of the weeke.

2 They that set themselves to needlesse, worldly, and servile affaires upon the Sunday, or suffer those over whom they have authoritie (as being their Husbands, Parents, Masters, or lawfull Governours) to doe the like, or any way to neglect the holy duties of the day.

3 They that spend it away in idle and vaine sports; that eate and drink, or discourse, or sleepe it away.

4 They that neglect to be duly present and assistant at the publike Service of the Church, whereby God hath this day his solemne Homage and worship done him.

5 They that refuse to give their almes, and do other the works of mercie and charitie, according to their owne power, and the necessitie of other good Christians.

6 They that under a pretence of serving God more strictly than others (especially for hearing and meditating of Sermons,) doe by their Fasts, and certaine Judaizing observations, condemne the joyfull Festivitie of this High & Holy day, which the Church allowes, aswell for the necessary recreation of the Body in due time, as for spirituall exercises of the soule.

9 idle and vain: idle vain *6*
15–16 other the works: other works *6*
21 *om.* certaine *6*
23–25 allowes, aswell . . . soule.: allowes, first, for the spirituall exercises of the soul, & then for the lawfull and convenient recreation of the bodie in due time. *3 8*: allow's; First, (*then as 3 8*) *6*

The Duties of the fifth Commandement.

5. *Honour thy Father and thy Mother, &c.*

TO love, honour, and obey our Father and Mother with all lowlines and reverence.

2 To succour, help, and serve them at their need.

3 In like manner, faithfully to serve, honour, and humbly obey the King; to reverence his sacred power, and his Soveraigne Authoritie over us.

4 To live by his lawes and commandements, according to Gods blessed Word and Ordinance, and not at our owne pleasure, to doe what we will.

5 To live in an orderly and quiet subjection to the Kings subordinate Magistrates; to our Husbands, Masters, Tuters, and Governours, with all fidelitie.

6 To submit our selves lowly and reverently to them that are our spirituall Guides, and Fathers, the Prelates and Priests of Gods Church.

7 Finally, to carrie our selves meekly to all, and humbly to them that bee our Betters in any kind or degree whatsoever; not denying them their due love and regard that be our inferiours, or under our authoritie.

Offenders against the fifth Commandement.

THey that disobey the lawfull commands of their Father or Mother.

2 They that neglect, or despise, or grieve their persons.

3 They that murmure, mutine, rebell, and dishonour the King, either by denying reverence to his Person, or obedience to his Lawes, or due maintenance to his State.

4 They that are undutifull to their Husbands, Masters, and Governours in such matters as bee within their power and authoritie.

5 They that neither reverence the persons, nor obey the precepts, nor care for the authoritie of their Ecclesiasticall Governours.

6 They that give offence by disregard of any, specially of them that are more aged, & better then themselves.

7 They that are unthankful to their Benefactors.

8 They that neglect to give unto their wives, their children, their kinred, their neighbors, or any their inferiours, that love and regard which severally belongs unto them.

The Duties of the sixth Commandement.

6. *Thou shalt do no murther.*

TO protect and preserve, as much as in us lies, the person or the life of any man whatsoever.

2 To procure peace & love among all sorts of people.

Offenders against the 6. Commandement.

THey that murder themselves, or study and use meanes to hasten their owne death.

2 They that destroy the lives of other men, or consent to have them destroyed; and offer any violence or hurt to their persons.

3 They that beare any anger, envie, hatred, malice, uncharitablenesse, or any kind of mischievous indignation against others.

4 They that be sowers of strife and sedition among any men whatsoever.

5 They that are given to revenge and oppression.

6 They that are privie to any conspiracies against the lives or bodies of other men, and reveale them not.

7 They that feed or clothe not him who is ready to perish with hunger and cold.

8 They that may, and assist him not, who at any time is in danger of hurt, or of the losse of his life.

9 They that have no care of their owne health and being.

10 They that procure, or consent to the procuring of Abortive children.

The Duties of the seventh Commandement.

7. *Thou shalt not commit adultery.*

TO keep our bodies in temperance, sobriety, and chastitie.

Offenders against the 7. Commandement.

THey that by adultery, incest, fornication, or any other uncleanenesse defile the body.

2 They that are lascivious in their speech, wanton in their gesture, and immodest in their attire.

3 They that be uncleane and lustfull in their thoughts.

4 They that delight in lewd and wanton company, in idle and unchast songs, in fond and filthy discourse.

5 They that are luxurious in their diet, and abuse their bodies, either by gluttony or drunkennesse.

6 They that keepe open or private stewes, that sollicit, or consent unto the fond love, or uncleanenesse of others.

7 They that presume to doe any thing beyond the bounds of modestie and shamefastnesse.

The Duties of the eighth Commandement.

8. *Thou shalt not steale.*

TO preserve our neighbors goods, and to suffer every man to enjoy what is his own quietly and fairely to himselfe.

Offenders against the eighth Commandement.

THey that go about to hurt and impaire other mens estates, either by open wrong and violence, as by spoiling and robbing men of their goods; or by secret purloyning and deceit, as by cheating and cunning in bargaines, by false weights and measures, by all kind of beguiling contracts, and by unlawfull suites or tricks at the Law.

2 They that be inordinate in gaming, and in unnecessarie consuming or spending of their goods.

3 They that be immoderate in running into debt, to the losse and hinderance of their owne, or of any other mans estate.

4 They that by any violence or fraud detaine and keepe other mens goods unto themselves.

5 They that are covetous, unjust, given to usurie and oppression.

6 They that deteine, or defraud the King of his subsidies and other duties, the Priest of his Tithes and offerings, the Orphans, &c. of their Legacies, the Servant of his wages, and the like.

23 deteine: *deceive 2 3 4 5 6*

The Duties of the ninth Commandement.

9. *Thou shalt not beare false witnesse, &c.*

TO preserve every mans good name, to beare witnes to the truth, and to speake well of them that deserve not otherwise.

Offenders against the ninth Commandement.

THey that bring in false witnesse, or unjust accusations against any man.

2 They that openly slander, or secretly detract from his credit and estimation.

3 They that are given to flatterie, and to telling of lies, or false tales.

4 They that inordinately divulge, or blaze abroad other mens faults and infirmities.

5 They that conceale the truth to the prejudice of another, being required by justice or charity, to give testimonie thereunto.

The Duties of the tenth Commandement.

10. *Thou shalt not covet thy neighbours, &c.*

TO content our selves with what we have of our owne, and with that estate of life whereunto God hath called us.

2 To covet nothing that belongs to other men.

Offenders against the tenth Commandement.

THey who though they unjustly possesse not, yet covet and desire that which is another mans, as his Wife, his Fortunes and the like.

2 They that envy other mens wealth and prosperitie.

3 They that with greedinesse hunt after the riches, pleasures, and honors of this world.

4 They that having food and rayment, are over-sollicitous and disquieted in their minds for more.

☞ *Many other offences there be against Gods Commandements; some so obvious that they need not, and some so enormious that they would not be named: but both the one and other easie to bee reduced unto these that have been already specified.*

THE TWO PRECEPTS OF CHARITY,

Or

The Lawes of Nature.

TO love God above all, for his own sake. Matth. 22.

2 To love all men as our selves for Gods sake, and to doe unto others, as we would they should do unto us.

The Precepts of the Church.

TO observe the **Festivals* and Holy dayes appointed. *The Church Calendar.

2 To keep the **Fasting dayes* with devotion and abstinence. *The Rubrick after the *Nicen Creed.*

3 To observe the **Ecclesiasticall Customes* and *Ceremonies* established, and that without frowardnesse or contradiction. *Can. 6. and the Preface of Ceremonies.

15 Matth. 22.: Matth. 2. 2. *2 3 4 5*: *om. 6*
19 *only 2 3 6 give the stars* (*) *for reference*

*Preface to the Book of Common Prayer.

*Rubrick at the end of the *Communion.*

4 To *repaire unto the publike Service of the Church for *Mattens* and *Evensong*, with other *holy offices* at times appointed, unlesse there be a just and an unfeigned cause to the contrary.

*The second Exhortation to be read before the *Communion.*

*Bishop *Overals*, and Bishop *Andrewes* Articles in the Visitation of their Diocesse.

5 To receive the **Blessed Sacrament* of the *Body* and *Blood* of Christ with frequent devotion, and three times a yeere at least, of which times *Easter* to be alwaies one. *And for better preparation thereunto, as occasion is, to disburthen and quit our consciences of those sins that may grieve us, or scruples that may trouble us, to a learned and discreet Priest, and from him to receive advise, and the benefit of *Absolution.*

The Sacraments of the Church.

a Catech. *of the Sacram.* S. Aug ep. 118 Articles of Relig. Artic. 25. Acts 8. Joh 20. 1. Tim 4. Ephes 5. James 5.

THe principall, and truly so called, (as generally necessary to salvation) [a]are *Baptisme* and *The Lords Supper.*

The other five, that is to say, *Confirmation*, *Penitence*, *Orders*, *Matrimonie*, and *Visitation of the sicke*, or *Extreme Unction*, though they be somtimes called, & have the name of Sacraments, yet have they not the like nature that the Two principall and true Sacraments have.

The three Theologicall Virtues.

1. Cor. 13. Faith, Hope, and Charitie.

Three kinds of Good Works.

Matth. 6. Fasting, Prayer, and Almesdeeds.

2 *Evensong*, with other: *Evensong*, *for *Sermons*, & other *the star referring to marginal note* *Rubrick . . . *Communion.* *2 3 4 5 6*

9 quit: quiet *7 8* 9 *om.* our *6*

12 advise: advice *2 3 4 5 6 7 8*

14 The Principall, and truly so called: The Two truly so called *8*

15 *only 4 and 5 give the* [a] *for reference*

19–20 though they be somtimes called, . . . Sacraments,: though they have been by some late Authors called by the name of sacraments (and so numbered) *8*

23 1. Cor. 13.: 1. Cor. 23. *6*

Seven Gifts of the Holy Ghost.

1. The Spirit of Wisedome, 2. and Understanding. 3. The Spirit of Counsell, 4. and Ghostly Strength. 5. The Spirit of Knowledge, 6. and Pietie. 7. The spirit of a holy & a godly Feare. Esay 11. The 1. Prayer in the forme of our Confirmation.

The Twelve Fruits of the Holy Ghost.

Love, Joy, Peace, Patience, Mercy, Goodnesse, Long-suffering, Meeknes, Faith, Modestie, Shamefastnesse, Sobriety. Gal. 5.

The Spirituall works of Mercy.

1. To instruct the Ignorant. Matth. 18.
2. To correct offenders. Jam. 5.
3. To counsell the doubtfull. Gal. 6.
4. To comfort the afflicted. Prov. 27.
5. To suffer injuries with patience. Eccles. 5.
6. To forgive offences and wrongs. Rom. 15.
7. To pray for others. Mark. 11.

The Corporall works of mercy.

1. To feed the hungry and to give drinke to the thirstie. Matth. 15.
2. To clothe the naked. Matth. 25.
3. To harbor the stranger & needy. Tob. 1.
4. To visit the sicke. Esay 58.
5. To minister unto prisoners and captives. Tob. 12.
6. To bury the dead.

The eight Beatitudes.

BLessed are the poore in spirit for theirs is the Kingdome of Heaven. Matth. 5.

2. Blessed are they that mourne, for they shall receive comfort.

3. Blessed are the meeke, for they shall receive the inheritance of the earth.

4. Blessed are they that hunger and thirst after righteousnesse, for they shal be satisfied.

5. Blessed are the mercifull, for they shall obtaine mercy.

6. Blessed are the pure in heart, for they shall see God.

7. Blessed are the Peacemakers, for they shall bee called the Children of God.

8. Blessed are they that suffer persecution for righteousnesse sake; for theirs is the Kingdome of Heaven.

Seven deadly Sinnes.

Gal. 5. 1. Pride, 2. Covetousnes, 3. Luxurie, 4. Envy, 5. Gluttonie, 6. Anger. 7. Sloth.

The Contrary vertues.

1. Humility, 2. Liberalitie, 3. Chastitie, 4. Gentlenesse, 5. Temperance, 6. Patience. 7. Devout and earnest serving of God.

QUATUOR NOVISSIMA,

OR,

The foure last things that befall any men.

Matth. 25. Death. Hell or

Heb. 9 Judgement. Heaven.

12 *Seven deadly Sinnes.*: *Seven deadly sinnes, as they are commonly so called.* *2 3 4 5 6 8*

A
COLLECTION
OF
PRIVATE DEVOTIONS,
FOR
THE HOURES
OF
PRAYER.

[ornament]

LONDON,
Printed *Anno* 1627.

OF THE ANCIENT AND ACCUSTOMED TIMES OF PRAYER in generall.

AT all times, and in all places to give thanks and praise unto Almighty God our heavenly Father, with all manner of devout Prayer and Supplication, is no more than our very meet, right, and bounden Duety. [a]*But in as much as the common employments of most, and the naturall infirmities of all sorts of people be so great, that whiles they have this body of flesh upon them, they cannot possibly attend the heavenly Exercise of Prayer and Thanks-giving without any Intermission at all: it hath therefore been the custome of religious and godly persons in all ages, to appoint themselves certaine set* Times *and* Houres *of the day, wherein to performe their Devotions. By which meanes it came to passe, that as other* [b]*carelesse people spent the whole day either in their owne affaires, or pleasures, these men bestowed it, or the chiefe and more eminent parts of it at least, in the affaires and service of God.*

a S. *Basil* in Regu. Interr. 37.

b S. *Chrysost.* hom. 59. ad pop. Antioch.

They that understood Christ's Parable so, as if *men ought alwaies to pray, *and to doe nothing else, mistooke the matter, and were put into the* [c]*Catalogue of Heretickes for their labour. They on the other side, that went about to take away all set Times of Prayer, to maintaine their affected libertie, and to doe it onely when they list, have deserved no lesse blame, and incurred no milder censure. Wise men have gone an even path, and expounding the Scripture, for continuall Prayer, by the*

*Luc. 18. 1.

c S. *Aug.* de hæres. I. 57 & epist. 121. ad Prob.

Isid. de eccl. off. l. 1 cap. 22.

9 Interr. 37.: Interr. 7. *3 4 5 6*

continuall Practice of the Church, have neither one way, nor other, offered any violence to Devotion.

d Psal. 55. 18.
e Psal. 119.
Dan. 6. 10.

The Practice then of old hath been, so to keepe up Prayer, that men might keepe up themselves withall. [d]Three *times a day to performe this Dutie; and otherwhiles* [e]Seven *times a day to doe it, was K.* DAVIDS *sacred resolution; but* Three *times a day, howsoever,* [at Evening, & Morning, and at Noon day,] *was his custom to pray, and that* [instantly,] *in solemne and devout manner. After him, the great Prophet of God that lived in* Babylon *accustomed himselfe to kneele upon his knees, and in his chamber to pray* three times *a day towards* Jerusalem, [f]*(saith the story)* as hee was alwaies wont to doe.

g Num. 28
Isid. etym. lib. 6. c. ult.
h S. *Sypr.* de orat. dom. in fine.

From which holy Examples, it afterwards came to passe, that what was by them so religiously observed under the Law, three times *a day (at least) to offer up prayers and thankes-giving to Almighty God, besides the* [g]Morning *and the* Evening sacrifice, *was by Christians as piously continued and practised under the Gospell also; both Jewes and Christians being in this duty but equall servants to the same* Trinitie, *the God both of Law and Gospell.* It is from the Prophet DANIEL (*saith S.* [h]CYPRIAN) that we Christians have our THIRD, our SIXT, and our NINTH houre of Prayer, which we duly observe in reverence of the BLESSED TRINITIE.

S. *Ambr.* lib. 3. de Virgin.
i S. *Cypr.* ibid.

Besides these (such was the ardor of ancient pietie) they added yet more, and aswell in imitation of King DAVIDS *holy Resolutions before mentioned, as also in honour of those times which the speciall Actions of God, and of our Saviour had in a manner made sacred unto them, they* augmented their houres of Prayer, ([i]*saith that old godly Father*) *and made their Devotions more frequent and fervent than they were before.*

Such are these Houres *and* Prayers *that hereafter follow;*

12 f Dan. 6. 10.: *om.* 10 *1 2*: *the verse incorrectly as* 20 *3 5*

which be not now set forth for the countenancing of their Novelties that put any trust in the bare recitall onely of a few Prayers, or place any vertue in the beadroll or certaine number of them at such and such set-houres; but for the heartie imitation of that Ancient and Christian pietie, to whom the distinction of Houres *was but an orderly and usefull, no superstitious or wanton performance of their dueties.*

And surely, so small a part of our Time taken up from other common actions, if not perhaps from doing ill, or doing nothing; and so small a Taske, though but voluntarily imposed upon our selves for Gods service, will never undoe us, nor ever prove to be an abridgement of our Christian libertie, who say, our delight is to be *numbred with the Saints *of old, and professe every day, that* [a]Gods service is perfect freedome.

*In the *Te Deum.*

a In the 2. Coll for Morn. Pr.

2 *of a few*: *of few 6*
11 *ever*: *never 6*

CERTAINE CHOICE SENTENCES OUT OF HOLY SCRIPTURE,

Whereby the frequency of Prayer and Devotion is highly commended *unto us.*

PSAL. 34. 15.

THe Eyes of the Lord are over the righteous, and his Eares are open unto their Prayers.

MATTH. 7. 7.

Aske, and it shalbe given you; seeke, and yee shall find; knock, and it shall be opened unto you.

MARK. 13. 35.

Watch and pray, for yee know not, at what houre the Lord will come.

LUK. 11. 8.

Because of his importunitie, hee will rise, and give him what he needeth.

LUK. 18. 1.

It behoveth alwayes to pray, and not to be weary.

LUK. 18. 7.

And shall not God heare, and avenge his servants, that pray night and day unto him?

EPHES. 6. 18.

Pray alwaies with all maner of Prayer and Supplication in the Spirit, and watch thereunto with all instance and supplication for all Saints.

I. THES. 5. 17.

Pray without ceasing. And in all things give thankes: for this is the will of God in Christ Jesus.

I. TIM. 2. I.

I will therfore that first of all Prayers and Supplications, Intercessions and Giving of Thankes bee made for all men; for Kings, and for all that are in authority, that we may leade a quiet and a peaceable life in all godlinesse and honestie: for this is good, and acceptable in the sight of God our Father, who will have all men to bee saved, and to come to the knowledge of his truth.

JAM. 5. 16.

The effectuall fervent Prayer of a righteous man availeth much.

REVEL. 5. 8.

The Prayers of the Saints are like the golden vials, that are full of sweete Odours.

S. GREG. NYSSEN. *hom. de orat.*

PRayer is a worke of the same dignitie and honour, wherein the Angels and Saints of Heaven themselves are imployed. It is an Advocate for the guiltie, a Redemption for the captive, a Rest for the wearied, & a

Comfort for the sorrowfull. It is our watchtowre whilest we sleepe, and our safeguard whilest we are awake.

S. CHRYSOST. *de orando Deum.*

When I see a man that loveth not his Prayers, and is not frequent at his Devotions, I shall presently conclude him to be a miserable creature, and to have nothing in him at all, that is worthy of commendation.

IDEM. *ibid.*

As the light of the Sunne is to the Eye of the Body; so is Prayer to the Soule.

IDEM. *ibid.*

I cannot but admire and wonder at the great love of God towards man, for vouchsafing him so high an honor, as familiarly to speake unto him by Prayer.

IDEM. *Homil. contra Pseudo-Proph.*

Heare how the blessed Apostle cryeth out unto us to bee instant in Prayer, to pray without ceasing; that is, though not every minute of our life without intermission, yet that as long as we live, and upon all occasions, we never give over prayer, but still and still continue in it. Pray therefore when thou art at home in thy house, and when thou art abroad in thy journey. Pray when thou lyest downe, and when thou risest up. But when thou prayest, pray with humilitie. &c.

PIOUS EJACULATIONS,

OR,

Short PRAYERS, to be committed unto perfect memorie, for our first Holy Exercise *in the beginning of the Day.*

According to the direction of S. AMBROSE in his third Book *de virgin.*

When we first awake.

LIghten mine eyes, O Lord, that I sleepe not in death. Psal. 13.
Awake thou that sleepest, and arise from death, and Christ shal give thee light. Ephes. 5.

Open thou mine Eyes, O Lord, that I may see the wonders of thy Law. Psal. 119.

At our uprising.

IN the Name of the Father, and of the Sonne, and of the Holy Ghost, *Amen.* Blessed bee the holy and undivided Trinitie, now, and for evermore.

Or this.

IN the Name of our Lord Jesus Christ, who was crucified for me, I arise from mine owne rest, to do him service. He by his Crosse and Passion, save me, blesse me, governe mee, and keepe mee this day and for ever. *Amen.*

I layd me downe and slept, and rose up againe, for the Lord hath susteyned me. Psal. 3.

At our Apparrelling.

According to the direction of S. BASIL, *orat. in Martyr.* JULIT.

CLothe me, O Lord, with the Ornaments of thy heavenly Grace, & cover me with the Robes of righteousnesse.

Rom. 13. Put yee on the Lord Jesus Christ, and make no provision for the flesh to fulfill the lusts thereof.

At the washing of our hands.

Psal. 51. WAsh me cleane, O Lord, from my wickednesse, and purge me from my sinnes.

Cleanse me, O God, by the bright fountaine of thy mercy, and water me with the dew of thine abundant grace, that being purified from my sinnes, I may grow up in good workes, truly serving thee in holines and righteousnes all the dayes of my life.

And then humbly commending ourselves to Gods protection, upon our knees.

INto the hands of thy blessed protection and unspeakeable mercy, O Lord, I commend this day my soule and my body, with all the faculties, powers, and actions of them both, beseeching thee to bee ever with me, to direct, sanctifie, and governe mee in the wayes of thy Lawes, and in the workes of thy Commandements; that through thy most mighty protection, both here and ever I may be preserved in body and soule, to serve thee the only true God, through Jesus Christ our Lord. *Amen.*

At our going abroad.

SHew me thy waies, O Lord, and teach me thy pathes. Psal. 25.

Lead mee, O God, in the way of thy truth, and guide me for thy mercies sake. Psal. 5.

O give thine Angels charge over me, to keepe me in all my waies. Psal. 91.

When wee heare the Clock at any houre of the day.

TEach me, O Lord, to number my dayes, that I may applie my heart unto wisedome. Psal. 90.

Our time passeth away like a shadow, and we bring our dayes to an end, like a tale that is told.

Have mercy upon mee, O Lord, now, and at the houre of death.

At our entrance into the Church.

AS for me, I will goe into thy House, O Lord, in the multitude of thy mercies, and in thy feare will I worship thee in thy Holy Temple. Psal. 5.

Lord, I have loved the habitation of thine house, and the place where thine honour dwelleth.

My soule hath a desire and longing to enter into the Courts of the Lord.

When wee are come into the Quire.

O How amiable are thy dwellings, thou Lord of Hosts! one day in thy Courts is better than a thousand. Psal. 84.

Blessed are they that dwell in thy House, they wilbe alwaies praising thee.

When wee fall downe to worship and adore before the presence of God.

Revel. 4. HOly, Holy, Holy, Lord God Almighty, which was, and is, and is to come, we worship him that liveth for ever, and cast our selves before his Throne.

Thou art worthy, O Lord our God, to receive Glory and Honour, and Power, for thou hast created all things, and for thy wils sake they are, and were created.

A DIVINE HYMNE,
preparative to *Prayer*.

WHen to thy God thou speak'st,
O creature meane,
Lift up pure hands,
lay downe all foule desires:
Fixe thoughts on heaven,
present a conscience cleane;
Such holy balme
to Mercies throne aspires;
Confesse faults guilt,
crave pardon for thy sinne:
Tread holy pathes,
call grace to guide therein.

It is the Spirit
with reverence must obey
Our Makers will,
to practise what he taught.
Make not the flesh
thy Counsell when thou pray,
'Tis enemy
to every vertuous thought:
It is the foe
we daily feed and cloath,
It is the prison
that the soule doth loath.

Even as Elias
mounting to the skie,
Did cast his Mantle
to the earth behind:

So when the heart
  presents the prayer on high,
Exclude the world
  from traffick with the mind.
Lips neere to God,
  and ranging heart within,
Is but vaine babling
  and converts to sinne.

Like Abraham
  ascending up the hill
To sacrifice,
  his servants left below,
That he might act
  the Great Commanders will,
Without impeach
  to his obedient blow;
Even so the soule
  remote from earthly things
Should mount salvation's shelter,
  mercie's wings.

Nothing more gratefull
  in the Highest Eyes;
Nothing more firme
  in danger to protect us;
Nothing more forcible
  to pierce the skies,
And not depart
  till mercy doe respect us.
And as the soule
  life to the body gives,
So Prayer revives
  the soule, by Prayer it lives.

THE HOURES OF PRAYER.

[ornament]

LONDON,
Printed by *R.Y.* 1627.

AN ADVERTISEMENT
CONCERNING THE DIVISION
OF
THE HOURES
following.

IT appeareth both by the Histories of the Jews, and by plaine observations out of the new Testament, that the space of the day from the Morning to the Evening was solemnely divided into foure equall parts, which they called Houres [to wit,] the First, the Third, the Sixth, and the Ninth. The First Houre comprehended the whole space from the Sunne being risen, about sixe of the clocke in the Morning after our account, till Nine, or thereabouts. The Third Houre began from thence, and lasted till high-Noone with us. The Sixth, from thence to our three of the clocke after noone. The Ninth, from that houre, to the Vespers, or Evensong, about sixe in the Evening, or Sun-set. And what was done in any part of these foure spaces was indifferently taken, and said to bee done in that Houre, whereunto every space of time was allotted. In which respect, S. MARKE, *chap.* 15. 25. *saith,* It was the THIRD Houre when they crucified Christ: *and yet* S. JOHN, *chap.* 19. 14. *saith,* It was about the SIXT Houre *before he was yet crucified. Nor is there any contradiction at all betweene these two Evangelists;* S. MARKE *understanding the last part of the* Third *Houre, which was now at the very end; and* S. JOHN *meaning, that it was now neere upon the beginning of the* Sixt *Houre, which was immediately to follow; the ending of the Third, and the beginning of the Sixt being both one, and the same point of time.*

THE

FIRST HOURE,

OR,

THE MORNING PRAYERS.

☞ Which have beene distinguished but of late times, being anciently both one Houre of Prayer. RADUL. DE RIVO. *in lib. de Can. observ. propos.* 14.

THE ANTIQUITIE OF *THE* MATTINS,

OR,

MORNING PRAYER.

Deduced aswell from the Testimony of the sacred Scriptures, as from the holy Fathers of the Church.

IN *the Primitive Church it was daily the first speech which those good Christians used, and the first thing they did,* Ante omnia adoremus Dominum, qui fecit nos, (i) [*Before we do any thing, let us fall down & worship the Lord that made us.*] *They would serve God first, and then serve themselves; as* S. JEROME, *tells the story of* HILARION; *when hee and his company were somewhat early invited to their Mornings Refection in a vineyard,* Maledictus sit (*saith the Holy Man*) qui prius Refectionem Corporis, quam Animæ quæsierit, reddamus Domino officium, oremus, psallemus, & sic properabimus, &c. (i) [*Let him not prosper that seekes to feede his Body, before he hath refreshed his Soule, or doth any thing, before he hath offered up his Prayers and Prayses with all Devotion to Almighty God, &c.*] *And many are the sacred directions, and pious examples of holy men in all ages before us, whose custome it was every day to begin Gods service, when the day itselfe began; and to set apart the first houre of their* Morning *for the more cheerfull performance of their heavenly Devotions, as by these subsequent testimonies may at large appeare.*

Psal. 95. 6.

S. *Hieron.* in vit. Hil.

11 Psal. 95. 6.: *om.* *2 3 4 5 6*
27 *Devotions*: *Devotion 6*

FROM THE HOLY SCRIPTURES.

EXOD. 36. 3.

ANd they brought their offerings unto him every MORNING.

NUMB. 28. 2.

My sacrifices for a sweet savour, yee shall observe to offer me in their *due season.* The offering of the MORNING is for a continuall, and a daily offering.

I. SAM. I. 19.

And they arose up EARLY IN THE MORNING, & worshipped before the Lord, and so returned to their house.

I. CHRON. 23. 30.

Their office was to waite and to stand every MORNING, to thanke and praise the Lord.

JOB 38. 7.

The MORNING Starres sang together, and all the Sonnes of GOD shouted for joy.

PSAL. 5. 3.

My voyce shalt thou heare *betimes*, O Lord, early in the MORNING wil I direct my prayer unto Thee.

PSAL. 59. 16.

As for me I will sing of thy power, and will prayse thy mercy betimes in the MORNING.

PSAL. 63. I.

O God, thou art my God, EARLY wil I seeke thee.

PSAL. 88. 13.

Unto thee have I cryed, O Lord, & early in the MORNING shall my prayer come before thee.

PSAL. 92. 12.

It is a good thing to give thanks unto thee, O Lord, and to tell of thy loving kindnes early in the MORNING.

PSAL. 130. 6.

My soule flyeth unto the Lord before the MORNING watch, I say, before the MORNING watch.

ESAY 26. 9.

With my soule have I desired thee, and with my spirit will I seeke thee early in the MORNING.

LAMENT. 2. 19.

Arise, and in the *beginning* of the watches, powre out thine heart like water before the Lord.

ECCLUS. 39. 5.

A wise man will give his heart early in the MORNING to the Lord that made him, and will pray before the most high.

WISD. 16. 28.

That it might be knowne, we must prevent the Sun to give thee thankes, O Lord, and at the *day-spring* to praise thee.

MARK. I. 35.

And in the MORNING, JESUS rising up before day, went into a solitarie place, and there prayed.

25 MARK. I. 35.: MARK 35. I. *6*

MARK. 13. 35.

Watch ye therefore, for ye know not at what houre the Lord will come, whether in the MORNING, &c.

MATTH. 20. I.

The Kingdome of Heaven is like unto a man, which went out early in the MORNING to hire Labourers into his vineyard.

LUK. I. 10.

And the whole multitude of the people were praying without, at the time of incense, *which was in the* MORNING.

MATTH. 26. I.

When the MORNING was come, all the chiefe Priests and Elders of the people took counsell against JESUS, to put him unto death. ☞ *Which the Fathers make one reason, why Christians use to pray in the morning, that as Christs enemies did lose no time for their wicked designes against him; so Christs servants should make like benefit of the same time to do him honour and service.*

THE 4. EVANGELISTS.

It was early in the MORNING when JESUS arose from the dead.

FROM THE FATHERS.

CONST. APOST. LIB. 8. CAP. 34.

LEt every Christian begin his daies worke with Devotion; praying first, and giving thanks to God for his renewing of the MORNING light.

15 unto: *to 7 8*

Tertul. Apologet. Cap. 2.

Of the ancient Christians, in the Emperour TRAJAN'S dayes, his Vicegerent PLINY had no worse thing to say, then that *their custome was to meet together at the DAWNING OF THE DAY, & to worship Christ with Hymns and Prayers as a God.

**Pli. Secund.* li. 10. ep. 97.

S. Cyprian *de Orat. Dom.

*In fine.

Besides the Houres which were anciently used, the Times of Prayer, and the Mysteries of Religion are now much encreased. We are up betimes in the MORNING, that by our daily devotions, the memory of our Lords Resurrection may be preserved and celebrated among us.

S. Athanas. de Meditat.

Let the *Sun* when it RISETH, see the Psalter, or thy Prayer-Booke in thine hands.

S. Basil. in Reg. fus. disp. Q. 37.
Rup. de divin. Off. cap. 2.

Before we do any thing else, be we carefull to consecrate the *first-fruits* of the DAY, & the very BEGINNINGS of our holy thoughts unto the service of God.

Id. Ibid.

Let not the day when it commeth finde us sleeping in our beddes, but awaken, and up, and ready at our Prayers, according to his custome, whose *Eyes prevented the night-watches, &c.* Psal. 119.

Idem Epist. 63.

It is the common custome and unanimous consent of all our Churches, to be up early in the MORNING; and when with earnest and devout teares they have made confession of their sinnes unto Almighty God, at length with Hymnes and Psalmes to prayse him for his mercies.

IDEM IN EPIST. I. AD NAZIANZEN.

What greater blisse and happinesse can there be, than thus on earth to imitate the Angels that are in Heaven, every MORNING to honour and worship him that made us all?

S. CHRYS. DE OR. DEUM. L. I.

It behooveth us therefore to RISE before the Sunne be up, and so to order our time, that the course of our Prayers may equall and answer the course of the day. For tell me, with what face can wee behold the Sunne, unlesse we worship him first, that hath made so glorious a light for us?

S. AMBROS. IN EXAMER. LIB. 5. CAP. 12.

Who blusheth not to heare the birds every MORNING, how sweetly and solemnely they sing out their praises unto God, and is so dull himselfe as not to doe the like?

IDEM DE VIRG. LIB. 3.

The Lords Prayer and the Apostles Creed, which doe seale up our hearts unto the service and love of God, are daily to be repeated every MORNING.

S. HIERON. AD LAETAM.

Let there bee one of good life and sound Religion set over thy daughter, who by continuall example may both teach and allure her to rise up betimes to Prayer, and to sing the MORNING Hymns, to the glorious praise of God.

15 EXAMER.: *hexamer. 6*

IDEM AD EUSTOCHIUM.

Who is it that knoweth not the ordinary Houres of Prayer to bee the Third, the Sixt, & the Ninth Houre, with the MORNING and the Evening?

RAB. MAUR. DE INST. CLER. LIB. 2. CAP. 9.

This HOURE of Prayer is universally observed by the Church of Christ.

1 IDEM AD EUSTOCHIUM.: *om. 6*

PREPARATORIE PRAYERS

To all the HOURES that follow.

God be in my head & understanding.
God be in my eyes and in my seeing.
God be in my mouth & in my speaking.
God be in my heart & in my thinking.
God be at my end and my departing.
AMEN.

PRevent mee, O Lord, in all my doings with thy most gracious favour, & further me with thy continuall helpe, that in all my works begun, continued, and ended in thee, I may glorifie thy holy Name, and finally by thy mercy obtaine everlasting life, through Jesus Christ our Lord. *Amen.*

THE CONFESSION.

ALmighty and most mercifull father, I have erred and strayed from thy wayes like a lost sheepe: I have followed too much the devices and desires of mine owne heart: I have offended against thy Holy lawes: I have left undone those things which I ought to have done, & I have done those things which I ought not to have done, and there is no health in me, but thou, O Lord, have mercy upon me miserable offender. Spare thou mee, O God, which confesse my faults. Restore thou mee that am penitent, according to thy promises declared unto mankinde, in Christ Jesus our Lord; and grant, O most mercifull Father, for his sake, that I may hereafter

11 works begun: works, begun *3*

live a godly, righteous, and sober life, to the glory of thy holy name. *Amen.*

The Prayer.

ALmighty God, the Father of our Lord Jesus Christ, who desirest not the death of a sinner, but that he may turne from his wickednesse, and live, and hast promised to pardon them that truly repent, and unfeignedly beleeve thy holy Gospell; of thy mercy I beseech thee to grant mee true repentance and thy holy Spirit, that those things may please thee which I doe at this present, and that the rest of my life hereafter may bee pure and holy, so that at the last I may come to thine eternall joy, through Jesus Christ our Lord. *Amen.*

THE MATTINS,
OR
MORNING PRAYER,
For the first HOURE of the DAY.

OUr Father which art in Heaven, hallowed be thy Name. Thy Kingdom come. Thy wil be done in earth, as it is in heaven. Give us this day our daily bread. And forgive us our trespasses, as we forgive them that trespasse against us. And leade us not into temptation. But deliver us from evill. *Amen.*

THE VERSICLES.

Vers. O Lord open thou my lips.
Resp. And my mouth shall shew forth thy praise.
V. O God make speed to save me.
R. O Lord make hast to help me.

Glory be to the Father, and to the Sonne : and to the holy Ghost.
As it was in the beginning, is now, and ever shall be : world without end. *Amen.*

ALLELUIAH. Praise the Lord.

11 evill. *Amen.*: evill. &c. *Amen. 3*: evill, &c. *4*: evil. For thine is the Kingdom, and the Power, and the Glory, for ever and ever. *Amen. 7 8*

The Venite. Psal. 95.

Serm. de Deip.

[With which S. Ambrose saith, it was the use of the Church in his time to begin their service.]

O Come, let us sing unto the Lord : let us heartily rejoyce in the strength of our salvation.

Let us come before his presence with thankesgiving : and shew our selves glad in him with Psalmes.

For the Lord is a great God : and a great King above all gods.

In his hand are all the corners of the earth : and the strength of the hills is his also.

The sea is his, & he made it : and his hands prepared the dry land.

O come, let us worship, and fall downe : and kneele before the Lord our Maker.

For he is the Lord our God : and we are the people of his pasture, and the sheepe of his hands.

To day if yee will heare his voyce, harden not your heartes : as in the provocation, and as in the day of temptation in the wildernesse.

When your fathers tempted me : proved mee, and saw my workes.

Fortie yeeres long was I grieved with this generation, and said : it is a people that doth erre in their hearts, for they have not knowne my wayes.

Unto whom I sware in my wrath : that they should not enter into my rest.

Glory be to the Father, and to the Sonne : and to the holy Ghost.

As it was in the beginning, is now, and ever shall be : world without end. *Amen.*

THE HYMNE.

Jam lucis orto Sidere.

NOw that the Day-star doth arise,
Beg we of God with humble cries
Hurtfull things to keep away,
While we duly spend the day.
Our tongues to guide so, that no strife
May breed disquiet in our life:
To shut and close the wandring eye,
Least it let in vanitie:
To keepe the heart as pure and free
From fond and troubled fantasie:
To tame proud flesh, while we deny it
A full cup, and wanton diet.
That when the Day-light shall go out,
Time bringing on the night about,
We by leaving worldly waies
May in silence sing Gods praise.
AMEN.

THE ANTIPHONA.

AS long as I live will I magnifie thee on this manner, and lift up my hands in thy Name.

PSAL. 8.

O Lord our Governor, how excellent is thy Name in all the world : thou that hast set thy glory above the heavens.

2 Out of the mouth of very babes and sucklings hast thou ordained strength, because of thine enemies : that thou mightest still the enemie and the avenger.

21 live will I: live, I will *4*

3 For I will consider the heavens, even the workes of thy fingers : the Moone and the Starres which thou hast ordained.

4 What is man that thou art mindfull of him : and the sonne of man that thou visitest him?

5 Thou madest him lower then the Angels : to crowne him with glory and worship.

6 Thou makest him to have dominion of the workes of thy hands : & thou hast put all things in subjection under his feete.

7 All sheepe and oxen : yea, and the beasts of the field.

8 The foules of the ayre, and the fishes of the sea : and whatsoever walketh through the pathes of the seas.

9 O Lord our Governour : how excellent is thy Name in all the World?

Glory bee to the Father, and to the Sonne : and to the holy Ghost.

As it was in the beginning, is now, and ever shall be : world without end. *Amen.*

PSAL. 19.

THe heavens declare the glorie of God : and the firmament sheweth his handy worke.

2 One day telleth another : and one night certifieth another.

3 There is neither speech nor language : but their voyces are heard among them.

4 Their sound is gone out into all lands : and their words unto the ends of the World.

5 In them hath he set a tabernacle for the Sunne : which commeth forth as a Bridegroome out of his chamber, and rejoyceth as a Gyant to runne his course.

6 It goeth forth from the uttermost part of the Heaven, and runneth about unto the end of it againe : and there is nothing hid from the heate thereof.

7 The Law of the Lord is an undefiled Law, converting the soule : the testimony of the Lord is sure, and giveth wisdome unto the simple.

8 The Statutes of the Lord are right, and rejoyce the heart : the Commandement of the Lord is pure, and giveth light unto the eyes.

9 The feare of the Lord is cleane, and endureth for ever : the Judgments of the Lord are true, and righteous altogether.

10 More to be desired are they than gold, yea, than much fine gold : sweeter also than hony, and the hony combe.

11 Moreover, by them is thy servant taught : and in keeping of them there is great reward.

12 Who can tell how oft he offendeth : O cleanse thou me from my secret faults.

13 Keepe thy servant also from presumptuous sins, lest they get the dominion over me : so shall I be undefiled, and innocent from the great offence.

14 Let the words of my mouth, and the meditation of my heart : be alway acceptable in thy sight.

15 O Lord : my Strength, and my Redeemer.

Glory bee to the Father, and to the Sonne : and to the holy Ghost.

As it was in the beginning, is now and ever shall be : world without end. *Amen.*

PSAL. 24.

THe earth is the Lords, and all that therein is : the compasse of the World, and they that dwell therein.

2 For hee hath founded it upon the seas : and prepared it upon the floods.

3 Who shall ascend into the hill of the Lord : or who shall rise up in his holy Place?

4 Even hee that hath cleane hands, and a pure heart : and that hath not lift up his mind unto vanity, nor sworne to deceive his neighbour.

5 He shall receive the blessing from the Lord : and righteousnes from the God of his salvation.

6 This is the generation of them that seeke him : even of them that seeke thy face, O Jacob.

7 Lift up your heads, O yee gates, and be yee lift up yee everlasting doores : and the King of glory shall come in.

8 Who is the King of glory : it is the Lord strong and mightie, even the Lord mightie in battell.

9 Lift up your heads, O yee gates, and be yee lift by yee everlasting doores : and the King of glorie shall come in.

10 Who is the King of glorie : even the Lord of hosts, hee is the King of glory.

Glory bee to the Father, and to the Sonne : and to the holy Ghost.

As it was in the beginning, is now, and ever shall bee : world without end. *Amen.*

THE ANTIPHONA.

AS long as I live will I magnifie thee on this manner, and lift up my hands in thy Name.

THE BENEDICTION.

BLessed are those that be undefiled in the way, and walke in the Law of the Lord.

THE LESSON,

OUT OF THE PROVERBS OF SALOMON.

THe feare of the Lord is the beginning of wisedome. If sinners entise thee, doe not Thou consent unto them. These sixe things doth the Lord hate, yea, seven are an abomination unto him: A proud Looke, and a lying Tongue, and Hands that shed innocent blood, an Heart that deviseth wicked imaginations, Feet that be swift in running to mischiefe, a false witnesse that speaketh not the truth, and him that soweth discord among Brethren. In the multitude of words there will be sinne: but he that refraineth his tongue is wise. Fear God, and the King, and meddle not with them that are seditious. Keepe innocency, and doe the thing that is **Psal. 37.** right, for that will bring a man peace at the last.

Vers. Thy Testimonies are my delight, O Lord, and my Counsellors.

Resp. O Give me understanding, that I may learne thy Commandements.

17 Psal. 37.: *om. 6*

THE SONG OF S. AMBROSE,

DIVINELY COMPOSED WHEN S. AUGUSTINE was baptized by him, AND SUNG BY THEM BOTH in profession of their Faith, and honour of the blessed TRINITIE.

Te Deum laudamus.

WE praise thee, O God : we knowledge thee to be the Lord.

All the earth doth worship thee : the Father everlasting.

To thee all Angels cry aloud : the heavens and all the powers therein.

To thee Cherubin and Seraphin : continually doe cry.

Holy, holy, holy : Lord God of Sabaoth.

Heaven and earth are full of the majestie : of thy glory.

The glorious company of the Apostles : prayse thee.

The goodly fellowship of the Prophets : praise thee.

The noble armie of Martyrs : prayse thee.

The holy Church throughout all the world : doth knowledge thee.

The Father : of an infinite Majestie.

Thy honourable : true, and only Sonne.

Also the holy Ghost : the Comforter.

Thou art the King of glory : O Christ.

Thou art the everlasting Son : of the Father.

When thou tookest upon thee to deliver man : thou diddest not abhorre the Virgins wombe.

When thou haddest overcome the sharpenesse of

death : thou diddest open the Kingdome of Heaven to all beleevers.

Thou sittest on the right hand of God : in the glory of the Father.

Wee beleeve that thou shalt come : to be our Judge.

Wee therefore pray thee helpe thy servants : whom thou hast redeemed with thy precious blood.

Make them to bee numbred with thy Saints : in glory everlasting.

O Lord save thy people : and blesse thine heritage.

Governe them : and lift them up for ever.

Day by day : wee magnifie thee.

And we worship thy Name : ever world without end.

Vouchsafe, O Lord, to keepe us this day without sinne.

O Lord have mercy upon us : have mercy upon us.

O Lord let thy mercy lighten upon us : as our trust is in thee.

O Lord in thee have I trusted : let me never be confounded.

THE LAUDES,

OR

THE PRAISES AT MORNING PRAYER.

ALLELUIA. Prayse the Lord.

THE ANTIPHONA.

BLessed are they that dwell in thy house, they will be alwayes praising thee.

PSAL. 148.

O Praise the Lord of Heaven : prayse him in the height.

2 Prayse him all yee Angels of his : prayse him all his hoste.

3 Prayse him Sunne and Moone : prayse him all yee starres and light.

4 Prayse him all yee Heavens : and yee waters that be above the Heavens.

5 Let them prayse the Name of the Lord : for he spake the word, and they were made, he commanded, and they were created.

6 He hath made them fast for ever & ever : hee hath given them a Law which shall not be broken.

7 Praise the Lord upon earth : yee Dragons and all Deepes.

8 Fire and Haile, Snow and Vapours : Winde and Storme, fulfilling his Word.

9 Mountaines and all Hills : fruitfull Trees, and all Cedars.

10 Beasts and all Cattell : Wormes and feathered Foules.

11 Kings of the earth, and all people : Princes, and all Judges of the World.

12 Young Men and Maidens, old Men and Children, prayse the Name of the Lord : for his Name onely is excellent, and his prayse above heaven and earth.

13 He shall exalt the horne of his people; all his Saints shall prayse him : even the children of Israel, even the people that serveth him.

1 PSAL. 148.: PSAL. 149. *6*

Glory bee to the Father, and to the Sonne : and to the holy Ghost.

As it was in the beginning, is now, and ever shall be : world without end. *Amen.*

PSAL. 149.

O Sing unto the Lord a new song : let the congregation of Saints prayse him.

2 Let Israel rejoyce in him that made him : and let the children of Sion be joyfull in their King.

3 Let them prayse his Name in the dance : let them sing praises unto him with Tabret and Harp.

4 For the Lord hath pleasure in his people : and helpeth the meeke hearted.

5 Let the Saints bee joyfull with glory : let them rejoyce in their beds.

6 Let the prayses of God bee in their mouth : and a two edged sword in their hands.

7 To bee avenged of the Heathen : and to rebuke the people.

8 To binde their Kings in chaines : and their Nobles with linkes of yron.

9 That they may be avenged of them, as it is written : such honor have all his Saints.

Glory bee to the Father, and to the Sonne : and to the holy Ghost.

As it was in the beginning, is now, and ever shall bee : world without end. *Amen.*

PSAL. 150.

O Prayse God in his holinesse : prayse him in the firmament of his power.

2 Prayse him in his Noble actes : prayse him according to his excellent greatnesse.

3 Praise him in the sound of the Trumpet : prayse him upon the Lute and Harpe.

4 Prayse him in the Cymbals and Dances : prayse him upon the Strings and Pipe.

5 Prayse him upon the well tuned Cymbals : prayse him upon the loud Cymbals.

6 Let every thing that hath breath : prayse the Lord.

Glory bee to the Father, and to the Sonne : and to the holy Ghost.

As it was in the beginning, is now, and ever shall bee : world without end. *Amen.*

THE ANTIPHONA.

LEt my mouth be filled with thy prayse, that I may sing of thy glory and honour all the day long.

OR,

THE SONG OF THE THREE CHILDREN,

CALLED BENEDICITE.

O All yee workes of the Lord, blesse yee the Lord : prayse him, and magnifie him for ever.

O yee Angels of the Lord, blesse yee the Lord : praise him and magnifie him for ever.

O yee Heavens, blesse yee the Lord : prayse him and magnifie him for ever.

O yee Waters that be above the firmament, blesse ye the Lord : prayse him and magnifie him for ever.

O all yee powers of the Lord, blesse yee the Lord : prayse him and magnifie him for ever.

O ye Sunne and Moone, blesse yee the Lord : praise him and magnifie him for ever.

O yee Stares of heaven, blesse ye the Lord : prayse him and magnifie him for ever.

O yee Showres and dew, blesse yee the Lord : praise him and magnifie him for ever.

O yee Windes of God, blesse ye the Lord : prayse him and magnifie him for ever.

O yee Fire and Heate, blesse ye the Lord : praise him and magnifie him for ever.

O yee Winter and Summer, blesse yee the Lord : prayse him and magnifie him for ever.

O yee Dewes and Frosts, blesse yee the Lord : praise him and magnifie him for ever.

O yee Frost and Cold, blesse ye the Lord : praise him and magnifie him for ever.

O yee Ice and Snow, blesse ye the Lord : praise him and magnifie him for ever.

O yee Nights and Dayes, blesse yee the Lord : prayse him and magnifie him for ever.

O yee Light and Darknesse, blesse yee the Lord : prayse him and magnifie him for ever.

O yee Lightnings and Clouds, blesse yee the Lord : prayse him and magnifie him for ever.

O let the earth blesse the Lord : yea, let it prayse him, and magnifie him for ever.

O yee Mountaines and hills, blesse yee the Lord : prayse him and magnifie him for ever.

O all yee greene things upon the earth, blesse ye the Lord : praise him and magnifie him for ever.

O yee Wells, blesse yee the Lord : prayse him and magnifie him for ever.

O yee Seas and Floods, blesse ye the Lord : praise him and magnifie him for ever.

O yee Whales, and all that moove in the waters, blesse yee the Lord : prayse him and magnifie him for ever.

O all yee Foules of the Ayre, blesse yee the Lord : prayse him and magnifie him for ever.

O all yee Beasts and Cattell, blesse yee the Lord : prayse him and magnifie him for ever.

O yee Children of men, blesse yee the Lord : prayse him and magnifie him for ever.

O let Israel blesse the Lord : prayse him and magnifie him for ever.

O yee Priests of the Lord, blesse yee the Lord : prayse him and magnifie him for ever.

O yee Servants of the Lord, blesse yee the Lord : prayse him and magnifie him for ever.

O yee Spirits and Soules of the righteous, blesse yee the Lord : prayse him and magnifie him for ever.

O yee holy and humble Men of heart, blesse yee the Lord : prayse him and magnifie him for ever.

O Ananias, Azarias and Misael, blesse ye the Lord : prayse him and magnifie him for ever.

Glory bee to the Father, and to the Sonne : and to the holy Ghost.

As it was in the beginning, is now, and ever shall be : world without end. *Amen.*

THE BENEDICTION.

BLessed is the wombe that bare Thee, O Lord, and the pappes that gave Thee suck.

THE LESSON.

MAT. 5. 3.

BLessed are the poore in spirit, for theirs is the Kingdome of heaven. Blessed are they that mourne, for they shall receive comfort. Blessed are the meeke, for they shall receive the inheritance of the earth. Blessed are they that hunger and thirst after righteousnes, for they shall be satisfied. Blessed are the mercifull, for they shall obtaine mercy. Blessed are the pure in heart, for they shall see God. Blessed are the peace-makers, for they shall bee called the Children of God. Blessed are they which suffer persecution for righteousnesse sake, for theirs is the Kingdome of Heaven.

Vers. Make me to goe in the path of thy Commandements.

Resp. For therein is my desire.

THE SONG OF ZACHARY THE PRIEST,

CALLED BENEDICTUS.

BLessed be the Lord God of Israel : for hee hath visited and redeemed his people.

And hath raised up a mightie salvation for us : in the house of his servant David.

As he spake by the mouth of his holy Prophets : which have been since the world began.

That we should be saved from our enemies : and from the hands of all that hate us.

To performe the mercy promised to our forefathers : and to remember his holy Covenant.

To performe the oath which he sware to our fore-father Abraham : that he would give us.

That we being delivered out of the hands of our enemies : might serve him without feare.

In holines & righteousnes before him : all the dayes of our life.

And thou Child shalt be called the Prophet of the Highest : for thou shalt goe before the face of the Lord, to prepare his wayes.

To give knowledge of salvation unto his people : for the remission of their sinnes.

Through the tender mercy of our God : whereby the Day-spring from on high hath visited us.

To give light to them that sit in darknesse, and in the shadow of death : and to guide our feet into the way of peace.

Glory bee to the Father, and to the Sonne : and to the holy Ghost.

As it was in the beginning, is now and ever shall be : world without end. *Amen.*

THE CREED.

I Beleeve in God the Father Almightie, Maker of heaven and earth. And in Jesus Christ his only Sonne our Lord, which was conceived by the holy Ghost, borne of the Virgin Mary, suffered under Pontius Pilate, was crucified, dead, and buried, he descended into hell, the third day he rose againe from the dead, he ascended into heaven, and sitteth on the right hand of God the Father Almightie: from thence hee shall come to judge both the quick and the dead. I beleeve in the holy Ghost, the holy Catholik Church, the Communion of Saints, the forgivenesse of sinnes, the resurrection of the body, and the life everlasting. *Amen.*

THE PRAYERS.

Lord have mercy upon us.
Christ have mercy upon us.
Lord have mercy upon us.

OUr Father which art in Heaven, hallowed be thy Name. Thy Kingdom come. Thy wil be done in earth, as it is in heaven. Give us this day our daily bread. And forgive us our trespasses, as we forgive them that trespasse against us. And leade us not into temptation. But deliver us from evill. *Amen.*

Vers. O Lord shew thy mercy upon us.
Resp. And grant us thy salvation.
Vers. O Lord save the King.
Resp. And mercifully heare us when we call upon thee.
Vers. Endue thy Ministers with righteousnesse.
Resp. And make thy chosen people joyfull.
Vers. O Lord save thy people.
Resp. And blesse thine inheritance.
Vers. Give peace in our time, O Lord.
Resp. Because there is none other that fighteth for us, but onely thou, O God.
Vers. O Lord, make cleane our hearts within us.
Resp. And take not thy holy Spirit from us.
Vers. O Lord heare my prayer.
Resp. And let my crying come unto thee.

4 PRAYERS: PRAYER *3*
13 evill. *Amen.*: evill, &c. *Amen. 3*

Then the COLLECTS proper for the weeke, with these Prayers following.

THE SECOND COLLECT FOR PEACE.

O God which art the Author of peace, and lover of concord, in knowledge of whom standeth our eternal life, whose service is perfect freedome: defend us thy humble servants in all the assaults of our enemies, that wee surely trusting in thy defence, may not feare the power of any adversaries, through the might of Jesus Christ our Lord. *Amen.*

THE THIRD COLLECT FOR GRACE.

O Lord our heavenly Father, Almightie and everlasting God, which hast safely brought us to the beginning of this day: defend us in the same with thy mightie power, & grant that this day we fall into no sin, neither runne into any kind of danger, but that all our doings may bee ordered by thy governance, to doe alwaies that that is righteous in thy sight, through Jesus Christ our Lord. *Amen.*

A DEVOUT PRAYER, WHICH MAY BE USED AT ALL TIMES.

I.

GRant me, gracious Lord, a pure intention of my heart, and a stedfast regard to thy glory in all my actions. Possesse my mind continually with thy

18 any kind of: any of *6*   20 that that: that which *6*: that *7 8*

presence, and ravish it with thy love, that my onely delight may be, to bee embraced in the armes of thy Protection.

II.

BE Thou a Light unto mine eyes, musick to mine eares, sweetenesse to my taste, and a full contentment to my heart. Bee thou my Sunshine in the day, my Food at the table, my Repose in the night, my cloathing in nakednesse, and my succour in all necessities.

III.

LOrd Jesu, I give thee my body, my soule, my substance, my fame, my friends, my liberty, and my life: dispose of mee, and of all that is mine, as it seemeth best to thee, and to the glory of thy blessed Name.

IV.

I Am not now mine, but thine. Therefore claime mee as thy right, keepe me as thy charge, and love me as thy childe. Fight for me when I am assaulted, heale me when I am wounded, and revive me when I am destroyed.

V.

MY Lord and my God, I beseech thee to give mee patience in troubles, humilitie in comforts, constancie in temptations, and victorie against all my ghostly enemies. Grant mee sorrow for my sinnes, thankefulnesse for thy benefits, feare of thy Judgements, love of thy mercies, and mindfulnesse of thy presence for evermore.

9 all necessities: all my necessities *6*

VI.

MAke me humble to my Superiours, and friendly to my equals: make me ready to pleasure all, and loth to offend any: make me loving to my friends, and charitable to mine enemies.

VII.

GIve me modesty in my countenance, gravity in my behaviour, deliberation in my speech, holinesse in my thoughts, & righteousnesse in all my actions. Let thy mercie cleanse me from my sinnes, and let thy Grace bring forth in me the fruites of everlasting life.

VIII.

LOrd, let me be obedient without arguing, humble without fayning, patient without grudging, pure without corruption, merrie without lightnesse, sad without mistrust, sober without dulnesse, true without doublenes, fearing thee without desperation, and trusting in thee without presumption.

IX.

LEt me be joyfull for nothing, but that which pleaseth thee: nor sorrowfull for any thing, but that which doth displease thee. Let my Labour be my delight, which is for thee: and let all Rest wearie me, which is not in thee.

X.

GIve me a waking spirit, and a diligent soule, that I may seek to know thy will, and when I know it truly, may performe it faithfully, to the honour and glory of thy ever blessed Name. *Amen.*

13–14 humble . . . grudging: humble without grudging *6*

THE FINALL PRAYERS.

ASsist us mercifully, O Lord, in these our supplications and prayers, and dispose the way of thy servants, toward the attainement of everlasting salvation, that among all the changes and chances of this mortall life, they may ever bee defended by thy most gracious and ready helpe, through Christ our Lord. *Amen.*

ALmighty Lord and everliving GOD, vouchsafe wee beseech thee, to direct, sanctifie, and governe both our hearts and bodies in the waies of thy Lawes, & in the works of thy Commandements, that through thy most mighty protection, both here and ever, wee may be preserved in body and soule, through our Lord and Saviour Jesus Christ. *Amen.*

THE DOXOLOGIE.

NOw unto the King Eternall, the immortall, invisible, and onely wise God, be honor and glory for ever and ever. *Amen.* 1. Tim. 1. 17.

THE END OF THE MATTINS, OR FIRST HOURE OF PRAYER.

16 1. Tim. 1. 17.: *om. 3*

THE THIRD HOURE OF PRAYERS, OR THE MIDDLE SPACE BETWEENE SUNNE-RISING AND NOONE.

THE ANCIENT USE OF PRAYERS AT THE THIRD HOURE.

*STEPH. DUR. de Rit.

THe THIRD HOURE *of the Day is commonly called by the* Italians, *THE GOLDEN HOURE; *and in the Decrees of the Church*, Distin. 44. can. fin. *it is termed*, THE HOLY HOURE. *A Time in a manner made sacred to Christians, even by the holy Ghost himselfe, saith* RUPERTUS: as

ACTS 2.

THey were all with one accord in one place; and suddenly there came a sound from heaven, and they were all filled with the holy Ghost.
☞ *Where at the fifteenth verse by those words of* S. PETER [It is but the Third houre of the day] *it appeareth, that this descent of the holy Ghost was at the Third houre of Prayer, at which time and godly exercise, the Apostles were then assembled.*

MARK. 15.

PILATE said unto them, What will you that I doe to the King of the Jewes? They cryed againe, Crucifie him, crucifie him, &c. And it was the THIRD HOURE. VERS. 25.

DAN. 6.

And hee kneeled three times a day before the Lord. *The first of which times (saith* S. CYPRIAN *and* S. HIEROM) *hath been alwayes understood to be the* THIRD HOURE *of Prayer*.

---

4 Italians: Italian *6*
4–5 *and in the Decrees*: *and the decrees 6*
4 *STEPH. DUR. de Rit.: *om. 8*
6 *A Time*: *Time 6*

USE OF PRAIERS AT THE THIRD HOURE

CONST. CLEM. LIB. 8 CAP. 34.

LEt your Prayers bee made at the THIRD HOURE also; for then it was when PILATE gave sentence upon our Lord and Saviour to have him crucified. MARK. 15.

TERTUL. DE JEJUN. CAP. 10.

The THIRD, the *sixth*, and the *ninth* HOURES, as they are the more eminent parts of the day, to distribute and distinguish the publike affaires of men; so have they been accounted the most solemne times of Prayer and divine duties in the Church of God. For at this THIRD HOURE were the holy Apostles met together at their devotions, and filled with the power of the holy Ghost.

S. CYPRIAN DE ORAT. DOM.

In the Exercise of Devotion and Praier, we reade, that the THREE CHILDREN, and the Prophet DANIEL, men strong in Faith, and victorious in Captivitie, observed the THIRD HOURE of the day; a Mysterie no doubt of the Holy and Blessed TRINITY, which was afterwards to be made manifest; and a Type of the Holy Ghost's descent at THAT VERY HOURE.

S. BASIL. IN REG. FUS. DISP. INT. 37.

At the THIRD HOURE of the day, let us give our selves to holy Supplications and Prayers, having in continuall remembrance, the most glorious Gift of the Holy Ghost, which was then bestowed upon the Apostles of Christ, as they were devoutly met together at their

1 CONST. CLEM. LIB. 8 CAP. 34.: *om. 6*   11 this THIRD: the Third *8*

Prayers and holy Exercises. And let us beseech Almighty God, that we also may bee made fit to receive the like blessed Sanctification of the Spirit, to bee our Director and Instructor in all things that we doe.

S. Hieron. ad Eustoch.

Who knoweth not that the THIRD HOURE is one of those times, which are allotted to Prayer?

Idem de obitu Paulae.

At the THIRD, *sixth*, and *ninth* HOURE she said her *Psalter*, and orderly performed her Devotions.

Isid. de eccl. off. lib. I. c. 19.

For the service of the Holy and undivided TRINITY, are these THREE HOURES devoted to Prayer.

PRAYERS FOR THE THIRD HOURE.

OUr Father which art in heaven. Hallowed be thy Name. Thy kingdom come. Thy will be done in earth as it is in heaven. Give us this day our daily bread. And forgive us our trespasses, as we forgive them that trespasse against us. And leade us not into temptation: but deliver us from evill. *Amen.*

Vers. O God make speed to save me.
Resp. O Lord make hast to help me.

21 evill. *Amen*,: evill. &c. *Amen.* *3*: evil,. For thine is . . . *Amen.* *7 8*

Glory be to the Father, and to the Sonne: and to the holy Ghost.

As it was in the beginning, is now, and ever shall be: world without end. *Amen.*

ALLELUIAH. Praise the Lord.

THE HYMNE.

VENI CREATOR.

COme Holy Ghost; our soules inspire,
And lighten with celestiall fire.
Thou the anointing Spirit art,
Who dost thy seven-fold gifts impart:
Thy blessed unction from above
Is comfort, life, and fire of love;
Enable with perpetuall light
The dulnesse of our blinded sight.
Anoint and cheere our soyled face
With the abundance of thy grace.
Keep far our foes: give peace at home;
Where thou art guide, no ill can come.
Teach us to know the Father, Sonne,
And Thee of Both to be but One.
That through the Ages all along
This may be our endlesse Song.
Praise to thy eternall merit,
Father, Sonne, and Holy Spirit.
Amen.

THE ANTIPHONA.

SHew thy servant the light of thy countenance, and save me for thy mercies sake.

PSAL. 15.

LOrd, who shal dwell in thy Tabernacle : or who shall rest in thy holy hill?

2 Even he that leadeth an uncorrupt life : and doth the thing that is right, and speaketh the truth from his heart.

3 Hee that hath used no deceit in his tongue, nor done evill to his neighbour : and hath not slandred his neighbours.

4 He that setteth not by himselfe, but is lowly in his owne eyes : and maketh much of them that feare the Lord.

5 He that sweareth unto his neighbour, and disappointeth him not : though it were to his owne hinderance.

6 He that hath not given his money upon usurie : nor taken reward against the innocent.

7 Whoso doth these things : shall never fall.

Glory bee to the Father, and to the Sonne : and to the holy Ghost.

As it was in the beginning, is now and ever shall be : world without end. *Amen.*

PSAL. 25.

UNto thee, O Lord, will I lift up my soule, my God, I have put my trust in thee : O let me not bee confounded : neither let mine enemies triumph over me.

2 For all they that hope in thee, shall not bee ashamed : but such as transgresse without a cause, shall be put to confusion.

3 Shew mee thy wayes, O Lord : and teach me thy pathes.

4 Leade me forth in thy truth, and learne mee : for thou art the God of my salvation, in thee hath been my hope all the day long.

5 Call to remembrance, O Lord, thy tender mercies : and thy loving kindnesse which hath been ever of old.

6 Oh remember not the sins and offences of my youth : but according to thy mercie thinke thou upon me (O Lord) for thy goodnesse.

7 Gracious and righteous is the Lord : therefore will he teach sinners in the way.

8 Them that be meeke shall he guide in judgement : and such as be gentle, them shall hee learne his way.

9 All the pathes of the Lord are mercie and truth : unto such as keepe his Covenant and his testimonies.

10 For thy Names sake, O Lord : bee mercifull unto my sin, for it is great.

11 What man is hee that feareth the Lord : him shall hee teach in the way that he shall chuse.

12 His soule shall dwell at ease : and his seed shall inherit the land.

13 The secret of the Lord is among them that feare him : and he will shew them his Covenant.

14 Mine eyes are ever looking unto the Lord : for hee shall pluck my feete out of the net.

15 Turne thee unto me, and have mercy upon me : for I am desolate and in miserie.

16 The sorrowes of my heart are enlarged : O bring thou me out of my troubles.

17 Looke upon mine adversitie and miserie : and forgive mee all my sinne.

18 Consider mine enemies how many they are : and they beare a tyrannous hate against me.

19 O keepe my soule, and deliver me : let me not be confounded, for I have put my trust in thee.

20 Let perfectnesse and righteous dealing waite upon mee : for mine hope hath beene in thee.

21 Deliver Israel, O God : out of all his troubles.

Glory bee to the Father, and to the Sonne : and to the holy Ghost.

As it was in the beginning, is now, and ever shall bee : world without end. *Amen.*

PSAL. 145.

I Wil magnifie thee O God, my King : and I will prayse thy Name for ever and ever.

2 Everie day will I give thankes unto thee : and prayse thy Name for ever and ever.

3 Great is the Lord, and marveilous worthy to bee praised : there is no end of his greatnes.

4 One generation shall praise thy workes unto another: and declare thy power.

5 As for me, I will be talking of thy worship : thy glorie, thy praise, and wondrous workes.

6 So that men shall speake of the might of thy marveilous acts : and I will also tell of thy greatnesse.

7 The memoriall of thine abundant kindnesse shall be shewed : and men shall sing of thy righteousnesse.

8 The Lord is gracious and mercifull : long suffering, and of great goodnesse.

9 The Lord is loving unto everie man : and his mercy is over all his workes.

10 All thy workes praise thee, O Lord : and thy Saints give thankes unto thee.

11 They shew the glory of thy Kingdome : and talke of thy power.

12 That thy power, thy glorie, and mightinesse of thy kingdom : might be knowne unto men.

13 Thy Kingdome is an everlasting Kingdome : and thy dominion endureth throughout all Ages.

14 The Lord upholdeth all such as fall : and lifteth up all those that be downe.

15 The eies of all wait upon thee, O Lord : and thou givest them their meate in due season.

16 Thou openest thine hand : and fillest all things living with plenteousnesse.

17 The Lord is righteous in all his waies : and holy in all his workes.

18 The Lord is nigh unto all them that call upon him : yea, all such as call upon him faithfully.

19 He will fulfill the desire of them that feare him : he also will heare their crie, and will helpe them.

20 The Lord preserveth all them that love him : but scattereth abroad all the ungodly.

21 My mouth shall speake the praise of the Lord : and let all flesh give thanks unto his holy Name for ever and ever.

Glory bee to the Father, and to the Sonne : and to the holy Ghost.
As it was in the beginning, is now, and ever shall bee : world without end. *Amen.*

THE BENEDICTION.

BLessed be the Lord God of Israel from everlasting, & world without end.

THE LESSON.

EPHES. 6.

TAke unto you the whole Armour of God, that yee may be able to resist the evill day, and stand perfect in all things. Stand therefore, and your loynes gird with the truth, having on the Brest-plate of righteousnesse, and having shooes on your feete, that yee may be prepared for the Gospell of peace. Above all, take to you the shield of Faith, wherewith yee may quench all the fiery darts of the wicked one. Take the Helmet of Salvation, and the sword of the Spirit, which is the Word of God. And pray alwaies with all manner of prayer and supplication in the spirit: and watch thereunto with instance.

Vers. O Lord heare my prayer.
Resp. And let my cry come unto thee.

THE PRAYERS.

I.

ALmightie God, which as about this Houre didst instruct, and replenish the hearts of thy faithfull Servants, by sending downe upon them the Light of thy holy Spirit: Grant me by the same Spirit to have a right judgement in all things, that I may both perceive, and know what I ought to doe, and also have grace and power faithfully to fulfill the same: through the merits of our Lord Jesus Christ, who was also at this Houre contented to receive the bitter sentence of death for us, and now liveth and reigneth with Thee in the unitie of the same blessed Spirit, one God world without end. *Amen.*

II.

ALmightie God, the fountaine of all goodnesse, and the welspring of divine Graces, who hast vouchsafed to regenerate me, being borne in sinne, by water and the Holy Ghost in the blessed Laver of Baptisme, thereby receiving me into the number of thine elect Children, and making mee an Heire of everlasting life, in the Communion of thy glorious Saints: strengthen me, I beseech thee, O Lord, with that blessed Spirit of thine, the Ghostly Comforter: and daily increase in mee thy manifold Gifts of Grace, the Spirit of Wisedome and Understanding, the Spirit of Councell and Ghostly Strength, the Spirit of Knowledge and true Godlinesse, and fulfill me, O Lord, with the spirit of thy Holy Feare, even through him who hath sent down the Spirit upon his Church, Jesus Christ our Lord. *Amen.*

The Lords Name be praysed, from the rising up of the Sunne, unto the going downe thereof.

THE END OF THE THIRD HOURE.

6–7 thine elect Children,: thy Children, *3*: thy Children *6*
17 rising up of: rising of *6*

THE SIXTH HOURE OF PRAYER, OR MID-DAY.

THE ANCIENT CUSTOME OF PRAYER AT THE SIXTH HOURE, OR NOONE-DAY.

For many reasons (saith S. *CYPRIAN) *is the* SIXTH HOURE *of Prayer observed by devout Christians, as being a Time that hath beene specially consecrated and advanced therunto, both in the old and new Testament.*

*De orat. Dom.

PSAL. 55. 18.

And at NOONE-TIME will I pray, and that instantly, and he shall heare my voyce.

MATTH. 27.

There they crucified him; and it was about the SIXTH HOURE. ☞ *At which time our Saviour offered his last prayers upon the Altar of his Crosse.*

ACTS 10. 9.

PETER went up into his house to pray about the SIXTH HOURE.

CLEM. CONST. LIB. 8. CAP. 34.

Let your Prayers bee made also at the SIXTH HOURE, for at that time was our Lord and Saviour crucified upon the Crosse for us.

TERTUL. DE JEJUN. CAP. 10.

The SIXTH HOURE hath been ever accounted a solemne time for Devotion and Prayer.

S. CYPRIAN DE ORAT. DOM.

Besides, wee observe the SIXTH HOURE, not onely for that we find holy men before us to have done the like; both in the *Old* Testament, as DANIEL in his chamber; and in the *New*, as PETER upon his house; but also for that our Lord JESUS CHRIST was at THIS HOURE exalted upon the Crosse, like the Serpent in the wildernes, that whosoever turneth to him might bee healed.

S. BAS. IN REG. FUS. DISP. INT. 37.

When we pray at the SIXTH HOURE, we imitate that holy Saint, who said, *And at* NOONE-TIME *will I call upon Thee.* There is an Arrow that flyeth about, and a Devill that destroyeth in the NOON-DAY; fit it is we should then seeke, and take heed to be delivered from them.

S. ATHANAS. DE MEDITAT.

Be instant at Praiers with God, and worship him that hung upon the crosse for thee at the SIXTH HOURE of the day.

S. ISIDOR. LIB. 6. ETYM. CAP. ULT.

The *Third*, the SIXTH, and the *Ninth* HOURES, they divide the day into even spaces of time, and are therefore allotted to Prayer, that whilest we are perhaps intent upon other businesse, and may forget our duties towards God, the VERY HOURE when it comes, may put us in mind thereof. And how can we doe lesse, than THREE times in the day at least (besides Morning and Evening, which will invite us to prayer of themselves) fall downe and worship the Blessed TRINITY, *Father*, *Sonne*, and *Holy Ghost*?

PRAYERS FOR THE SIXTH HOURE.

OUr Father which art in heaven. Hallowed be thy Name. Thy kingdom come. Thy will be done in earth as it is in heaven. Give us this day our daily bread. And forgive us our trespasses, as we forgive them that trespasse against us. And leade us not into temptation: but deliver us from evill. *Amen.*

Vers. O God make speed to save me.
Resp. O Lord make hast to help me.

Glory bee to the Father, and to the Sonne : and to the holy Ghost.
As it was in the beginning, is now and ever shall be : world without end. *Amen.*

ALLELUIA. Praise the Lord.

THE HYMNE.

WHo more can crave
  than God for me hath done?
To free a slave
  that gave his onely Sonne.

14 evill. *Amen.*: evill. &c. *Amen.* *3*: evil. For thine is . . . *Amen.* *7 8*
19–20 now . . . *Amen.*: now, and shall be, &c. *4*

Blest be that houre
 when he repair'd my losse,
I never will
 forget my Saviours Crosse.

Whose death revives
 my soule; Once was I dead,
But now I'le raise
 againe my drooping head.
And singing say,
 and saying sing for ever,
Blest be my Lord
 that did my soule deliver. *Amen.*

THE ANTIPHONA.

THe Lord hath redeemed me from all my sinnes.

PSAL. 103.

PRaise the Lord, O my soule : and all that is within me, praise his holy Name.

2 Prayse the Lord, O my soule : and forget not all his benefits.

3 Which forgiveth all thy sin : and healeth all thine infirmities.

4 Which saveth thy life from destruction : and crowneth thee with mercy and loving kindnes.

5 Which satisfieth thy mouth with good things : making thee young and lustie as an Eagle.

6 The Lord executeth righteousnesse and judgement : for all them that are oppressed with wrong.

7 He shewed his wayes unto Moses : his workes unto the children of Israel.

8 The Lord is full of compassion and mercy : long suffering and of great goodnesse.

9 Hee will not bee alway chiding : neither keepeth hee his anger for ever.

10 He hath not dealt with us after our sinnes : nor rewarded us according to our wickednesse.

11 For looke how high the heaven is in comparison of the earth : so great is his mercy also toward them that feare him.

12 Looke how wide also the East is from the West : so farre hath he set our sinnes from us.

13 Yea, like as a father pittieth his owne children : even so is the Lord merciful unto them that feare him.

14 For he knoweth whereof we be made : he remembreth that we are but dust.

15 The dayes of man are but as grasse : for hee flourisheth as a floure of the field.

16 For assoone as the winde goeth over it, it is gone : and the place thereof shall know it no more.

17 But the mercifull goodnesse of the Lord endureth for ever and ever, upon them that feare him : and his righteousnesse upon childrens children.

18 Even upon such as keepe his Covenant : and thinke upon his Commandements to doe them.

19 The Lord hath prepared his Seate in heaven : and his Kingdome ruleth over all.

20 O prayse the Lord yee Angels of his, yee that excell in strength : yee that fulfill his Commandements, and hearken unto the voyce of his words.

21 O prayse the Lord, all yee his hosts : yee servants of his that doe his pleasure.

22 O speake good of the Lord, all yee works of his, in all places of his dominion : prayse thou the Lord, O my soule.

Glory bee to the Father, and to the Sonne : and to the holy Ghost.

As it was in the beginning, is now, and ever shall be : world without end. *Amen.*

PSAL. 116.

I Am well pleased : that the Lord hath heard the voyce of my prayer.

2 That he hath enclined his eare unto me : therefore will I call upon him as long as I live.

3 The snares of death compassed me round about : & the paines of hell gate hold upon me.

4 I shall find trouble and heavinesse, and I shall call upon the Name of the Lord : O Lord, I beseech thee, deliver my soule.

5 Gracious is the Lord and righteous : yea, our God is mercifull.

6 The Lord preserveth the simple : I was in miserie, and he helped me.

7 Turne againe then unto thy rest, O my soule : for the Lord hath rewarded thee.

8 And why? Thou hast delivered my soule from death : mine eyes from teares, and my feete from falling.

9 I will walk before the Lord: in the Land of the living.

10 I beleeved, and therefore will I speak, but I was sore troubled : I said in my haste, All men are lyars.

11 What reward shall I give unto the Lord : for all the benefits that he hath done unto me?

12 I will receive the cup of salvation : and call upon the name of the Lord.

13 I will pay my vowes now in the presence of all his people : right deare in the sight of the Lord is the death of his Saints.

14 Behold (O Lord) how that I am thy servant : I am thy servant, and the sonne of thine handmaid, thou hast broken my bonds in sunder.

15 I will offer unto thee the sacrifice of thankesgiving : and will call upon the Name of the Lord.

16 I will pay my vowes unto the Lord in the sight of all his people : in the Courts of the Lords house, even in the middest of thee, O Hierusalem, Prayse the Lord.

Glory bee to the Father, and to the Sonne : and to the holy Ghost.

As it was in the beginning, is now, and ever shall be : world without end. *Amen.*

PSAL. 117.

O Prayse the Lord, all yee heathen : prayse him, all ye Nations.

2 For his mercifull kindnesse is ever more and more toward us : and the truth of the Lord endureth for ever. Prayse the Lord.

Glory bee to the Father, and to the Sonne : and to the holy Ghost.

As it was in the beginning, is now, and ever shall be : world without end. *Amen.*

THE BENEDICTION.

BLessed is he whose unrighteousnesse is forgiven, and whose sin is covered.

THE LESSON.

PHIL. 2.

LEt the same mind bee in you, that was in Christ Jesus, who when hee was in the shape of God, yet made himselfe of no reputation, but humbled himselfe, and became obedient to the death, even to the death of the Crosse. Wherefore God hath also exalted him on high, and given him a Name which is above all Names, that at the NAME OF JESUS every knee should bow, both of things in heaven, and things in earth, and things under the earth, and that all tongues should confesse, that Jesus Christ is the Lord, unto the prayse of God the Father.

Vers. I will make my prayer unto thee, O Lord.
Resp. In an acceptable time.

THE PRAYERS.

I.

SAve us, O Blessed Saviour of the World, who by thy Crosse and precious blood: hast redeemed us, helpe us, we beseech thee, O God of our salvation.

II.

O Lord Jesus Christ, the blessed Sonne of God, who hast suffered death for mee upon the Crosse, that I might thereby be brought unto eternall life: have mercie on me, I beseech thee, both now and at the houre of death: and grant unto mee thy humble servant, with

18–20 Save us, . . . us, helpe us, we . . . our salvation : Save me, . . . me: helpe me, I . . . my salvation *2 3 4 5 6*
19 blood: hast: blood, hast *2 3 6*: Bloud hast *4 5 7 8*

all other good people that have this thy blessed Passion in devout remembrance, a prosperous and godly life in this present World, and through thy Grace eternall glory in the World to come, where, with the Father and the Holy Ghost, thou livest and reignest ever one God World without end. *Amen.*

THe Lords Name be praised from the rising of the Sunne, unto the going downe thereof.

THE END OF THE
SIXTH HOURE.

7 rising of: rising up of *3*

THE

NINTH HOURE

OF

PRAYER,

OR

MID-SPACE BETWEENE
NOONE AND SUN-SET.

THE ANCIENT USE OF PRAYERS AT THE NINTH HOURE.

THat the NINTH HOURE *also hath ever been a chosen and a solemne time for Devout Prayer, these places of the Holy Scripture, and the Old Fathers, will give sufficient Testimony.*

ACTS 3.

PETER and JOHN went up into the Temple at the NINTH HOURE of Praier, [*or*] at THAT HOURE of Prayer, which is called the NINTH HOURE.

ACT. 10. 2.

CORNELIUS was a devout man, and one that feared God with all his house, who gave much Almes to the people, and prayed to God continually. He saw in a manifest Vision, and it was at the NINTH HOURE of the day, an Angel of God comming unto him, who said; CORNELIUS, thy Prayers and thine Alms are come up for a memoriall before God.

MAT. 27. 50.

And at the NINTH HOURE, JESUS cryed with a loud voyce, and yeelded up the Ghost.

---

20 MAT. 27. 50.: S. MATTH. 27. 46, 50. *7 8*

USE OF PRAYER AT THE NINTH HOURE

Clem. Const. lib. 8. cap. 34.

WEe observe also the NINTH HOURE of Prayer, for that at this time the Sunne was darkened, and the earth shaken with horror, as being not able to suffer, or to looke upon those bitter cruelties of the Jewes, wherewith the God of Heaven and Earth was despighted.

S. Cypr. de orat. Dom.

Our Lord and Saviour was exalted upon his Crosse at the sixth Houre of the day, and there being tormented three long houres together, at the NINTH HOURE hee made perfect our Redemption, and yeelded up his owne life, to save ours. So mysterious were these Times of praier, which holy men of old had chosen for the exercise of their pietie.

S. Basil. in reg. Int. 37.

The Apostles themselves have taught us how fit and needfull our Prayers are at the NINTH HOURE of the day; an Houre which PETER and JOHN observed, wherein to goe up to the very Temple and pray: it beeing a sacred memoriall also of that time when our Lord JESUS was put to death, that he might keepe us from death.

S. Hier. in Dan. 6.

The Church hath ever been accustomed, to interpret one of the Prophets Times of Prayer, to bee the NINTH HOURE, and to observe it accordingly.

RAB. MAUR. L. 2. DE INST. CL. CAP. 6.

The NINTH HOURE of the day is therefore accounted a solemne and a sacred time among us, that remembring how Christ at THIS HOURE commended up his Spirit into the hands of his Father, we also with devout Prayers and Supplications might yeeld up unto him both our soules and bodies as a living sacrifice, &c.

RUP. LIB. I. DE DIV. OFF. CAP. 5.

At THIS HOURE did the Sacraments of the Church flow from the side of our Saviour; the Blood whereby wee are redeemed, and the Water wherewith we are regenerate: JESUS yeelded up the ghost; the Thiefe was admitted into Paradise; the Labourers sent into the Vineyard; and forgivenesse of sinnes promised to them that repent and come unto Christ, even at the LAST HOURE of the day. Pray wee therefore with all Supplication, &c.

PRAYERS FOR THE NINTH HOURE.

OUr Father which art in heaven. Hallowed be thy Name. Thy kingdom come. Thy will be done in earth as it is in heaven. Give us this day our daily bread. And forgive us our trespasses, as we forgive them that trespasse against us. And leade us not into temptation: but deliver us from evill. *Amen.*

Vers. O God make speed to save me.
Resp. O Lord make hast to help me.

25 evill. *Amen.*: evill. &c. *Amen.* *3*: evil. For thine is . . . *Amen.* *7 8*

Glory bee to the Father, and to the Sonne : and to the holy Ghost.

As it was in the beginning, is now and ever shall be : world without end. *Amen.*

ALLELUIA. Praise the Lord.

THE HYMNE.

O Thou God Almightie,
Father of all mercy,
Fountaine of all pitty,
Grant we beseech thee,
Of thy great clemency,
On us to have mercy,
Now and at the houre of death.
Amen.

THE ANTIPHONA.

ANd now Lord, what is my hope: Truely my hope is even in thee.

PSAL. 34.

I Will alway give thankes unto the Lord : his prayse shal ever be in my mouth.

2 My soule shall make her boast of the Lord : the humble shall heare thereof, and be glad.

3 O prayse the Lord with me : and let us magnifie his Name together.

4 I sought the Lord, and hee heard me : yea, hee delivered mee out of all my feare.

5 They had an eye unto him, and were lightned : and their faces were not ashamed.

6 Loe, the poore cryeth, and the Lord heareth him : yea, and saveth him out of all his troubles.

7 The Angell of the Lord tarieth round about them that feare him : and delivereth them.

8 O taste and see how gracious the Lord is : blessed is the man that trusteth in him.

9 O feare the Lord, yee that be his Saints : for they that feare him lacke nothing.

10 The Lyons doe lacke, and suffer hunger : but they which seek the Lord, shall want no manner of thing that is good.

11 Come yee children, and hearken unto mee : I will teach you the feare of the Lord.

12 What man is hee that lusteth to live, and would faine see good dayes : keepe thy tongue from evill, and thy lips that they speake no guile.

13 Eschew evill, and doe good : seeke peace, and ensue it.

14 The eyes of the Lord are over the righteous : and his eares are open unto their prayers.

15 The countenance of the Lord is against them that doe evill : to roote out the remembrance of them from the earth.

16 The righteous crie, and the Lord heareth them : and delivereth them out of all their troubles.

17 The Lord is nigh unto them that are of a contrite heart : and will save such as be of an humble spirit.

18 Great are the troubles of the righteous : but the Lord delivereth him out of all.

19 He keepeth all his bones : so that not one of them is broken.

20 But misfortune shall slay the ungodly : and they that hate the righteous shall be desolate.

21 The Lord delivereth the soules of his servants : and all they that put their trust in him, shall not be destitute.

Glory be to the Father, and to the Sonne : and to the holy Ghost.
As it was in the beginning, is now, and ever shall be : world without end. *Amen.*

PSAL. 46.

GOd is our hope and strength : a verie present helpe in trouble.

2 Therefore will wee not feare though the earth be mooved : and though the hills bee carried into the midst of the Sea.

3 Though the waters thereof rage, and swell : and though the mountaines shake at the tempest of the same.

4 The Rivers of the floods thereof shall make glad the Citie of God : the holy place of the Tabernacle of the most Highest.

5 God is in the middest of her, therefore shall she not bee remooved : God shall helpe her, and that right early.

6 The heathen make much adoe, and the Kingdomes are mooved : but God hath shewed his voyce, and the earth shall melt away.

7 The Lord of hosts is with us : the God of Jacob is our refuge.

8 O come hither, and behold the workes of the Lord : what destruction hee hath brought upon the earth.

9 He maketh warres to cease in all the World : he breaketh the bow, and knappeth the speare in sunder, and burneth the chariots in the fire.

10 Bee still then, and know that I am God : I will bee exalted among the heathen, and I will be exalted in the earth.

11 The Lord of hosts is with us : the God of Jacob is our refuge.

Glory bee to the Father, and to the Sonne : and to the holy Ghost.

As it was in the beginning, is now and ever shall be : world without end. *Amen.*

PSAL. 54.

SAve mee, O God, for thy Names sake : & avenge me in thy strength.

2 Heare my prayer, O God : and hearken unto the words of my mouth.

3 For strangers are risen up against me : and tyrants (which have not God before their eyes) seeke after my soule.

4 Behold, God is my helper : the Lord is with them that uphold my soule.

5 He shall reward evill unto mine enemies : destroy thou them in thy truth.

6 An offering of a free heart will I give thee : and praise thy Name (O Lord) because it is so comfortable.

7 For hee hath delivered mee out of all my trouble : and mine eye hath seene his desire upon mine enemies.

Glory bee to the Father, and to the Sonne : and to the holy Ghost.

As it was in the beginning, is now, and ever shall bee : world without end. *Amen.*

THE BENEDICTION.

BLessed are the mercifull, for they shall obtaine mercie.

THE LESSON.

EPHES. 5. ROM. 12.

BE yee followers of God as deere children: and walke in love, even as Christ loved us, and gave himselfe for us an offering, and a sacrifice of a sweete savour unto God. Offer up your bodies as a living sacrifice, holy and acceptable unto God, which is your reasonable service of God. And fashion not your selves like unto this World.

Vers. The Lord is loving unto everie man.
Resp. And his mercy is over all his workes.

THE PRAYERS.

I.

HEare me, O Lord, and remember now that houre, in which thou diddest once commend thy blessed Spirit into the hands of thy heavenly Father: when with a torne Body, and a broken Heart thou didst shew forth the bowels of thy mercie, & die for us. I beseech thee, O Thou Brightnesse and Image of God, so to assist me by this thy most precious death, that being dead unto the World, I may live onely unto thee: and at the last houre of my departing from this mortall life, I may commend my soule into thy hands, and thou mayest receive me into life immortall, there to reigne with Thee for ever and ever. *Amen.*

II.

ALmighty God, who of thy tender love towards man, hast sent our Saviour Christ to suffer death upon the Crosse for us, that all mankind should follow the example of his great humility: mercifully grant that we, who have this his most precious Death and Passion in continuall remembrance, may both follow the example of his patience, and be made partakers of his glorie, through the same Jesus Christ our Lord. *Amen.*

The Lords Name be praysed.

THE END OF THE
NINTH HOURE.

PRAYERS
AT
THE VESPERS,
OR
TIME OF EVENSONG.

THE ANCIENT USE OF EVENING PRAYER.

T*He* MORNING *began, the* THREE HOURES *continued, and the* EVENING *ends our day. Neither is any worke wee take in hand like to prosper, unlesse it be begun, continued, and ended in Him, who must prevent us with his gracious favour, and further us with his continuall helpe.*

In which regard, the very Heathens, who knew not how to serve God aright, yet thus much they knew, that in the MORNING *and the* *EVENING *there was a service to bee given him, and they acknowledged it every mans duty to performe the same.*

*PLA. 10. de legibus.

Besides, in the *Old *Law, the* EVENING *was a speciall time appointed by God himselfe for the offering up of solemne Sacrifice: and in the* *New, *Christ chose it for the institution of his Blessed Supper; a Time also wherin his bruised* **Body was taken downe from the Crosse, and laid up in the Grave. Which being all the sacred mysteries of our Christian Religion, and the* **Time it selfe most naturally inviting, and admonishing us to Contemplation and Prayer; needs must they bee either indevout, or somewhat worse, that will not duly observe* THIS HOURE *of Gods service. The Testimonies and Examples of Holy men are these.*

*Exo. 12. 6 Nu. 28. 4.

*Mat. 26. 20.

*Mat. 27. 57.

*ISID. *Etym. lib.* 6.

GEN. 24. 63.

ANd ISAAC went out to meditate, or to pray, in the EVENING.

EXOD. 12. 6.

And the whole multitude of the people shall offer it in sacrifice at the EVENING.

NUMB. 28. 2. & 4.

My Sacrifices yee shall observe to offer to me in their due season : in the EVENING ye shall offer, &c.

PSAL. 55. 18.

In the EVENING will I pray, and he shall heare my voyce.

PSAL. 65. 8.

Who makest the outgoings of the morning, and EVENING to praise thee.

PSAL. 14. I. 2.

Let my prayer be set forth in thy sight as the Incense : and let the lifting up of my hands be as an EVENING SACRIFICE.

MAT. 26. 20.

In the EVENING he sate downe with the Twelve. And whilest they were at supper, JESUS tooke Bread and blessed it, &c.

MARK. 13. 35.

Watch yee therefore, for yee know not when the Lord of the house will come, whether in the EVENING, or at midnight, &c.

CLEM. CONST. LIB. 8. CAP. 34.

LEt your devout Prayers bee made also in the EVENING with thanksgiving unto God, who hath given you THE NIGHT, wherein to rest from your daily labours.

4 PSAL. 55. 18.: PSAL. 55. 17. *7 8*

CONCIL. LAODIC. CAN. 18.

And fit it is, the same order of Prayer should be observed in the VESPERS, or the EVEN-SONG of the Church.

S. BASIL. ORAT. IN S. JULIT.

When thou lookest upon the Heavens, and beholdest the beautie of the Starres, adore Him that in his wisedome made them all for thee. When the day is ended, and THE NIGHT approcheth on, fall downe and worship Him, who made both the day and THE NIGHT, to give thee joy and rest.

S. AMBROS. LIB. 3. EP. II.

I began to think upon that *Versicle*, which wee had used a little before in our EVEN-SONG.

S. HIER. AD EUSTOCH.

The EVENING is a common and usuall Time of Prayer with all men.

ISID. CAP. 20. DE ECCL. OFF. L. I.

In honour and memory of those great Mysteries, which at THIS TIME have been performed for us, do we present our selves with the Sacrifice of Prayers and Thanksgiving, before the presence of Almightie God.

PRAYERS FOR THE EVENING.

OUr Father which art in heaven. Hallowed be thy Name. Thy kingdom come. Thy will be done in earth as it is in heaven. Give us this day our daily bread.

And forgive us our trespasses, as we forgive them that trespasse against us. And leade us not into temptation: but deliver us from evill. *Amen.*

Vers. O God make speed to save me.
Resp. O Lord make hast to help me.

Glory bee to the Father, and to the Sonne: and to the holy Ghost.
As it was in the beginning, is now and ever shall be: world without end. *Amen.*

ALLELUIA. Praise the Lord.

THE HYMNE.

Salvator mundi Domine.

BLessed Saviour, Lord of all;
Vouchsafe to heare us when we call:
And now to those propitious be,
That in Prayer bow to Thee,
Still to be kept from miserie.

Great Ruler of the Day and Night,
On our darknesse cast thy Light:
And let thy Passion pardon winne
For what we have offended in
Thought, or word, or deed of sinne.

And as thy Mercy wipes away
What we have done amisse to day:
So now the night returnes againe,
Our Bodies & our Soules refraine,
From being soyld with sinful staine.

3 evill. *Amen.*: evill. &c. *Amen.* *3*: evil. For thine is . . . *Amen.* *7 8*

Let not dull sleepe oppresse our eyes,
Nor us the enemie surprise:
  Nor feareful dreames our minds affright,
  While the blacknes of the Night,
  Holds from us the cheareful Light.

To Thee who dost by Rest renue
Our wasted strength, we humbly sue,
  That when we shal unclose our eies,
  Pure and chast we may arise,
  And make our Morning Sacrifice.

Honour, Lord, to thee be done,
O Thou Blessed Virgins Sonne,
  With the Father, and the Spirit,
  As is thine eternall merit,
  Ever and ever to inherit.

Amen.

The Antiphona.

HE hath made the out-goings of the Morning and Evening to prayse Him.

Psal. III.

I Will give thanks unto the Lord with my whole heart : secretly among the faithfull, and in the Congregation.

2 The workes of the Lord are great : sought out of all them that have pleasure therein.

3 His worke is worthy to bee praysed, and had in honour : and his righteousnesse endureth for ever.

4 The mercifull and gracious Lord hath so done his marveilous workes : that they ought to be had in remembrance.

5 Hee hath given meate unto them that feare him : he shall ever be mindfull of his Covenant.

6 He hath shewed his people the power of his workes : that he may give them the heritage of the Heathen.

7 The workes of his hands are Veritie and Judgement : all his Commandements are true.

8 They stand fast for ever and ever : and are done in truth and equitie.

9 Hee sent redemption unto his people : hee hath commanded his Covenant for ever, holy and reverent is his Name.

10 The feare of the Lord is the beginning of wisedome : a good understanding have all they that do thereafter, the prayse of it endureth for ever.

Glory bee to the Father, and to the Sonne : and to the holy Ghost.

As it was in the beginning, is now, and ever shall be : world without end. *Amen.*

PSAL. 112.

BLessed is the man that feareth the Lord : he hath great delight in his commandements.

2 His seed shall be mightie upon earth : the generation of the faithful shall be blessed.

3 Riches and plenteousnesse shall bee in his house : and his righteousnesse endureth for ever.

4 Unto the godly there ariseth up light in the darkenesse : hee is mercifull, loving and righteous.

5 A good man is mercifull, and lendeth : and will guide his words with discretion.

6 For he shall never bee mooved : and the righteous shall bee had in an everlasting remembrance.

10 reverent: reverend *7 8*

7 Hee will not bee afraid for any evill tidings : for his heart standeth fast, and beleeveth in the Lord.

8 His heart is stablished and will not shrinke : untill he see his desire upon his enemies.

9 Hee hath disperced abroad, and given to the poore : and his righteousnesse remaineth for ever, his horne shall bee exalted with honor.

10 The ungodly shall see it, and it shall grieve him : he shall gnash with his teeth, & consume away, the desire of the ungodly shall perish.

Glory bee to the Father, and to the Sonne : and to the holy Ghost.

As it was in the beginning, is now, and ever shall be : world without end. *Amen.*

PSAL. 141.

LOrd, I call upon thee, haste thee unto mee : and consider my voyce when I crie unto thee.

2 Let my prayer be set forth in thy sight as the incense : and let the lifting up of my hands bee an evening sacrifice.

3 Set a watch (O Lord) before my mouth : and keepe the doore of my lips.

4 O let not mine heart be enclined to any evill thing : let mee not bee occupied in ungodly workes with the men that worke wickednesse, lest I eate of such things as please them.

5 Let the righteous rather smite me friendly : and reproove me.

6 But let not their precious balmes breake mine head : yea, I will pray yet against their wickednesse.

7 Let their Judges bee overthrowne in stony places : that they may heare my words, for they are sweet.

8 Our bones lie scattered before the pit : like as when one breaketh and heweth wood upon the earth.

9 But mine eyes looke unto thee, O Lord God : in thee is my trust, O cast not out my soule.

10 Keepe me from the snare which they have laid for me : and from the traps of the wicked dooers.

11 Let the ungodly fall into their owne nets together : and let me ever escape them.

Glory bee to the Father, and to the Sonne : and to the holy Ghost.

As it was in the beginning, is now, and ever shall bee : world without end. *Amen.*

THE BENEDICTION.

BLessed are the pure in heart, for they shall see God.

THE LESSON.

MARK. 13.

TAke heed, watch and pray: for yee know not when the time is. For the Sonne of Man is as one taking a farre journey, who left his house, and gave authoritie to his servants, and to everie man his worke, and commanded the Porter to watch. Watch yee therefore, for ye know not, when the Master of the house will come, at Even, or at Mid-night, or at the Cock-crowing, or in the Morning: lest if hee come suddenly, hee find you sleeping. And what I say unto you, I say unto all, Watch. *At that time Jesus said: Come unto mee all yee that are laboured, and sore travailed, and I will give

*MAT. 11.

you Rest. Take my yoke upon you, (my yoke is easie, and my burden light,) and learne of me, for I am meeke and lowly in heart, and yee shall find rest unto your soules.

THE MAGNIFICAT
OF THE
BLESSED VIRGIN MARIE.

MY soule doth magnifie the Lord : and my spirit hath rejoyced in God my Saviour.

For he hath regarded: the lowlines of his handmaiden.

For behold from henceforth : all generations shall call me blessed.

For hee that is mightie hath magnified mee : and holy is his Name.

And his mercy is on them that feare him : thorowout all generations.

He hath shewed strength with his arme : he hath scattered the proud in the imagination of their hearts.

He hath put downe the mighty from their seate : and hath exalted the humble and meeke.

He hath filled the hungry with good things : and the rich hee hath sent emptie away.

Hee remembring his mercy hath holpen his servant Israel : as hee promised to our forefathers, Abraham, and his seed for ever.

Glory bee to the Father, and to the Sonne : and to the holy Ghost.

As it was in the beginning, is now, and ever shall be : world without end. *Amen.*

2 burden light: burden is light *6*

THE PRAYERS.

I.

O God from whom all holy desires, all good counsels, and all just works do proceed, give unto thy servants that peace which the world cannot give, that both our hearts may bee set to obey thy commandements, and also that by thee we being defended from the feare of our enemies, may passe our time in rest and quietnes, through the merits of Jesus Christ our Saviour. *Amen.*

II.

ALmightie God, the Fountaine of all wisedome, which knowest our necessities before we ask, and our ignorance in asking, we beseech thee to have compassion upon our infirmities, and those things which for our unworthinesse wee dare not, and for our blindnesse we cannot aske, vouchsafe to give us for the worthines of thy Sonne Jesus Christ our Lord. *Amen.*

III.

O Lord our heavenly Father, Almightie and everliving God, by whose providence both the day and the night are governed: vouchsafe, we beseech thee, as thou hast this day preserved us by thy goodnesse, so still this night to shadow us under the blessed wings of thy most mightie protection, and to cover us with thy heavenly mercy, that neither the Princes of darkenesse may have any power over us, nor the workes of darkenesse overwhelme us, but that wee being armed with thy defence, may bee preserved from all adversities which may hurt the body, & from all wicked thoughts which may assault and defile the soule, through Jesus Christ our Lord. *Amen.*

IV.

O Thou that art the Light eternall, and the Sonne of Righteousnesse, evermore arising, and never going downe, giving life, and food, and gladnesse unto all things: mercifully vouchsafe to shine upon me, and cast thy blessed beames upon the darkenesse of my understanding, and the blacke mists of my sinnes and errors, for thy onely merits, who art alone my Saviour Jesus Christ our Lord. *Amen.*

THe Lords Name is praised from the rising up of the Sunne, unto the going downe thereof.

THE END OF THE
PRAYERS AT EVENING.

THE COMPLINE,

OR

FINAL PRAYERS TO BE SAID BEFORE BED-TIME.

PSAL. 132. 4.

I Will not suffer mine eies to SLEEPE, nor mine eie-lids to SLUMBER, nor the temples of my head to take any REST; untill I find out a place for the habitation of the Lord.

S. CHRYS. LIB. I. DE ORANDO DEUM.

Tell me, with what confidence canst thou lie downe to SLEEPE, and passe away the black darknes of the NIGHT? With what feareful and ougly dreames shall thy soule (thinkest thou) be troubled, unlesse thou shalt first arme thy selfe against such delusions and feares, by strong and devout Prayers? Let the wicked Spirits find thee without such a guard, and presently thou becommest a prey unto them: Let them but spie thee at thy Prayers, and presently like frighted Theeves they runne away.

THE PRAYERS.

THE ANTIPHONA.

GOd bee mercifull unto us, and blesse us, and shew us the light of his countenance, and be mercifull unto us.

PSAL. 91.

☞ To be said at this time, according to the direction of Saint BASIL, *in reg.*

WHo so dwelleth under the defence of the most High : shall abide under the shadow of the Almightie.

2 I will say unto the Lord, Thou art my hope, and my strong hold : my God, in him will I trust.

3 For he shall deliver thee from the snare of the hunter : and from the noisome Pestilence.

4 Hee shall defend thee under his wings, and thou shalt bee safe under his feathers : his faithfulnesse and truth shall bee thy shield and buckler.

5 Thou shalt not bee afraid for any terror by night : nor for the arrow that flyeth by day.

6 For the Pestilence that walketh in the darkenesse : nor for the sicknes that destroyeth in the noone-day.

Glory be to the Father, and to the Sonne : and to the Holy Ghost.

As it was in the beginning, is now, and ever shall be : world without end. *Amen.*

THE LESSON.

I. PETER.

BE sober and watch, because your adversarie the divell goeth about like a roaring Lion, seeking whom he may devoure. And the day of the Lord will come as a thiefe in the night, in the which the Heavens shall passe away with a great noise, and the Elements shall melt with fervent heate. Seeing then that all these things shalbe disolved, what manner of persons ought we to bee in all holy conversation and godlinesse?

THE SONG OF SIMEON,

CALLED

NUNC DIMITTIS.

LOrd, now lettest thou thy servant depart in peace : according to thy Word.

For mine eyes have seene : thy salvation.

Which thou hast prepared : before the face of all people.

To bee a Light to lighten the Gentiles : and to be the Glory of thy people Israel.

Glory bee to the Father, and to the Sonne : and to the holy Ghost.

As it was in the beginning, is now, and ever shall bee : world without end. *Amen.*

THE CREED.

I Beleeve in God the Father Almightie, Maker of heaven and earth. And in Jesus Christ his only Sonne our Lord, which was conceived by the holy Ghost, borne of the Virgin Mary, suffered under Pontius Pilate, was crucified, dead, and buried, he descended into hell, the third day he rose againe from the dead, he ascended into heaven, and sitteth on the right hand of God the Father Almightie: from thence hee shall come to judge both the quick and the dead. I beleeve in the holy Ghost, the holy Catholik Church, the Communion of Saints, the forgivenesse of sinnes, the resurrection of the body, and the life everlasting. *Amen.*

Lord have mercy upon us.
Christ have mercy upon us.
Lord have mercy upon us.

OUr Father which art in Heaven, hallowed be thy Name. Thy Kingdom come. Thy wil be done in earth, as it is in heaven. Give us this day our daily bread. And forgive us our trespasses, as we forgive them that trespasse against us. And leade us not into temptation. But deliver us from evill. *Amen.*

THe Day is thine, and the Night is thine: Thou art worthy, O Lord to receive honour, and prayse, and worship for evermore.

THE PRAYERS.

I.

MErcifull Lord, who of thine abundant goodnesse towards us, hast made the day to travaile in, and ordained the Night wherein to take our rest: grant us such Rest of body, that wee may continually have a waking soule, to watch for the time when our Lord shall appeare to deliver us from this mortall life. Let no vaine or wandring fancie trouble us: let our ghostly enemies have no power over us, but let our minds be set wholly upon thy presence, to love, and feare, and rest in Thee alone: that being refreshed with a moderate and sober sleepe, wee may rise up againe with chearefull strength and gladnesse, to serve thee in all good workes, through Jesus Christ our Lord. *Amen.*

1–3 *add* V. / R. / V. / *at the versicles* 2 3 4 5 6
9 evill. *Amen.*: evill. &c. 2: evill. &c. *Amen.* 3
10 *add* Vers. *before* THe Day is . . . 2 3 5 6
11 Lord to: Lord, to 2 3 5
13 THE PRAYERS.: *om.* 6: *at head of the versicles* 2 3 4 5

II.

LIghten our darkenesse, wee beseech thee (O Lord) and by thy great mercy defend us from all perils and dangers of this night, for the love of thy onely Son our Saviour Jesus Christ. *Amen.*

THE BENEDICTION.

GOd the Father blesse me: God the Sonne defend me: God the holy Ghost preserve me now and for ever. *Amen.*

PRAYERS AT BED-TIME.

AN ADMONITION

BEFORE WE GOE TO SLEEPE.

PErmit not sluggish sleepe
to close your waking eye,
Till that with judgement deepe,
your daily deeds you trye.
He that his sins in conscience keepes,
when he to quiet goes
More desperate is than he that sleepes
amidst his mortall foes.

WHEN WE ENTER INTO OUR BED.

IN the Name of our Lord Jesus Christ (who was crucified upon his Crosse, and laid into his grave for me,) I lay me downe to rest; He blesse mee, keepe mee, and save mee; raise me up againe, and bring me at last to life eternall. *Amen.*

AS WE LIE DOWNE TO SLEEPE.

AT Night lie downe,
prepare to have
Thy sleepe thy death,
thy bed thy grave.

1–2 PRAYERS AT BED-TIME.: *add* To be committed unto perfect memorie. *2 3 4 5 6*

Awake, arise,
  thinke that thou hast
Thy life but lent,
  thy breath a blast.

I.

I Will lay me downe in peace, and take my rest, for it is thou Lord onely that makest mee dwell in safety.

II.

HAve mercy upon me, O Lord, now, and at the houre of death.

III.

PReserve mee while I am waking, and defend mee when I am sleeping, that my soule may continually watch for thee, and both body and soule may rest in thy peace for ever. *Amen*, *Amen*, *Amen*.

THE END OF THE
LAST HOURE AT NIGHT.

THE SEVEN PENITENTIALL PSALMES,

WITH

THE LETANIE

AND

SUFFRAGES.

THE SEVEN PENITENTIALL PSALMES,

To be used in times of Penance, Fasting, Affliction, or Trouble; or, at any other time, as private Devotion shall move us.

THE ANTIPHONA.

REmember not, Lord, our offences, nor the offences of our forefathers, neither take thou vengeance of our sinnes : spare us good Lord, spare thy people, whom thou hast redeemed with thy most precious blood, and be not angry with us for ever.

PSAL. 6.

Domine ne in furore.

O Lord, rebuke me not in thine indignation : neither chasten mee in thy displeasure.

2 Have mercy upon me, O Lord, for I am weake : O Lord heale me, for my bones are vexed.

3 My soule is also sore troubled : but Lord, how long wilt thou punish me?

4 Turne thee, O Lord, and deliver my soule : O save me for thy mercies sake.

5 For in death no man remembreth thee : and who will give thee thankes in the pit?

6 I am wearie of my groaning, every night wash I my bed: and water my couch with my teares.

7 My beautie is gone for very trouble : and worne away, because of all mine enemies.

8 Away from me, all yee that worke vanitie : for the Lord hath heard the voyce of my weeping.

9 The Lord hath heard my petition : the Lord will receive my prayer.

10 All mine enemies shall bee confounded and sore vexed : they shall be turned backe, and put to shame suddenly.

Glory bee to the Father, and to the Sonne : and to the holy Ghost.

As it was in the beginning, is now, and ever shall be : world without end. *Amen.*

PSAL. 32.

Beati quorum.

BLessed is he whose unrighteousnesse is forgiven : and whose sinne is covered.

2 Blessed is the man, unto whom the Lord imputeth no sin : and in whose spirit there is no guile.

3 For while I held my tongue : my bones consumed away through my daily complaining.

4 For thy hand is heavie upon me day and night : and my moysture is like the drought in Summer.

5 I will knowledge my sinne unto thee : and mine unrighteousnesse have I not hid.

6 I said, I will confesse my sinnes unto the Lord : and so thou forgavest the wickednesse of my sinne.

7 For this shall every one that is godly, make his prayer unto thee in a time when thou mayest be found : but in the great water-floods they shall not come nigh him.

8 Thou art a place to hide mee in, thou shalt preserve me from trouble : thou shalt compasse mee about with songs of deliverance.

9 I will informe thee, and teach thee in the way wherein thou shalt goe : and I will guide thee with mine eye.

10 Be ye not like to Horse & Mule, which have no understanding : whose mouthes must be holden with bit and bridle, lest they fall upon thee.

11 Great plagues remaine for the ungodly : but whoso putteth his trust in the Lord, mercy embraceth him on every side.

12 Be glad, O ye righteous, and rejoyce in the Lord : and bee joyfull, all yee that are true of heart.

Glory bee to the Father, and to the Sonne : and to the holy Ghost.

As it was in the beginning, is now and ever shall be : world without end. *Amen.*

PSAL. 38.

Domine ne in furore.

PUt mee not to rebuke (O Lord) in thine anger : neither chasten mee in thine heavie displeasure.

2 For thine Arrowes sticke fast in me : and thy hand presseth me sore.

3 There is no health in my flesh, because of thy displeasure : neither is there any rest in my bones, by reason of my sinne.

4 For my wickednesses are gone over my head : and are like a sore burden, too heavie for me to beare.

5 My wounds stinke, and are corrupt : through my foolishnesse.

6 I am brought into so great trouble and miserie : that I goe mourning all the day long.

7 For my loines are filled with a sore disease : and there is no whole part in my body.

8 I am feeble and sore smitten : I have roared for the very disquietnesse of my heart.

9 Lord, thou knowest all my desire : and my groaning is not hid from thee.

10 My heart panteth, my strength hath failed me : and the sight of mine eies is gone from me.

11 My lovers and my neighbours did stand looking upon my trouble : and my kinsmen stood afarre off.

12 They also that sought after my life, laid snares for mee : and they that went about to doe mee evill, talked of wickednesse, and imagined deceit all the day long.

13 As for me, I was like a deafe man, and heard not : and as one that is dumbe, which doth not open his mouth.

14 I became even as a man that heareth not : and in whose mouth are no reproofes.

15 For in thee, O Lord, have I put my trust : thou shalt answer for me, O Lord, my God.

16 I have required that they (even mine enemies) should not triumph over mee : for when my foot slipt, they rejoyced greatly against me.

17 And I truly am set in the plague : and my heavinesse is ever in my sight.

18 For I will confesse my wickednesse : and bee sorrie for my sinne.

19 But mine enemies live, and are mightie : and they that hate me wrongfully, are many in number.

20 They also that reward evill for good, are against me : because I follow the thing that good is.

21 Forsake me not, O Lord my God : be not thou farre from me.

22 Haste thee to helpe me : O Lord God of my salvation.

Glory bee to the Father, and to the Sonne : and to the holy Ghost.

As it was in the beginning, is now and ever shall be : world without end. *Amen.*

PSAL. 51.

Miserere mei Deus.

HAve mercy upon me, O God, after thy great goodnesse : according to the multitude of thy mercies doe away mine offences.

2 Wash mee thorowly from my wickednesse : and cleanse me from my sinne.

3 For I knowledge my faults : and my sinne is ever before me.

4 Against thee onely have I sinned, and done this evill in thy sight : that thou mightest be justified in thy saying, and cleare when thou art judged.

5 Behold, I was shapen in wickednesse : and in sinne hath my mother conceived me.

6 But loe, thou requirest truth in the inward parts : and shalt make me to understand wisdome secretly.

7 Thou shalt purge me with hysope, and I shall be cleane : thou shalt wash me, and I shall be whiter than snow.

8 Thou shalt make me heare of joy and gladnesse : that the bones which thou hast broken may rejoyce.

9 Turne thy face from my sinnes : and put out all my misdeeds.

10 Make mee a cleane heart (O God :) and renew a right spirit within me.

11 Cast mee not away from thy presence : and take not thy holy Spirit from me.

12 O give mee the comfort of thy helpe againe : and stablish me with thy free Spirit.

13 Then shall I teach thy wayes unto the wicked : and sinners shalbe converted unto thee.

14 Deliver mee from blood-guiltinesse, O God, thou that art the God of my health : and my tongue shall sing of thy righteousnesse.

15 Thou shalt open my lippes (O Lord :) and my mouth shall shew forth thy prayse.

16 For thou desirest no sacrifice, else would I give it thee : but thou delightest not in burnt offerings.

17 The sacrifice of God is a troubled spirit : a broken and contrite heart (O God) shalt thou not despise.

18 O be favourable and gracious unto Sion, build thou the walls of Jerusalem.

19 Then shalt thou be pleased with the sacrifice of righteousnesse, with the burnt offerings and oblations, then shall they offer young bullocks upon thine Altar.

Glory bee to the Father, and to the Sonne : and to the holy Ghost.

As it was in the beginning, is now, and ever shall bee : world without end. *Amen.*

PSAL. 102.

Domine exaudi.

HEare my prayer, O Lord : and let my crying come unto thee.

2 Hide not thy face from me in the time of my trouble : encline thine eares unto mee when I call, O heare me, and that right soone.

3 For my dayes are consumed away like smoke : and my bones are burnt up as it were a fire-brand.

4 My heart is smitten downe, and withered like grasse : so that I forget to eate my bread.

5 For the voyce of my groaning : my bones will scarce cleave to my flesh.

6 I am become like a Pelicane in the Wildernesse : and like an Owle that is in the Desart.

7 I have watched, and am even as it were a Sparrow : that sitteth alone upon the house top.

8 Mine enemies revile me all the day long : and they that are mad upon me, are sworne together against me.

9 For I have eaten ashes as it were bread : and mingled my drinke with weeping.

10 And that because of thine indignation and wrath : for thou hast taken mee up, and cast mee downe.

11 My dayes are gone like a shadow : and I am withered like grasse.

12 But thou (O Lord) shalt endure for ever : and thy remembrance throughout all generations.

13 Thou shalt arise and have mercy on Sion : for it is time that thou have mercy upon her, yea, the time is come.

14 And why? thy servants thinke upon her stones : and it pittieth them to see her in the dust.

15 The heathen shall feare thy Name, O Lord : and all the kings of the earth thy Majestie.

16 When the Lord shall build up Sion : and when his glory shal appeare.

17 When he turneth him unto the prayer of the poore destitute : and despiseth not their desire.

18 This shall bee written for those that come after : and the people which shall be borne, shall praise the Lord.

19 For he hath looked downe from his Sanctuarie : out of the Heavens did the Lord behold the earth.

20 That hee might heare the mournings of such as bee in captivitie : and deliver the children appointed unto death.

21 That they may declare the Name of the Lord in Sion : and his worship at Jerusalem.

22 When the people are gathered together : and the kingdomes also to serve the Lord.

23 Hee brought downe my strength in my journey : and shortned my dayes.

24 But I said, O my God, take me not away in the midst of my age : as for thy yeares, they endure throughout all generations.

25 Thou Lord in the beginning hast laid the foundation of the earth : and the Heavens are the worke of thy hands.

26 They shall perish, but thou shalt endure : they all shall ware old as doth a garment.

27 And as a vesture shalt thou change them, and they shall bee changed : but thou art the same, and thy yeeres shall not faile.

28 The children of thy servants shall continue : and their seed shall stand fast in thy sight.

Glory be to the Father, and to the Sonne : and to the holy Ghost.

As it was in the beginning, is now, and ever shall be : world without end. *Amen.*

Psal. 130.

De profundis.

OUt of the Deepe have I called unto thee (O Lord :) Lord heare my voyce.

2 O let thine eares consider well : the voyce of my complaint.

3 If thou, Lord, wilt bee extreame to marke what is done amisse : O Lord who may abide it?

4 For there is mercy with thee : therefore shalt thou bee feared.

5 I looke for the Lord, my soule doth waite for him : in his Word is my trust.

6 My soule fleeth unto the Lord : before the morning watch, I say, before the morning watch.

7 O Israel, trust in the Lord, for with the Lord there is mercy : and with him is plenteous redemption.

8 And he shall redeeme Israel : from all his sinnes.

Glory bee to the Father, and to the Sonne : and to the holy Ghost.

As it was in the beginning, is now, and ever shall be : world without end. *Amen.*

Psal. 143.

Domine exaudi.

HEare my prayer, O Lord, and consider my desire : hearken unto me for thy truth and righteousnes sake.

2 And enter not into judgement with thy servant : for in thy sight shall no man living be justified.

3 For the enemie hath persecuted my soule, hee hath smitten my life downe to the ground : hee hath laid me in the darkenesse, as the men that have been long dead.

4 Therefore is my spirit vexed within mee : and my heart within me is desolate.

5 Yet do I remember the time past, I muse upon all thy works : yea, I exercise my selfe in the workes of thy hands.

6 I stretch forth my hands unto thee : my soule gaspeth unto thee as a thirstie land.

7 Heare me, O Lord, and that soone, for my spirit waxeth faint : hide not thy face from me, lest I be like unto them that go downe into the pit.

8 O let me heare thy loving kindnes betimes in the morning, for in thee is my trust : shew thou mee the way that I should walk in, for I lift up my soule unto thee.

9 Deliver me, O Lord, from mine enemies : for I flee unto thee to hide me.

10 Teach me to doe the thing that pleaseth thee, for thou art my God : let thy loving Spirit leade me forth into the land of righteousnesse.

11 Quicken me, O Lord, for thy Names sake, and for thy righteousnes sake bring my soule out of trouble.

12 And of thy goodnesse slay mine enemies : and destroy all them that vexe my soule, for I am thy servant.

Glory bee to the Father, and to the Sonne : and to the holy Ghost.

As it was in the beginning, is now, and ever shall be : world without end. *Amen.*

THE ANTIPHONA.

REmember not, Lord, our offences, nor the offences of our forefathers, neither take thou vengeance of our sinnes: spare us good Lord, spare thy people, whom thou hast redeemed with thy most precious blood, and be not angry with us for ever.

THE LETANY,
TO BEE USED ON SUNDAIES, WEDNESDAIES, AND FRIDAIES

after the Morning Prayers, or any other Houre of Devotion:

AS ALSO UPON THE ROGATION AND FASTING

daies; and in the time of Plague, Famine, Warre, and other Calamities.

SUch miseries as being present or imminent, all men are apt to bewaile with their teares, they that bee religious and wise, wil ever seeke to prevent, or avert with their prayers. In regard whereof these LETANIES were at first composed by the Fathers in the **Primitive Church*, solemnely to be used for the appeasing of Gods wrath in publike evils, and for the procuring of his mercy in common benefits.

At the first they were not so large as now they are, being augmented by MAMERCUS Bishop of *Vienna*, and by *SIDONIUS APOLLINARIS, Bishop of *Averna*, and afterwards by S. GREGORIE the Great, Bish. of *Rome*, in whose times there was much affliction and trouble throughout the World.

From their dayes they have beene brought downe to ours; and in the meane while got some rust: the Addition and Invocation of the SAINTS names,

*Antiq. Liturg. Iren. *lib. 2. cap. 57.* Prosp. *de vocat. Gent. cap. 4.* Tertul. *lib. 2, ad uxor.* S. Hieron. *ad* Eustoch. S. Basil. *epist. 63.* Ruffin *hist. lib. 2. cap. 23.*

*Sidon. Apoll. *Ep. ad* Mamer. *&* Apium.

14 *add in margin* R. H. *l.* 5. 2 3 4 5 6

*Wal. Strabo *de reb. Eccl. cap.* de Letaniis.

which some men have thereunto annexed, being by *WALAFRIDE STRABO's owne confession, but a Noveltie; and therefore are not inserted into these *our Letanies*: which being lately by our owne Church brought into that absolute perfection, both for matter and forme, as not any Church besides can shew the like, so compleate and full, needs must they be *upbraided either with error, or somewhat worse, whom in all parts this principal and excellent Prayer doth not fully satisfie.

*R. H. *l.* 5.

THE LETANIE.

O God the Father of Heaven : have mercie upon us miserable sinners.

O God the Father of Heaven : have mercy upon us miserable sinners.

O God the Sonne, Redeemer of the World : have mercie upon us miserable sinners.

O God the Sonne, Redeemer of the World : have mercy upon us miserable sinners.

O God the holy Ghost, proceeding from the Father and the Sonne, have mercie upon us miserable sinners.

O God the holy Ghost, proceeding from the Father and the Sonne, have mercy upon us miserable sinners.

O holy, blessed, and glorious Trinitie, three Persons and one God : have mercie upon us miserable sinners.

O holy, blessed, and glorious Trinitie, three Persons and one God : have mercie upon us miserable sinners.

1 which . . . annexed,: (which . . . annexed,) *2 3 4 5 6*

Remember not Lord our offences, nor the offences of our forefathers, neither take thou vengeance of our sinnes : spare us good Lord, spare thy people whom thou hast redeemed with thy most precious blood, and bee not angry with us for ever.

Spare us good Lord.

From all evill & mischiefe, from sin, from the crafts and assaults of the devill, from thy wrath and from everlasting damnation.

Good Lord deliver us.

From all blindnesse of heart, from pride, vaine-glory and hypocrisie, from envie, hatred, and malice, and all uncharitablenesse.

Good Lord deliver us.

From fornication, and all other deadly sinne, and from all the deceits of the world, the flesh and the devill.

Good Lord deliver us.

From lightning and tempest, from plague, pestilence and famine, from battell and murder, and from sudden death.

Good Lord deliver us.

From all sedition and privie conspiracie, from al false doctrine and heresie, from hardnesse of heart, and contempt of thy word and commandement.

Good Lord deliver us.

By the mysterie of thy holy Incarnation, by thy holy Nativitie and Circumcision, by thy Baptisme, Fasting and Temptation.

Good Lord deliver us.

By thine Agonie and bloodie Sweate, by thy Crosse and Passion, by thy precious Death and Buriall, by thy glorious Resurrection and Ascension, and by the comming of the holy Ghost.

Good Lord deliver us.

In all time of our tribulation, in all time of our wealth, in the houre of death, and in the day of Judgement.

Good Lord deliver us.

We sinners doe beseech thee to heare us (O Lord God) and that it may please thee to rule and governe the holy Church universally in the right way.

Wee beseech thee to heare us good Lord.

That it may please thee to keepe and strengthen in the true worshipping of thee, in righteousnesse and holinesse of life, thy servant *Charles*, our most gracious King and Governour.

We beseech thee to heare us good Lord.

That it may please thee to rule his heart in thy faith, feare and love, and that hee may evermore have affiance in thee, and ever seeke thy honour and glory.

We beseech thee to heare us good Lord.

That it may please thee to bee his defender & keeper, giving him the victory over all his enemies.

We beseech thee to heare us good Lord.

That it may please thee to blesse our most Gracious Queene *Marie*, *Frederick* the Prince Elector Palatine, and the Lady *Elizabeth* his wife, with their Princely Issue.

We beseech thee to heare us good Lord.

That it may please thee to illuminate all Bishops, Pastours and Ministers of the Church, with true knowledge and understanding of thy Word, and that both by their preaching and living they may set it forth, and shew it accordingly.

We beseech thee to heare us good Lord.

21–22 Queene *Marie* . . . Issue.: Queene *Marie*, Prince *Charles*, and the rest of the Royall Progenie, and the Lady *Elizabeth*, with her Princely Issue. *4 5*: Queen CATHERINE, MARY the Queen Mother, JAMES Duke of *York*, and all the Royal Family; *7*: Queen CATHERINE, JAMES Duke of *York*, and all the Royal Family. *8*

24–26 Bishops, . . . knowledge: Bishops, Priests and Deacons with true knowledge *7 8*

That it may please thee to endue the Lords of the Councell, and all the Nobilitie, with grace, wisedome, and understanding.

We beseech thee to heare us good Lord.

That it may please thee to blesse and keepe the Magistrates, giving them grace to execute justice, and to maintaine truth.

We beseech thee to heare us good Lord.

That it may please thee to blesse and keepe all thy [people.

We beseech thee to heare us good Lord.

That it may please thee to give to all Nations unitie, peace and concord.

We beseech thee to heare us good Lord.

That it may please thee to give us an heart to love and dread thee, and diligently to live after thy Commandements.

We beseech thee to heare us good Lord.

That it may please thee to give to all thy people increase of grace to heare meekely thy Word, and to receive it with pure affection, and to bring forth the fruits of the Spirit.

We beseech thee to heare us good Lord.

That it may please thee to bring into the way of truth, all such as have erred, and are deceived.

We beseech thee to heare us good Lord.

That it may please thee to strengthen such as doe stand, and to comfort and helpe the weake-hearted, and to raise up them that fall, and finally to beate downe Satan under our feete.

We beseech thee to heare us good Lord.

That it may please thee to succour, help, & comfort all that be in danger, necessitie and tribulation.

We beseech thee to heare us good Lord.

That it may please thee to preserve all that travell by land or by water, all women labouring of child, all sicke persons and young children, and to shew thy pitie upon all prisoners and captives.

We beseech thee to heare us good Lord.

That it may please thee to defend & provide for the fatherlesse children and widows, and all that be desolate and oppressed.

We beseech thee to heare us good Lord.

That it may please thee to have mercie upon all men.

We beseech thee to heare us good Lord.

That it may please thee to forgive our enemies, persecuters and slanderers, and to turne their hearts.

We beseech thee to heare us good Lord.

That it may please thee to give and preserve to our use, the kindly fruits of the earth, so as in due time we may enjoy them.

Wee beseech thee to heare us good Lord.

That it may please thee to give us true repentance, to forgive us all our sinnes, negligences and ignorances, and to endue us with the grace of thy holy Spirit, to amend our lives according to thy holy Word.

We beseech thee to heare us good Lord.

Sonne of God : we beseech thee to heare us.

Sonne of God : we beseech thee to heare us.

O Lambe of God, that takest away the sinnes of the World.

Grant us thy peace.

O Lambe of God, that takest away the sinnes of the World.

Have mercy upon us.

O Christ heare us.

O Christ heare us.

Lord have mercie upon us.
Lord have mercy upon us.
Christ have mercie upon us.
Christ have mercie upon us.
Lord have mercie upon us.
Lord have mercie upon us.

OUr Father which art in heaven. Hallowed be thy Name. Thy kingdom come. Thy will be done in earth as it is in heaven. Give us this day our daily bread. And forgive us our trespasses, as we forgive them that trespasse against us. And leade us not into temptation: but deliver us from evill. *Amen.*

Vers. O Lord deale not with us after our sinnes.
Resp. Neither reward us after our iniquities.

Let us pray.

O God mercifull Father, that despisest not the sighing of a contrite heart, nor the desire of such as bee sorrowfull, mercifully assist our prayers, that we make before thee in all our troubles and adversities whensoever they oppresse us: and graciously heare us, that those evils which the craft and subtiltie of the devill, or man worketh against us, be brought to nought, and by the providence of thy goodnesse they may be dispersed, that we thy servants being hurt by no persecutions, may evermore give thankes unto thee in thy holy Church, through Jesus Christ our Lord.

O Lord arise, helpe us, and deliver us for thy Names sake.

12 evill. *Amen.*: evill, &c. *2*: evill, &c. *Amen. 3*

O God, we have heard with our eares, and our fathers have declared unto us the noble works that thou diddest in their dayes, and in the old time before them.

O Lord, arise, helpe us, and deliver us for thine honour.

Glory bee to the Father, and to the Sonne : and to the holy Ghost.

As it was in the beginning, is now, and ever shall be : world without end. *Amen.*

From our enemies defend us O Christ.

Graciously looke upon our afflictions.

Pitifully behold the sorrowes of our hearts.

Mercifully forgive the sinnes of thy people.

Favourably with mercy heare our prayers.

O Sonne of David, have mercy upon us.

Both now and ever vouchsafe to heare us, O Christ.

Graciously heare us, O Christ : graciously heare us, O Lord Christ.

Vers. O Lord, let thy mercy be shewed upon us.

Resp. As wee doe put our trust in thee.

Let us pray.

WE humbly beseech thee, O Father, mercifully to looke upon our infirmities: and for the glorie of thy Names sake, turne from us all those evils, that wee most righteously have deserved: and grant, that in all our troubles we may put our whole trust and confidence in thy mercie, and evermore serve thee in holinesse and purenesse of living, to thy honour and glorie, through our onely Mediatour and Advocate Jesus Christ our Lord. *Amen.*

23 thy Names sake,: thy Name *7 8*

O GOD, whose nature and propertie is ever to have mercy and to forgive, receive our humble petitions: and though we bee tied and bound with the chaine of our sins, yet let the pitifulnes of thy great mercy loose us, for the honour of Jesus Christs sake, our Mediator and Advocate. *Amen.*

THe grace of our Lord Jesus Christ, and the love of God, and the fellowship of the holy Ghost, be with us all evermore. *Amen.*

1–6 O GOD . . . *Amen.*: *om. 7 8 substitute A Prayer of S.* Chrysostom.
7 *before the blessing* 2. Cor. 13. *2 4 5 6*: 2 Corinth. 13. 14. *7 8*

THE COLLECTS
FOR
THE SUNDAYES
AND
HOLY-DAYES
THROUGHOUT THE
WHOLE YEERE.

THE COLLECTS FOR THE SUNDAYES AND HOLIDAYES THROUGHOUT THE YEERE.

ADVENT SUNDAY.

THe foure Sundayes in *Advent*, are to the great Feast of *Christmas*, as the *Vigills* or *Eves* are to every *Saints day*, and *Lent* to the Feast of *Easter*, a solemne time of preparation to the blessed *Birth* of our Saviour, which Christians have been used to call his *Advent*, or *Comming* to us in the flesh.

It is the peculiar Computation of the Church, to begin her yeare, and to renew the annuall course of her Holy and Divine Service at this *Advent*; herein differing from all other Accounts & Revolutions of Time whatsoever. And it is to let the world know, that she neither numbreth her dayes, nor measureth her seasons so much by the motion of the *Sunne*, as by the Course of her *Saviour*, beginning and continuing on the yeere with Him, who being the true *Sonne of Righteousnesse*, began now to rise upon the World, and as the Day-starre from on high, to enlighten them that sate in spirituall darkenesse.

THE COLLECT FOR THE FIRST SUNDAY IN ADVENT.

ALmighty God, give us grace that wee may cast away the workes of darkenesse, and put on the armour of light, now in the time of this mortall life

25 put on: put upon us *7 8*

(in the which thy Sonne Jesus Christ came to visite us in great humilitie) that in the last day, when hee shall come againe in his glorious Majestie, to judge both the quicke and the dead, we may rise to life immortall, through him, who liveth and reigneth with thee and the holy Ghost now and ever. *Amen.*

The Collect for the second Sunday in Advent.

BLessed Lord, which hast caused all the holy Scriptures to bee written for our learning, grant that we may in such wise heare them, read, marke, learne, and inwardly digest them, that by patience and comfort of thy holy Word, wee may embrace, and ever hold fast the blessed hope of everlasting life, which thou hast given us in our Saviour Jesus Christ. *Amen.*

The Collect for the third Sunday in Advent.

LOrd, we beseech thee, give eare to our prayers, and by thy gracious visitation lighten the darknes of our hearts by our Lord Jesus Christ. *Amen.*

The Collect for the fourth Sunday in Advent.

LOrd, raise up, we pray thee, thy power, and come among us, and with great might succour us, that whereas through our sinnes and wickednesse wee bee sore let and hindred, thy bountifull grace and mercy (through the satisfaction of thy Sonne our Lord)

1 *om* the *7 8* 4 *om* the *7 8*
8 which: who *7 8* 16–18 *for the reading of 7 8 see Appendix, p. 307.*
20 Lord: O Lord *7* 22 bee: are *7 8*
23 hindred, thy: hindred in running the race that is set before us, thy *7*
24 (through . . . Lord) *om. entirely 7 8*

may speedily deliver us, to whom with thee and the holy Ghost, be honor and glory, world without end. *Amen.*

The Collect for Christmas day.

ALmightie GOD, which hast given us thy onely begotten Sonne to take our nature upon him, and this day to be borne of a pure Virgin, grant that we being regenerate, and made thy children by adoption and grace, may daily bee renewed by thy holy Spirit, through the same our Lord Jesus Christ, who liveth and reigneth with thee and the holy Ghost now and ever. *Amen.*

The Collect for Saint Stevens day.

GRant us, O Lord, to learne to love our enemies by the example of thy Martyr S. Steven, who prayed for his persecutors, to thee which livest and reignest now and for ever, world without end. *Amen.*

The Collect for S. John the Evangelists day.

MErcifull Lord, wee beseech thee to cast thy bright beames of light upon thy Church, that it being lightened by the doctrine of the blessed Apostle and Evangelist John, may attaine to thy everlasting gifts, through Jesus Christ our Lord. *Amen.*

1 may speedily deliver us, to whom: may speedily help and deliver us, through the satisfaction of thy Son our Lord, to whom *7 8*

4 which: who *7 8*

6 this day: as at this time *7 8*

10 with . . . ever.: with thee and the same Spirit, ever one God, world without end. *7 8*

13–16 *for the reading of 7 8 see Appendix, p. 307.*

19–23 *for the reading of 7 8 see Appendix, p. 307.*

The Collect for Innocents day.

ALmighty God, whose prayse this day the young Innocents thy Witnesses, have confessed & shewed forth, not in speaking but in dying, mortifie and kill all vices in us, that in our conversation our life may expresse thy faith, which with our tongues wee doe confesse, through Jesus Christ our Lord.

The Collect for the Sunday after Christmas day.

ALmightie God, which hast given us thine only begotten Son to take, &c. *As upon Christmas day.*

The Collect for the Circumcision of Christ.

ALmighty God, which madest thy blessed Sonne to bee circumcised and obedient to the Law for man, grant us the true circumcision of the Spirit, that our hearts, and all our members being mortified from all worldly and carnall lusts, may in all things obey thy blessed will, through the same thy Sonne Jesus Christ our Lord.

The Collect for the Epiphany.

O God, which by the leading of a Starre, diddest manifest thy onely begotten Son to the Gentiles, mercifully grant, that we which know thee now by faith, may after this life have the fruition of thy glorious Godhead, through Jesus Christ our Lord.

2–7 *for the reading of 7 8 see Appendix, p. 308.*
10–11 *printed here in full (as for Christmas Day) 7 8* 14 which: who *7 8*
18 lusts, may: lusts, we may *7 8* 20 *add Amen. 7 8*
22 which: who *7 8* 26 *add Amen. 7 8*

The Collect for the first Sunday after the Epiphany.

LOrd, we beseech thee mercifully to receive the praiers of thy people, which call upon thee, and grant that they may both perceive and know what things they ought to doe, and also have grace and power faithfully to fulfill the same, through Jesus Christ our Lord.

The Collect for the second Sunday after the Epiphany.

ALmightie & everlasting God, which doest governe al things in heaven and earth, mercifully heare the supplications of thy people, and grant us thy peace all the dayes of our life.

The Collect for the third Sunday after the Epiphany.

ALmightie & everlasting God, mercifully looke upon our infirmities, and in all our dangers and necessities, stretch forth thy right hand to help and defend us, through Christ our Lord.

The Collect for the fourth Sunday after the Epiphany.

GOd which knowest us to bee set in the midst of so many and great dangers, that for mans frailenes we cannot alway stand upright: grant to us the health

3 LOrd: O Lord *7 8*
6 also have: also may have *7 8*
7 *add Amen. 7 8*
10 which: who *7 8*
13 life.: life, through *Jesus* Christ our Lord. *Amen. 7 8*
19 through Christ our Lord.: through *Jesus* Christ our Lord. *Amen. 7 8*
20–21 *for the reading of 7 8 see Appendix, p. 308.*

of body & soule, that all those things which we suffer for sinne, by thy helpe we may wel passe and overcome, through Christ our Lord.

The Collect for the fifth Sunday after the Epiphany.

LOrd wee beseech thee to keepe thy Church and houshold continually in thy true Religion, that they which doe leane onely upon the hope of thy heavenly grace, may evermore bee defended by thy mighty power, through Christ our Lord.

SEPTUAGESIMA SUNDAY.

SEPTUAGESIMA (so called from the number of *Seventie*) is a solemne beginning of a new Office, and a new Time, wherein our Holie Mother the Church hath taught us, by calling to mind the *Time* of the Jewes Captivitie from their Countrie, the better to remember and bewaile our owne Captivitie from ours, even that Heavenly Paradise which God at first created for us. For which purpose the LESSONS of the Church-Service (saith *S. BERNARD) are this day altered in their course, and the Storie of GENESIS (where both our first happinesse, and our first miseries are described) is alwaies begun to bee read in SEPTUAGESIMA.

**Serm. 1. in Septua.*

It is a time therefore that suddenly calls us back from our CHRISTMAS feasting and joy, to our LENTEN fasting and sorrow; from thinking how Christ came into the

6 LOrd: O Lord *7 8*   8 which: who *7 8*
10 through Christ our Lord.: through *Jesus* Christ our Lord. *Amen. 7 8*
10 *a collect for the sixth Sunday after the Epiphany is added here in 7 8 (see Appendix, p. 308)*
22 *om.* first *6*

World, to thinke upon our owne sins and miseries which brought him into the World; to think upon them, and to bewaile, or reforme them withall; considering that Hee came not to take away their sinnes, who are not weary of them, or be loth to part with them, and amend their lives themselves.

To this end there was a godly Ordinance in the ancient Church, (made by the old Councell of *AUXERRE, more than a thousand yeeres since) that in the end of the EPIPHANY, there should be certaine dayes appointed (such as THIS, and the *TWO SUNDAYES following are) wherein to prepare the people for their solemne fasting and penance, and to give them warning of their LENT before hand, that when it came, it might bee the more strictly and religiously observed.

*Can. 2.

*Sexa. and Quinqu. Sundayes.

And afterwards, through the varietie of Fasting in divers places, it came to passe, that these THREE SUNDAYES were made to bee Three severall Beginnings of the LENT-FAST, some extending their solemne humiliation and sorrow to a larger Time than ordinary, and others excepting from it those dayes of the weeke, whereupon many Christians had either no custome, or no leave to Fast: all agreeing in this, that whether wee begin at SEPTUAGESIMA, or any the SUNDAYES following, the LENT-FAST is duely to bee kept at One solemne time of the yeere, and religiously to bee continued on to the Great Feast of EASTER.

1–3 our owne sins . . . considering: our sins and to bewaile, or reform them: withal considering, *6*

11 *marginal note continues* Sundaies, so called *â rotundâ enumeratione*, being placed between *Septuag.* & *Quadrag.* Sundaies. *2 3 4 5 6*

16 *om.* the *6*

21 dayes: *daies + *in margin* *Thursdaies and Saturdaies. *2 3 4 5 6*

23 all: most *2 3 4 5 6*

24 or any: or at anie *6*

26 religiously: duely *2 3 4 5 6*

THE COLLECT FOR SEPTUAGESIMA SUNDAY.

O Lord, we beseech thee favourably to heare the prayers of thy people, that we which are justly punished for our offences, may bee mercifully delivered by thy goodnesse, for the glorie of thy Name, through Jesus Christ our Saviour, who liveth and reigneth, &c.

The Collect for Sexagesima Sunday.

LOrd God, which seest that wee put not our trust in any thing that we do, mercifully grant that by thy power wee may bee defended against all adversitie, through Jesus Christ our Lord.

The Collect for Quinquagesima Sunday.

O Lord, which doest teach us, that all our doings without charitie are nothing worth, send the holy Ghost, and powre into our hearts that most excellent gift of charitie, the very bond of peace and all vertues, without the which whosoever liveth, is counted dead before thee: grant this for thy onely Son Jesus Christs sake.

---

4 which: who *7 8*

7 reigneth, &c.: reigneth with thee and the holy Ghost, ever one God, world without end. *Amen.* *7 8*

9 LOrd: O Lord *7 8*

9 which: who *7 8*

12 *add* *Amen.* *7 8*

14 which doest teach: who hast taught *7 8*

15 the: thy *7 8*

17 and all: and of all *7 8*

18 *om.* the *7 8*

19 thy: thine *7 8*

19–20 Christs sake.: Christ's sake. *Amen.* *7 8*

THE FIRST DAY OF LENT.

BY the ancient Lawes and custome of the Church of Christ, we still observe a yeerely solemne time of Fasting & Prayer, which from the season wherein it falls, we call our *LENT *Fast*. A time wherein the Church commemorateth the miraculous Fasting of our Saviour, and by it commendeth the like ghostly and religious exercise unto us, as being the readiest meanes we can use against the temptations of the Divell, and the sinfull desires of our pampered flesh. Not as if she thought we were able to fast as Christ did, and live altogether without meate and drinke, or as if her meaning were to tye us unto any such scrupulous Abstinence, which refuseth some kindes of meates as being uncleane in themselves, but that as farre as our imperfections and infirmities would suffer us, wee should tye our selves to such a religious Fast and Abstinence, as therby eyther interrupting or otherwise abating not only the kind but the quantitie of our dyet, and so taking the lesse care of our bodily sustenance, we might the more earnestly hunger and thirst after righteousnesse, which is the food of our soules; and by mortifying of our sinfull flesh, fixe our mindes upon heavenlier and better desires. A LENT so kept, will conform us the better to our Saviours *Sufferings*,

** The Spring.*

4–5 yeerely . . . Prayer,: yeerly and more solemne time of Fasting and Prayer, than ordinarie; *2 3 4 5 6*

6 **The Spring*.: *Or *Spring Fast*. For Lent signifieth *the Spring* in the Saxon language. *2 3 4 5 6*

10 temptations: **temptations*+*in margin* * Whereupon the *Gospell* of *Christs Fasting*, and resisting of the *Divells temptation* is appointed for the *first Sunday* in *Lent*. *2 3 4 5 6*

23 mortifying: *mortifying+*in margin* *The Collect for the *first Sunday in Lent*. *2 3 4 5 6*

which are now remembred; and make us the more capable, and more sensible of the *Joy* which the Church expresseth in the joyfull solemnity of EASTER, as well in Commemoration of his, as in Hope of our glorious and gladsome *Resurrection.*

And after this manner hath it beene religiously observed throughout all ages, both in the *Greeke* and in the *Latine* Church.

For the *Greekes* first. It is mentioned by IGNATIUS, who was S. JOHNS disciple, in his Epistle to the *Philippians*, a writing unquestioned. By IRENAEUS, who was S. JOHNS scholler also but once removed. by ORIGEN, who lived not long after them, in his 10. *Homil.* upon *Leviticus*. By the famous Generall Councell of *NICE, not much above 300. yeares after Christ, where they mention the *Forty dayes of* LENT as a knowne thing, instituted and observed by all men long before their time. After them, by S. CYRILL in his *Catechisme*, and by S. CHRYSOSTOME in his Sermons upon *Genesis*, which were preached in this Time of LENT. By S. BASIL in his second Homily of *Fasting*, where hee tels us, that there was no age, nor no place, but both knew it and observed it. By ATHANASIUS in his Relation *ad Orthodox*. By S. GR. NYSSEN in his Sermon of *Baptisme*, & by NAZIANZEN surnamed the *Divine*, in his Sermon of *Almesdeeds*.

*Can. 5.

Then for the *Latins*. By TERTULLIAN first, who was the first of the *Latine Fathers*, and spake more concerning

3 expresseth: *expresseth + *in margin* *Both by the *Eucharist* and other *holy offices*. *2 3 4 5 6* 9 *Greekes*: *Greeke 5*
11 unquestioned.: unquestioned by most men. *2 3 4 5 6*
11 By IRENAEUS: Then by IRENAEUS *2 3 4 5 6*
12 also but: also, but *2 3 4 5 6*
12 removed. by ORIGEN: removed: by ORIGEN *2 3 4 5*: removed. By ORIGEN *6 7 8* 13 them: him *6*
16 *Forty dayes*: **Forty daies* + *in margin* **Quadragesima*. *2 3 4 5 6*
26 *Latins*. By: *Latins* by *2 3 4*: *Latins*, by *5 6*

the LENT FAST than perhaps the Church would have had him. By S. CYPRIAN after him, who was also his scholler. By S. AMBROSE, S. HIEROM, and S. AUGUSTINE in more than 40. severall places of their writings. After them by a whole cloud of *Witnesses*, even to our owne Times: All which being put together, will prove abundantly that THE LENT which we now keepe, is, and ever hath been an *Apostolicall Constitution*; as S. HIEROME said in his *Epistle* to MARCELLA. *Nos* UNAM QUADRAGESIMAM *secundum traditionem* APOSTOLORUM, *tempore nobis congruo jejunamus.* (that is) [*We observe a* LENT-FAST *of* FORTY DAIES, *as wee have bin taught to do by the* APOSTLES, *in a fit and seasonable time of the yeere.*] Wee adde out of S. AUGUSTIN in his 119. *Epistle* to JANUARIUS, a knowne place QUADRAGESIMA *Jejuniorum habet autoritatem &c.* [*The* LENTEN FAST (saith he) *is autorised both by the* OLD *and* NEW TESTAMENT; *there by* MOSES, *and here by* CHRIST. And out of CHRYSOLOGUS in his 11. Sermon. *Quod* QUADRAGESIMAM *jejunamus, non est humana inventio &c.* [*It is no* HUMANE INVENTION (as they call it) *but it comes from* DIVINE AUTHORITY *that wee Fast our* FORTY DAIES *in* LENT.]

THE COLLECT FOR ASHWENSDAY.

ALmighty & everlasting God, which hatest nothing that thou hast made, and doest forgive the sinnes of all them that be penitent, create and make in us new

8–9 *opposite* S. HIEROME said . . . *add marginal note* *S. *Hieron.* ep. ad Marcellam. *2 3 4 5 6*
15 QUADRAGESIMA: *QUADRAGESIMA + *in margin* *S. *Aug.* ep. 119 ad Jan. *2 3 4 5 6* 27 be: are *7 8*

and contrite hearts, that we worthily lamenting our sinnes, and knowledging our wretchednesse, may obtaine of thee the God of all mercy, perfect remission and forgivenesse, through Jesus Christ.

Three other Collects for this time of Lent.

O Lord, we beseech thee, mercifully heare our prayers, and spare all those which confesse their sinnes unto thee, that they, whose consciences by sinne are accused, by thy mercifull pardon may bee absolved, through Christ our Lord. *Amen.*

O Most mightie God and mercifull Father, which hast compassion of all men, and hatest nothing that thou hast made, which wouldest not the death of a sinner, but that hee should rather turne from sinne and bee saved: mercifully forgive us our trespasses, receive and comfort us, which be grieved and wearied with the burden of our sinnes. Thy propertie is to have mercy, to thee onely it appertaineth to forgive sinnes: spare us therefore, good Lord, spare thy people whom thou hast redeemed: enter not into judgement with thy servants, which be vile earth, and miserable sinners, but so turne thine ire from us, which meekely acknowledge

2 knowledging: acknowledging *7 8*
4 Jesus Christ.: Jesus, &c. *5*: Jesus Christ our Lord. *Amen. 7 8*
6 of Lent.: of Lent, as in the Commination, appointed to be used in the beginning of Lent. *2 3 4 5 6* 8 which: who *7 8*
12 which: who *7 8* 13 of: upon *7 8* 14 which: who *7 8*
15 from sinne: from his sinne *7 8* 17 which be: who are *7 8*
18 is to: is alwayes to *7 8* 22 which be: who are *7 8*
23 ire: anger *7 8* 23 which: who *7 8*

our vilenesse, and truly repent us of our faults: so make haste to helpe us in this world, that we may ever live with thee in the world to come, through Jesus Christ our Lord. *Amen.*

TUrne thou us, O good Lord, and so shall we be turned: bee favorable to thy people, O Lord, be favorable to thy people, which turne to thee in weeping, fasting, and praying: for thou art a mercifull God, full of compassion, long suffering, and of great pitie. Thou sparest when we deserve punishment, and in thy wrath thinkest upon mercy. Spare thy people, good Lord, spare them, and let not thine heritage be brought to confusion. Heare us, O Lord, for thy mercy is great, and after the multitude of thy mercies, looke upon us.

The Collect for the first Sunday in Lent.

O Lord, which for our sakes didst fast fortie dayes and fortie nights: give us grace to use such abstinence, that our flesh being subdued to the spirit, wee may ever obey thy godly motions in righteousnesse and true holinesse, to thy honour and glory, which livest and reignest, &c.

1 faults: so: faults, and so *7 8*

6 *om.* to thy people *7 8*

7 which: who *7 8*

14 us.: us, through Jesus Christ our Lord. *Amen. 2 3 4 5 6*: us, through the merits and mediation of thy blessed Son *Jesus* Christ our Lord. *Amen. 7 8*

17 which . . . sakes: who . . . sake *7 8*

21–22 which livest and reignest, &c.: which livest, &c. *4*: who livest and reignest with the Father and the holy Ghost, one God, world without end. *Amen. 7 8*

The Collect for the second Sunday in Lent.

ALmightie God, which doest see that we have no power of our selves to helpe our selves, keepe thou us both outwardly in our bodies, and inwardly in our soules, that we may be defended from all adversities which may happen to the body, and from all evil thoughts which may assault & hurt the soule, through Jesus, &c.

The Collect for the third Sunday in Lent.

WE beseech thee Almightie God, looke upon the hearty desires of thy humble servants, and stretch forth the right hand of thy Majestie, to bee our defence against all our enemies, through Jesus Christ our Lord. *Amen.*

The Collect for the fourth Sunday in Lent.

GRant we beseech thee Almighty God, that we which for our evill deeds are worthily punished, by the comfort of thy grace may mercifully bee relieved, thorough our Lord Jesus Christ.

The Collect for the fifth Sunday in Lent.

WE beseech thee, Almightie God, mercifully to look upon thy people, that by thy great goodnes, they may bee governed and preserved evermore both

3 which doest see: who seest *7 8* 4 *om.* thou *7 8*
9 Jesus, &c.: *Jesus* Christ our Lord. *Amen. 7 8* 20 which: who *7 8*
20 are worthily: do worthily deserve to be *7 8*
22 Lord Jesus Christ.: Lord and Saviour *Jesus* Christ. *Amen. 7 8*

in body and soule, through Jesus Christ our Lord. *Amen.*

THE WEEKE BEFORE EASTER.

THis *Last weeke* of LENT Christians have been used to call *The Holy & Great weeke*, or *The Passion weeke*, and more solemnely to observe it, than any of the rest before. For in it the Church doth commemorate and represent unto us for our greater humilitie and devotion, first the trayterous *Conspiracy* of the *Jewes* with *Judas* to betray Christ unto his death; as upon the WEDNESDAY before *Easter*. Then, the Institution of Christs *Blessed Supper*, and the *washing* of his Disciples feet, as upon MAUNDY THURSDAY. Next, the very *Crosse* and *Passion* of our Saviour, his precious *Death* and *Buriall* for us all, as upon GOOD FRIDAY. And lastly his *Rest* within the *Grave*, and his *Descent* also *into Hell*, as upon EASTER EVEN. And all these *in tempore suo*, in their owne *proper times* and seasons, upon the *very dayes* when they were done, and became the great and high mysteries of our Christian Religion. Which is the reason why *These Dayes*

6 *The Holy*: [a]*The Holy* + *in margin* [a]*Hebdomada sancta, magna, pœnosa: & Hebd. Passionis.* 2 3 4 5 6

11–12 WEDNESDAY: [b]WEDNESDAY + *in margin* [b]Wednesday *before* Easter. 2 3 4 5 6

14 MAUNDY THURSDAY: [c]MANDY THURSDAY + *in margin* [c]Mandy, Thursday (*or* Dies mandati) *so called from the words of Christ*, Mandatum dedi vobis, Joh. 13. *which is also the* Lesson *appointed to be read at the Kings solemne* Mandy, *and the washing of poore mens feet, upon this day.* 2 3 4 5 6

16 GOOD FRIDAY: [d]GOOD FRIDAY + *in margin* [d]Good Friday. 2 3 4 5 6

17–18 EASTER EVEN: [e]EASTER EVEN + *in margin* [e]Easter Even, *wherein the Grave and the Descent of Christ into Hell is commemorated, as appeareth by the Epistle and Gospell of this day.* 2 3 4 5 6

In the Table of Proper Lessons. *Clem. *Const. lib. 3.* *S. Aug. *ep.* 86. *ad Cas.*

are here and *elsewhere rank'd among the *Holy-dayes* of our Church, and a speciall Service appointed for them: as also *why all the *Wednesdayes* of the yeere have beene heretofore, and why the **Fridayes* and *Saturdayes* of every weeke besides are now continued and made common dayes of Abstinence and Prayer.

What the ancient Discipline and religious custome of the Church in this Holy weeke hath been of old, may appeare by this passage of EPIPHANIUS, HAERES. 75. *On Church Fasting Dayes, and especially* THE WEEK BEFORE EASTER, *when with us* (saith hee) *Custome admitteth nothing but lying downe upon the earth, abstinence from fleshly delights and pleasures, unsavoury and dry dyet, sorrow, prayer, watching, fasting, and all the medicines for our soules which holy affections can minister; other men (with whom the Discipline of the Church is in no regard) are up betimes in the morning to take in the strongest for the belly, and when their veynes are well swolne and growne big, they make themselves sport and laughter at this our Devout Service, wherewith wee are perswaded we please God.*

Surely SORROW for sinne is the proper and predominant affection of this Time, so taught us by the Church. And what can we resolve on lesse, than the Church now teacheth us? If He, in whom there was no sinne, was at this time above measure *sorrowfull* for our sinnes; shall not we whose sinnes they were, be in some measure touched with *sorrow* for them, especially at this *Time* of his *sorrow*? True it is that our Saviours *sufferings*, being the price of our Redemption, are the matter of our greatest JOY; but they are so, as they are joyned with his *Resurrection*, without which there had not been any

10 *On Church Fasting Dayes*: [1] *On Church fasting daies* + *in margin* [1] Epiphan. *hæres. 75* [2 3 4 5 6]

benefit or joy to us by them. His Church therefore even from the beginning judged this *Order* to bee most convenient and decent, That about the Time of *His Passion* we should have a sympathie, a *com-passion* and a fellow-feeling with him, being made comformable unto him herein by the exercises of Repentance, which are *The Passion* of every Christian, whereby he *dyeth* unto sinne; and that the solemne *Joy* of our *Redemption* should be put off till EASTER DAY, the day of his *Resurrection*, which is the Hope, & *Life*, and Glory of us all.

And hence must ever bee remembred, that the intent of the Church in the celebration of these her holy *Solemnities*, is not onely to *informe* us in the mysteries which are commemorated, but also, and that chiefly, to *conforme* us thereby unto Him, who is our Head, and the Substance of all our Solemnities whatsoever: that if wee be not thus affected with them, wee can neyther approve our selves to bee his followers and servants, nor any lively members of his Church.

THE COLLECT FOR THE SUNDAY NEXT BEFORE EASTER.

ALmightie and everlasting God, which of thy tender love towards man, hast sent our Saviour Jesus Christ to take upon him our flesh, and to suffer death

10 all.: all, fully expressed in the blessed Sacrament. *2 3 4 5 6*
11 hence: here it *2 3 4 5 6*
22 which: who *7 8*
23 man: mankind *7 8*
23 our Saviour: thy Son, our Saviour *7 8*

upon the Crosse, that all mankind should follow the example of his great humilitie: mercifully grant that we both follow the example of his patience, and be made partakers of his resurrection, through the same Jesus Christ our Lord.

Monday, Tuesday, Wednesday, and Thursday before Easter.

ALmightie & everlasting God, which of thy, &c. *as before.*

The Collects on good Friday.

ALmighty God, we beseech thee graciously to behold this thy family, for the which our Lord Jesus Christ was contented to bee betrayed, and given up into the hands of wicked men, and to suffer death upon the Crosse: who liveth and reigneth, &c.

ALmightie & everlasting God, by whose Spirit the whole body of the Church is governed and sanctified, receive our supplications and prayers which wee offer before thee, for all estates of men in thy holy Congregation, that every member of the same in his vocation and ministery, may truly and godly serve thee, through our Lord Jesus Christ, who liveth and reigneth, &c.

2–3 we both: we may both *7 8*
3 and be : and also be *7 8* 5 *add Amen. 7 8*
8 which: who *7 8* 12 *om.* the *7 8*
15 who . . . &c.: who now liveth and reigneth with thee and the holy Ghost, ever one God, world without end. *Amen. 7 8*
19–20 Congregation: Church *7 8*
21–22 through . . . &c.: through our Lord and Saviour *Jesus* Christ. *Amen. 7 8*

MErciful God, who hast made all men, and hatest nothing that thou hast made, nor wouldest the death of a sinner, but rather that he should be converted and live, have mercy upon all Jewes, Turkes, Infidels, and Heretickes, and take from them all ignorance, hardnesse of heart, and contempt of thy Word, and so fetch them home (blessed Lord) to thy flocke, that they may be saved among the remnant of the true Israelites, and be made one Fold under one Shepheard, Jesus Christ our Lord, who liveth and reigneth, &c.

EASTER DAY.

IT is a most solemne Festivall, as ancient as the glorious RESURRECTION OF CHRISTS selfe, by which it was *declared* & *instituted* to be kept holy (saith *S. AUGUSTINE) and by vertue of it, *All the* SUNDAIES of the yeere besides. Being for this cause called by the *Apostles* *THE LORDS DAY, and by the *Fathers*, *GOD'S OWNE EASTER DAY, and both by Them and our own Church, *THE DAY WHICH THE LORD HATH MADE. That what holy Institution soever the *other solemnities* of the yeare have received, some from the Apostles, and some from the Fathers of the Church in succeeding Ages, we may be sure that *this sacred Festivall* was instituted by the divine Authoritie of God and of Christ himselfe. In regard whereof, it ought to be no lesse to us, than it was of

***Ep.119.*

*Rev. 1. 10.

*Nazianz. *Orat.* 1. *in Pasch.*

*Psal. 118. 24. which is one of the *proper Lessons* for this day appointed.

1 MErciful: O Merciful *7 8*

10 reigneth, &c.: reigneth with thee and the holy Spirit, one God, world without end. *Amen. 7 8*

10 EASTER EVEN. Almighty & everlasting God, which of thy, &c. *As upon the Sunday before. 2 3 4 5 6: a special collect for Easter Even is added here in 7 8 (see Appendix, p. 309)*

12–13 the glorious RESURRECTION OF CHRISTS selfe, by which it: Christs glorious RESURRECTION it selfe, by which this day *2 3 4 5 6*

21 *Lessons*: *Psalmes 2 3 4 5*: *om. 6*

*S. Aug. *Epist.* 118. *S. Gr. Naz. *ubi supra.* *Const. *in ep. ad om. Eccl. apud* Euseb. *de vit. Const. lib.* 3. 1. Cor. 15. 17.

old to the Christians *all the world over, even *The Feast of all Feasts, and the Solemnitie of all Solemnities, the highest and the greatest that we have. *Which venerable Festivall we have received from our* SAVIOUR (saith *CONSTANTINE) *and by which we hold our hopes of immortalitie*; [we adde] And without which all that Christ had done for us besides, would have done us no good.

It is ever to be remembred, that this Holy Feast of joy followeth as Holy a Time of sorrow, that the *Feast* of EASTER commeth alwayes after the *Fast* of LENT, and therby we to learne, that if we will keepe this FEAST aright, if we will *rise* and reigne with Christ, we must *suffer* with him first; crucifie and kill those sinnes by repentance which be in us, that wee may be renewed by the power of that Spirit which is in him, and so being raised up to newnesse of life here, wee may be raised up (as this day He was) to the life of glorie hereafter.

THE ANTHEMES UPON EASTER DAY.

CHrist rising againe from the dead, now dieth not, death from henceforth hath no power upon him: for in that he dyed, hee dyed but once to put away sinne, but in that he liveth, he liveth unto God. And so likewise count your selves dead unto sinne, but living unto God, in Christ Jesus our Lord.

CHrist is risen againe, the first fruites of them that sleepe: for seeing that by man came death, by man also commeth the resurrection of the dead: for as by

10 *om.* alwayes *6* 11 we to learne: we learne *5*: we are to learne *6 8*
13 by: of *6* 16 *om. second* up *6*
18–19 *for the reading of 7 8 see Appendix, p. 309.*

Adam all men do die, so by Christ all men shall bee restored to life.

THE COLLECT FOR EASTER DAY.

ALmightie God, which through thine onely begotten Sonne Jesus Christ hast overcome death, & opened unto us the gate of everlasting life, wee humbly beseech thee, that as by thy speciall grace, preventing us, thou doest put in our minds good desires, so by thy continuall helpe, wee may bring the same to good effect, through Jesus Christ our Lord, who liveth and reigneth, &c.

MUNDAY AND TUESDAY IN EASTER WEEKE.

THese two Holy dayes have beene verie anciently annexed to the Feast of EASTER, and were the set dayes of a publick and solemne *Baptizing* of many multitudes of people together; which the good Christians then rather chose to administer and to receive at this *Time*, for that by the Sacrament of *Baptisme* the holy *Resurrection* of our Saviour is so lively set forth & commemorated in the Church. This was therefore one reason of their first institution in old time.

5 which: who *7 8*
9 in: into *7 8*
11 reigneth, &c.: reigneth with thee and the holy Ghost, ever one God, world without end. *Amen. 7 8*
15 were the set: were *in the Primitive Church the set + *in margin* **As in the Rubrick before* Publike Baptisme. *2 3 4 5 6*
18 then rather chose: then of old, rather chose *2 3 4 5 6*
18–19 and to receive at this *Time*,: and receive at this *Time* of Easter, *2 3 4 5 6*
21 *om.* therefore *2 3 4 5 6*

Another was (and it is the reason of their present continuance now) for that these two dayes might be a greater honour to the principall day of EASTER it selfe, whereupon they still attend: and being attendants upon it, have not, as other dayes, any proper name of their own.

*S. Aug. *de civit. Dei. l. 22. c. 8.* *Hom. 1 in Pasch.*

It was the Custome both of the ancient Latine and Greeke Churches to observe their EASTER after this manner. For the Latines, *S. AUGUSTINE is plaine, *In tertium Diem festi, &c.* (1.) [Upon the THIRD DAY of our most Holy Festivall.] And for the Greekes, *S. GR. NYSSEN is cleare, who expressely termeth it, *A Feast of* THREE *dayes.*

THE COLLECT FOR MONDAY IN EASTER WEEKE.

ALmighty God, which through thy &c. *As upon Easter day.*

The Collect for Tuseday in Easter weeke.

ALmighty Father, which hast given thine onely begotten Sonne to die for our sinnes, and to rise againe for our justification: grant us so to put away the leaven of malice and wickednesse, that wee may alway serve thee in purenesse of living and truth, through Jesus Christ our Lord. *Amen.*

---

16 which: who *7 8*
20–25 *substitute* Almighty God, who through, &c. *7 8*
22 *om.* so *6* 23 alway: alwaies *6*

THE FIRST SUNDAY AFTER EASTER.

IT was the Religious Custome of our Forefathers to observe the *Octaves* of their High and principall *Festivalls*. And this day is the *Octave*, or the *Eight day* after the Feast of EASTER. Upon everie *Octave* (which after seven dayes is a Returne to the first day) the use was to repeate some part of that Service and Devotion, which was performed upon the principall Feast it selfe. And this is the reason, that the *Collect* used upon EASTER DAY, is againe renewed upon this *Sunday*.

THE COLLECT FOR THE FIRST SUNDAY AFTER EASTER.

ALmighty God, which through thy &c. *As upon Easter day.*

The Collect for the second Sunday after Easter.

ALmighty God, which hast given thine onely Sonne to be unto us both a sacrifice for sinne, and also an example of good life, give us thy grace that wee may alway most thankfully receive that his inestimable benefit, and also daily endeavour our selves to follow the blessed steppes of his most holy life.

5 *Eight*: Eighth *7 8*
14 thy &c.: thine onely begotten Son Jesus Christ hast &c. *2 3 4 5 6*
14–15 *for the reading of 7 8 see Appendix, p. 310.*
18 which: who *7 8*
20 of good: for good *4 5*: of godly *7 8*
20 *om.* thy *7 8*
23 life.: life, through the same *Jesus* Christ our Lord. *Amen. 7 8*

The Collect for the third Sunday after Easter.

ALmighty God, which shewest unto all men that be in error, the light of thy truth, to the intent that they may returne into the way of righteousnesse, grant unto all them that be admitted into the fellowship of Christs Religion, that they may eschew those things that bee contrary to their profession, and follow al such things as bee agreeable to the same, through our Lord Jesus Christ.

The Collect for the fourth Sunday after Easter.

ALmightie GOD, which doest make the mindes of all faithfull men to bee of one will, grant unto thy people, that they may love the thing which thou commandest, and desire that which thou doest promise, that among the sundry and manifold changes of the world, our hearts may surely there be fixed, where as true joyes are to bee found, through Jesus Christ our Lord. *Amen.*

The Collect for the fifth Sunday after Easter.

LOrd, from whom all good things do come, grant us thy humble servants, that by thy holy inspiration wee may thinke those things that be good, and by thy

3 which . . . unto all men: who . . . to them *7 8* 6 be: are *7 8*
8 bee: are *7 8* 9 bee: are *7 8* 10 *add Amen.* *7 8*
13–14 ALmightie . . . will,: O Almighty God, who alone canst order the unruly wills and affections of sinful men; *7 8*
16–17 that among: that so among *7 8* 18 *om.* as *7 8*
23 LOrd: O Lord *7 8* 23 grant us: grant to us *7 8*

mercifull guiding may performe the same, through our Lord Jesus Christ. *Amen.*

The Collect for Ascension day.

GRant we beseech thee Almighty God, that like as we do beleeve thy onely begotten Sonne our Lord to have ascended into the Heavens: so wee may also in heart and mind thither ascend, and with him continually dwell.

The Collect for the Sunday after Ascension day.

O God the King of glory, which hast exalted thine only Son Jesus Christ with great triumph into thy Kingdome of heaven: we beseech thee leave us not comfortlesse, but send us thine holy Ghost to comfort us, and exalt us unto the same place whither our Saviour Christ is gone before, who liveth and reigneth, &c.

WHITSUNDAY, OR the Feast of PENTECOST.

THis *Day* hold we *holy* to the *holy Ghost*, by whom all *holy Dayes*, all *holy Persons*, & all *holy Things* whatsoever are made *Holy*. And wee observe it (as S. AUSTIN saith the old Church did **all the world over*,) in memorie of that day wherein the *Holy Spirit* of God after a

**Ep. 118. ad* Januar.

5–6 Lord to: Lord *Jesus* Christ to *7 8*

8 dwell.: dwell, who liveth and reigneth with thee and the holy Ghost, one God, world without end. *Amen. 7 8*

11 which: who *7 8*

12 into: unto *7 8*

13 of: in *7 8*

14 send us: send to us *7 8*

16 reigneth, &c.: reigneth with thee and the holy Ghost, one God, world without end. *Amen. 7 8*

*Acts 2.

wonderfull and mysterious maner *descended upon the Persons of the Apostles, for the founding, propagating, preserving & governing of Christs Catholike Church unto the end of the world.

*Cyril. *in Catech.*

*Munday *and* Tuesday *in Whitson weeke.*

*Rubr. *before publike Baptisme.*

Wee call it PENTECOST from the name it had at first, being 50 *dayes after* EASTER; and WHITSUNDAY from that glorious *Light* of Heaven, which was then sent down upon the Earth; as also for that it was the *custome of the ancient Christians to cloth themselves with a *White* Habit upon *This* and the *Two Attendant Holidayes* that are hereunto annexed: which they did, aswell to expresse the *Joy* they had, and the *Festivitie* they held for the visible descent of the *Holy Ghost* upon the Church at first, as for his mysterious descent now in the blessed Sacrament of *Baptisme*, which was *usually at this *Festivall* with great solemnity dispensed, and thereby many multitudes received into the number of Gods chosen people.

THE COLLECT FOR WHITSUNDAY.

GOd, which as upon this day, hast taught the hearts of thy faithfull people, by the sending to them the light of thy Holy Spirit, grant us by the same Spirit to have a right judgement in all things, and evermore to rejoyce in his holy comfort, through the merits of Jesus Christ our Saviour, who liveth and reigneth with thee in the unity of the same Spirit, one God, world without end. *Amen.*

1 *descended: *descending *6*　　8 also for that: also that *6*
9 cloth: reclothe *2 3 4 5 6*　　11 they did, aswell: they, aswell *6*
21 which . . . taught: who as at this time didst teach *7 8*

The Collect for Munday and Tuseday in Whitsun weeke.

GOd, which as upon this day, hast &c. *As upon Whitsunday.*

TRINITY SUNDAY.

IMmediately after the descent of Gods holy Spirit upon the Church, ensued the notice of the glorious and incomprehensible *Trinity*, the Father, Sonne, and Holy Ghost, which before that time was not so clearely knowne. This therefore is the order of the Church (& it is excellent to consider) that when by the revolution of the yeere, she hath solemnly commemorated al those sacred mysteries which *God the Father* had of his goodnes wrought for her, first by his *Blessed Sonne*, and then by his *Blessed Spirit*; now shee might end and perfect her Devotions, with a *Festivall* of holy Service to the whole *Blessed Trinity*.

THE COLLECT FOR TRINITY SUNDAY.

ALmightie and everlasting God, which hast given unto us thy servants grace by the confession of a true faith, to acknowledge the glory of the eternall Trinity, and in the power of thy divine Majestie to

3 which . . . &c.: who at this time didst, &c. *7 8*   20 which: who *7 8*
21 servants grace: servants, grace *4 5 6*: servants grace, *7 8*
23 thy: the *7 8*

worship the Unitie: we beseech thee that through the stedfastnesse of this faith, we may evermore be defended from all adversitie, which livest and reignest, &c.

The Collect for the first Sunday after Trinity.

GOd, the strength of all them that trust in thee, mercifully accept our prayers: and because the weakenesse of our mortall nature can do no good thing without thee, grant us the helpe of thy grace, that in keeping of thy commandements, wee may please thee both in will and deed, through Jesus Christ our Lord.

The Collect for the second Sunday after Trinity.

LOrd make us to have a perpetuall feare and love of thy holy Name: for thou never failest to helpe and governe them, whom thou doest bring up in thy stedfast love. Grant this &c.

The Collect for the third Sunday after Trinity.

LOrd, we beseech thee, mercifully to heare us, and unto whom thou hast given an hearty desire to pray, grant that by thy mightie ayde wee may bee defended, thorough Jesus Christ our Lord.

1–3 through . . . &c.: thou wouldest keep us stedfast in this faith, and evermore defend us from all adversities, who livest and reignest one God, world without end. *Amen.* *7 8*

6 GOd: O God *7 8*   6 that trust: that put their trust *7 8*

7 because the: because through the *7 8*

8 nature can: nature we can *7 8*

10 *om.* of *7 8*   11 *add Amen.* *7 8*

14–17 *for the reading of 7 8 see Appendix, p. 310.*

20–23 *for the reading of 7 8 see Appendix, p. 310.*

The Collect for the fourth Sunday after Trinity.

GOd, the protector of all that trust in thee, without whom nothing is strong, nothing is holy, increase and multiply upon us thy mercy, that thou being our Ruler & Guide, we may so passe through things temporall, that we finally lose not the things eternall: grant this heavenly Father, for Jesus Christs sake our Lord.

The Collect for the fifth Sunday after Trinity.

GRant, Lord, we beseech thee, that the course of this world may bee so peaceably ordered by thy governance, that thy Congregation may joyfully serve thee in all godly quietnesse, through Jesus Christ our Lord.

The Collect for the sixth Sunday after Trinity.

GOd which hast prepared to them that love thee, such good things as passe all mens understanding: powre into our hearts such love toward thee, that we loving thee in all things, may obtaine thy promises, which exceede all that we can desire, through Jesus Christ our Lord &c.

3 GOd: O God *7 8*
8 this heavenly: this, O heavenly *7 8*
8 *add Amen. 7 8*
11 GRant, Lord: GRant, O Lord *7 8*
13 Congregation: Church *7 8*
15 *add Amen. 7 8*
18 GOd which: O God, who *7 8*
18 to: for *7 8*
19 passe all mens: pass man's *7 8*
21 in: above *7 8*
23 Lord &c.: Lord. *Amen. 7 8*

The Collect for the seventh Sunday after Trinity.

LOrd of all power and might, which art the author and giver of all good things, graffe in our hearts the love of thy Name, increase in us true Religion, nourish us with all goodnesse, and of thy great mercy keepe us in the same, through Jesus Christ our Lord.

The Collect for the eight Sunday after Trinity.

GOd whose providence is never deceived, we humbly beseech thee, that thou wilt put away from us all hurtfull things, and give those things which be profitable for us, through Jesus Christ our Lord.

The Collect for the ninth Sunday after Trinity.

GRant us Lord, wee beseech thee, the Spirit to thinke and doe alwaies such things as bee rightfull, that we which cannot be without thee, may by thee be able to live according to thy will, through Jesus Christ our Lord.

The Collect for the tenth Sunday after Trinity.

LEt thy mercifull eares, O Lord, bee open to the prayers of thy humble servants: and that they may obtaine their petitions, make them to aske such things as shall please thee, through Jesus Christ our Lord.

3 which: who *7 8* 4 graffe: graft *7 8*
7 *add Amen. 7 8* 9 eight: eighth *2 3 4 5 7 8*
10–13 *for the reading of 7 8 see Appendix, pp. 310–11.*
16 GRant us: GRant to us *7 8*
18–19 which cannot be . . . able: who cannot doe any thing that is good . . . enabled *7 8* 20 *add Amen. 7 8* 26 *add Amen. 7 8*

The Collect for the eleventh Sunday after Trinity.

GOd which declarest thy Almighty power, most chiefely in shewing mercy and pitie: give unto us abundantly thy grace, that wee running to thy promises, may bee made partakers of thy heavenly treasure, through Jesus Christ our Lord.

The Collect for the twelfth Sunday after Trinity.

ALmightie and everlasting God, which art alwayes more ready to heare, than wee to pray, and art wont to give more than either we desire or deserve: powre downe upon us the abundance of thy mercy, forgiving us those things whereof our conscience is afraid, and giving unto us that, that our prayer dare not presume to aske, through Jesus Christ our Lord.

The Collect for the thirteenth Sunday after Trinity.

ALmighty and mercifull God, of whose onely gift it commeth, that thy faithfull people do unto thee, true and laudable service: Grant we beseech thee, that we may so runne to thy heavenly promises, that we faile not finally to attaine the same, through Jesus Christ our Lord.

3 GOd which: O God, who *7 8*

4–6 give . . . bee: mercifully grant unto us such a measure of thy grace, that we running the way of thy commandments, may obtain thy gracious promises, and be *7 8*   7 *add Amen. 7 8*   10 which: who *7 8*

15–16 unto . . . Lord.: us those good things which we are not worthy to ask, but through the merits and mediation of *Jesus* Christ thy Son our Lord. *Amen. 7 8*

22–23 runne . . . Lord.: faithfully serve thee in this life, that we fail not finally to attain thy heavenly promises, through the merits of *Jesus* Christ our Lord. *Amen. 7*: faithfully . . . nor finally . . . *Amen. 8*

The Collect for the fourteenth Sunday after Trinity.

ALmighty and everlasting God, give unto us the increase of faith, hope, and charitie, and that wee may obtaine that which thou doest promise, make us to love that which thou doest command, through Jesus Christ our Lord.

The Collect for the fifteenth Sunday after Trinity.

KEep we beseech thee, O Lord, thy Church with thy perpetuall mercy: and because the frailtie of man without thee cannot but fall, keepe us ever by thy helpe, and leade us to all things profitable to our salvation, through Jesus Christ our Lord.

The Collect for the sixteenth Sunday after Trinity.

LOrd, wee beseech thee, let thy continuall pitie cleanse and defend thy Congregation: and because it cannot continue in safetie without thy succour, preserve it evermore by thy help and goodnesse, through Jesus Christ our Lord.

7 *add Amen.* *7 8*
13 helpe, and: helpe from all things hurtful, and *7 8*
14 *add Amen.* *7 8*
17 LOrd: O Lord *7 8*
18 Congregation: Church *7 8*
21 *add Amen.* *7 8*

The Collect for the seventeenth Sunday after Trinity.

LOrd wee pray thee, that thy grace may alwayes prevent and follow us, and make us continually to bee given to all good workes, through Jesus Christ, &c.

The Collect for the eighteenth Sunday after Trinity.

LOrd we pray thee, grant thy people grace to avoid the infections of the devill, and with pure heart and mind to follow thee the onely God, thorough Jesus Christ our Lord.

The Collect for the nineteenth Sunday after Trinity.

O God, forasmuch as without thee we are not able to please thee, grant that the working of thy mercy, may in all things direct and rule our hearts, through Jesus Christ our Lord.

The Collect for the twentieth Sunday after Trinity.

ALmighty and mercifull God, of thy bountifull goodnesse, keepe us from all things that may hurt us: that we being ready both in body and soule, may

5–6 Christ, &c.: Christ our Lord. *Amen.* 7 8
9–12 *for the reading of* 7 8 *see Appendix, p. 311.*
16–17 grant . . . mercy,: mercifully grant that thy holy Spirit 7 8
18 *add Amen.* 7 8
21 ALmighty and mercifull: O Almighty and most mercifull 7 8
22 us from: us, we beseech thee, from 7 8

with free hearts accomplish those things that thou wouldest have done, through Jesus Christ our Lord.

The Collect for the 21. Sunday after Trinity.

GRant we beseech thee, mercifull Lord, to thy faithfull people, pardon and peace, that they may bee cleansed from all their sins, and serve thee with a quiet mind, through Jesus Christ our Lord.

The Collect for the 22. Sunday after Trinity.

LOrd, we beseech thee, to keepe thy houshold the Church in continuall godlines, that through thy protection it may be free from all adversities, and devoutly given to serve thee in good workes, to the glory of thy Name, through Jesus Christ our Lord.

The Collect for the 23. Sunday after Trinity.

GOd our refuge and strength, which art the author of all goodnesse, be ready to heare the devout prayers of the Church, and grant that those things which wee aske faithfully, we may obtaine effectually, through Jesus Christ our Lord.

1 with free hearts: chearfully *7 8* 2 *add Amen. 7 8*
8 *add Amen. 7 8*
15 *add Amen. 7 8* 18 GOd: O God, *7 8*
18 which: who *7 8*
19 goodnesse: godliness *7 8*
19 ready to: ready, we beseech thee, to *7 8*
20 the: thy *7 8* 22 *add Amen. 7 8*

The Collect for the 24. Sunday after Trinity.

LOrd, wee beseech thee, assoile thy people from their offences, that through thy bountifull goodnesse, wee may be delivered from the bonds of all those sins, which by our frailtie we have committed. Grant this, &c.

The Collect for the 25. Sunday after Trinity.

STirre up, we beseech thee, O Lord, the wills of thy faithfull people, that they plenteously bringing forth the fruite of good workes, may of thee bee plenteously rewarded, through Jesus Christ, &c.

COLLECTS PROPER FOR OTHER HOLYDAYES.

WHat the religious intention of the Church was at first, and what her meaning is still in the holy observation of these Saints dayes *that follow, may be seene in the* Preface *to the* Calendar *of this Booke.*

S. ANDREWS DAY.

SAint ANDREWS *day* beginneth the order of the Service for all the other *Saints dayes* of the yeere. And the reason is, because *his Feast* ever falleth out to be

3 LOrd: O Lord *7 8* 3 assoile: absolve *7 8*
5 may be: may all be *7 8* 5 bonds: bounds *8* 5 *om.* all: *7 8*
6–7 this, &c.: this, O heavenly Father, for Jesus Christ's sake, our blessed Lord and Saviour. *Amen. 7 8*
13 Christ, &c.: Christ our Lord. *Amen. 7 8*

Advent Sunday. either next before, or next after **that day*, wherewith the Church hath beene used to begin the whole course of her Ecclesiasticall yeere, and the order of her other solemne and daily Service.

THE COLLECT FOR S. ANDREWS DAY.

ALmighty God, which didst give such grace to thy holy Apostle S. Andrew, that hee readily obeyed the calling of thy Son Jesus Christ, and followed him without delay: Grant unto us all, that we being called by thy holy Word, may forthwith give over our selves obediently to follow thy holy Commandements, through the same Jesus Christ our Lord.

The Collect for S. Thomas day.

ALmighty & everliving God, which for the more confirmation of the Faith, didst suffer thy holy Apostle Thomas to be doubtfull in thy Sonnes resurrection: grant us so perfectly, and without all doubt to beleeve in thy Sonne Jesus Christ, that our faith in thy sight never bee reprooved. Heare us, O Lord, through the same Jesus Christ, to whom, &c.

7 which: who *7 8*
7 to: unto *7 8*
11 over: up *7 8*
12 follow: fulfill *7 8*
13 *add Amen. 7 8*
15 which: who *7 8*
21 whom, &c.: whom with thee and the holy Ghost be all honour and glory now and for evermore. *Amen. 7 8*

The Collect on the Conversion of Saint Paul.

GOd which hast taught all the world, through the preaching of thy blessed Apostle S. Paul, grant we beseech thee, that wee which have his wonderfull conversion in remembrance, may follow and fulfill the holy doctrine that hee taught, through Jesus Christ our Lord.

The Collect on the Purification of the blessed Virgin Mary.

ALmightie & everlasting God, we humbly beseech thy Majestie, that as thy onely begotten Sonne was this day presented in the Temple in the substance of our flesh: so grant that wee may be presented unto thee with pure and cleane minds by Jesus Christ our Lord.

The Collect for S. Matthias day.

ALmighty God, which in the place of the traitor Judas, diddest chuse thy faithfull servant Matthias, to be of the number of the twelve Apostles: Grant that thy Church being alway preserved from false Apostles, may bee ordered and guided by faithfull and true Pastors, through Jesus Christ our Lord.

3–8 *for the reading of 7 8 see Appendix, p. 311.*
11 everlasting: ever-living *7 8*
14 *om.* grant that *7 8*
15–16 minds . . . Lord.: hearts, by the same thy Son *Jesus* Christ our Lord. *Amen. 7 8*
18 ALmighty God, which in: O Almighty God, who into *7 8*
23 *add Amen. 7 8*

The Collect for the Anunciation of the Virgin Mary.

WE beseech thee, Lord, powre thy grace into our hearts, that as wee have knowne Christ thy Sonnes incarnation by the message of an Angel, so by his Crosse and Passion wee may bee brought unto the glory of his Resurrection, through the same Christ our Lord. *Amen.*

The Collect for S. Marks day.

ALmighty God, which hast instructed thy holy Church with the heavenly doctrine of the Evangelist S. Mark, give us grace that we be not like children caried away with every blast of vaine doctrine: but firmely to bee established in the truth of thy holy Gospel, through Jesus Christ, &c.

The Collect for S. Philip and S. James day.

ALmighty God, whom truly to know is everlasting life: grant us perfectly to know thy Son Jesus Christ to be the Way, the Truth, and the Life, as thou hast taught S. Philip, and other Apostles, through Jesus &c.

2 the Virgin: the blessed Virgin *2 3 4 5 6 7 8*   3 Lord: O Lord *7 8*
4–5 Christ . . . incarnation: the incarnation of thy Son *Jesus* Christ *7 8*
7 same Christ: same *Jesus* Christ *7 8*
10 ALmighty God, which: O Almighty God, who *7 8*
11 the Evangelist: thy Evangelist *7 8*   12 we be: being *7 8*
13 doctrine: but firmely to: doctrine, we may *7 8*
15 Christ, &c.: Christ our Lord. *Amen. 7 8*
18 ALmighty: O Almighty *7 8*
20–22 Life, . . . &c.: Life: that following the steps of thy holy Apostles S. *Philip* and S. *James*, we may stedfastly walk in the way that leadeth to eternal life, through the same thy Son *Jesus* Christ our Lord. *Amen. 7 8*

The Collect for S. Barnabe's day.

LOrd Almighty, which hast endued thy holy Apostle Barnabas with singular gifts of the holy Ghost: let us not be destitute of thy manifold gifts, nor yet of grace to use them alway to thine honour and glory, through &c.

The Collect for S. John Baptists day.

ALmighty God, by whose providence thy servant John Baptist was wonderfully borne, and sent to prepare the way of thy Sonne our Saviour, by preaching of penance: make us so to follow his doctrine and holy life, that we may truly repent: according to his preaching, and after his example, constantly speak the truth, boldly rebuke vice, and patiently suffer for the truths sake, through Jesus Christ, &c.

The Collect for S. Peters day.

ALmighty God, which by thy Sonne Jesus Christ, hast given to thy Apostle S. Peter many excellent gifts, and commandedst him earnestly to feed thy flock: make (wee beseech thee) all Bishops and Pastors diligently to preach thy holy Word, and the people obediently to follow the same, that they may receive the Crowne of everlasting glory, through Jesus Christ &c.

2 LOrd . . . endued: O Lord Almighty, who didst endue *7 8*
3–4 let us not be: leave us not, we beseech thee, *7 8*
5 thine: thy *7 8*
5–6 through &c.: through *Jesus* Christ our Lord. *Amen.* *7 8*
11 penance: : Repentance; *7 8* 12 repent: : repent *7 8*
15 Christ, &c.: Christ our Lord. *Amen.* *7 8*
17 ALmighty God, which: O Almighty God, who *7 8*
18 hast given: didst give *7 8*
23 Christ &c.: Christ our Lord. *Amen.* *7 8*

The Collect on S. James day.

GRant, O mercifull God, that as thy Apostle S. James, leaving his father and all that he had without delay, was obedient unto the calling of thy Son Jesus Christ, and followed him: so wee forsaking all worldly and carnall affections, may be evermore ready to follow thy Commandements, through Jesus Christ our Lord.

The Collect for S. Bartholomews day.

O Almighty and everlasting God, which hast given grace to thine Apostle Bartholomew, truly to beleeve and to preach thy word: Grant we beseech thee unto thy Church, both to love that hee beleeved, and to preach that hee taught, through Christ our Lord.

The Collect for S. Matthews day.

ALmighty God, which by thy blessed Son didst call Matthew from the receit of Custome, to be an Apostle and Evangelist: grant us grace to forsake all covetous desires, and inordinate love of riches, and to follow thy said Sonne Jesus Christ, who liveth and reigneth &c.

2 thy: thine holy *7 8* 3 had: had, *7 8*
4 delay,: delay *7 8*
7 thy Commandements: thy holy Commandements *7 8*
8 *add Amen. 7 8*
10–11 which . . . truly: who didst give to thine Apostle S. *Bartholomew* grace truely *7 8*
13–14 both to love . . . Lord.: to love that word which he believed, and both to preach and receive the same, through *Jesus* Christ our Lord. *Amen. 7 8*
16 ALmighty God, which: O Almighty God, who *7 8*
20 thy said: the same thy *7 8*
21 reigneth &c.: reigneth with thee and the holy Ghost, one God, world without end. *Amen. 7 8*

The Collect on S. Michael and All Angels.

EVerlasting God, which hast ordained and constituted the services of all Angels and men in a wonderfull order, mercifully grant that they which alway doe thee service in heaven, may by thy appointment succour and defend us in earth, through Jesus Christ our Lord.

The Collect for S. Lukes day.

ALmighty God, which calledst Luke the Physition, whose prayse is in the Gospel, to be a Physition of the soule, it may please thee by the wholesome medicines of his doctrine, to heale all the diseases of our soules, through thy Sonne Jesus &c.

The Collect for S. Simon and Judes day.

ALmighty God, which hast builded thy Congregation upon the foundation of the Apostles and Prophets, Jesus Christ himselfe being the head corner stone: grant us so to be joyned together in unitie of spirit by their doctrine, that wee may bee made an holy Temple acceptable unto thee, through Jesus Christ our Lord.

---

3 EVerlasting God, which: O Everlasting God, who *7 8*
4 *om.* all *7 8* 5 they which: as thy holy Angels *7 8*
6 may: so *7 8*
6–7 appointment succour: appointment they may succour *7 8*
7 in: on *7 8* 8 *add Amen. 7 8*
10–14 *for the reading of 7 8 see Appendix, p. 311.*
17–18 ALmighty . . . Congregation: O Almighty God, who hast built thy Church *7 8* 22 *add Amen. 7 8*

ALL-SAINTS DAY.

THe Reasons for the solemne observation of this great and general *Festival*, are set down in the *Preface* to the *Calendar* of this Booke.

THE COLLECT FOR ALL-SAINTS DAY.

ALmighty GOD, which hast knit together the Elect in one Communion and fellowship in the mysticall body of thy Sonne Jesus Christ our Lord: grant us grace so to follow thy holy Saints in all vertuous and godly living, that wee may come to those unspeakeable joyes, which thou hast prepared for them that unfainedly love thee, through Jesus &c.

7 ALmighty God, which: O Almighty God, who *7 8*
7 the: thine *7 8*
10 holy: blessed *7 8*
13 Jesus &c.: *Jesus* Christ our Lord. *Amen. 7 8*

DEVOUT PRAYERS
THAT MAY BE USED BEFORE AND AFTER THE RECEIVING OF CHRISTS HOLY SACRAMENT, HIS BLESSED BODY AND BLOOD.

7 HIS: OF HIS *6*

PRAYERS BEFORE THE RECEIVING OF THE BLESSED SACRAMENT.

When we enter into the Church.

I.

LOrd, I have loved the habitation of thine House, and the place where thine Honour dwelleth.

II.

I Will wash mine hands in innocency, O Lord, and so will I goe to thine Altar.

When we are prostrate before the Altar.

I.

THou art worthy, O Lord, to receive glory and honour and power, for thou hast created all things, and for thy wills sake they are, and were created.

II.

BLessing, and Glory, and Wisedome, and Thankes, and Honour, and Power and Might bee unto our God for evermore. *Amen.*

PSAL. 51.

HAve mercy upon me, O God, after thy great goodnesse : according to the multitude of thy mercies doe away mine offences.

Add marginal notes 6 Ps. 26. 8. *2 3 4 5* 9 Ps. 26. 6. *2 3 4 5* 14 Rev. 4. 11. *2 3 4 5 6* 18 Revel. 5. 13. *2 3 4 5*: Rev. 6. 13. *6*
20 *add* III. Revel. 4. Holy, Holy, Holy, Lord God Almightie, which was, and is, and is to come, receive my praier. *2 3 4 5*: *om.* Revel. 4. *6*

2 Wash mee thorowly from my wickednesse, and cleanse mee from my sinne.

3 For I know my faults : and my sinne is ever before me.

4 Against thee onely have I sinned, and done this evill in thy sight : that thou mightest be justified in thy saying, and cleare when thou art judged.

5 Behold, I was shapen in wickednesse : and in sinne hath my mother conceived me.

6 But loe, thou requirest truth in the inward parts, and shalt make me to understand wisedom secretly.

7 Thou shalt purge me with hysope, and I shall be cleane : thou shalt wash me, and I shall be whiter than snow.

8 Thou shalt make mee heare of joy and gladnesse : that the bones which thou hast broken may rejoyce.

9 Turne thy face from my sinnes : and put out all my misdeeds.

10 Make mee a cleane heart (O God :) and renew a right spirit within me.

11 Cast mee not away from thy presence : and take not thy holy Spirit from me.

12 O Give me the comfort of thy helpe againe : and stablish me with thy free spirit.

Glory bee to the Father, and to the Sonne: and to the holy Ghost.

As it was in the beginning, is now, and ever shall be : world without end. *Amen.*

At the Consecration.

Vers. I beleeve, Lord helpe my unbeliefe.

3 know: acknowledge *7 8*
24–25 Father, and . . . Ghost.: Father, &c. *4 5*
26–27 is . . . *Amen.*: &c. *4 5*
29 my: mine *7 8*

THE HYMNE.

A Speciall Theme of Praise is read,
True living and life giving Bread
Is now to be exhibited:
Within the Supper of the Lord
To twelve Disciples at his bord,
As doubtlesse 'twas delivered.

What at Supper *Christ* performed
To be done he straightly charged
For his eternall memorie.
Guided by his sacred orders
Heavenly food upon our Altars
For our soules we sanctifie.

Christians are by Faith assured
That by Faith Christ is received
Flesh and bloud most precious.
What no duller sense conceiveth
Firme and grounded Faith beleeveth;
In strange effects not curious.

THE PRAYER.

I.

ALmighty Lord, who hast of thine infinite mercy vouchsafed to ordaine this dreadfull Sacrament for a perpetuall memory of that blessed Sacrifice which once thou madest for us upon the Crosse: grant me with such diligent remembrance, and such due reverence to assist the holy celebration of so heavenly and wonderfull a Mystery, that I may be made worthy by thy grace to obtaine the vertue and fruits of the same, with all the

19 effects: effect, *6*

benefits of thy precious Death and Passion, even the remission of all my sins, and the fulnesse of all thy graces: which I beg for thy onely merits, who art my onely Saviour, God from everlasting, and world without end. *Amen.*

II.

O Lord our Heavenly Father, Almighty and everlasting God, regard, we beseech thee, the devotion of thy humble servants, who do now celebrate the memoriall which thy Sonne our Saviour hath commanded to be made in remembrance of his most blessed Passion and Sacrifice: that by the merits and power thereof now represented before thy divine Majesty, wee and all thy whole Church may obtaine remission of our sinnes, and bee made partakers of all other the benefits of his most precious Death & Passion, together with his mighty Resurrection from the earth, and his glorious Ascension into Heaven, who liveth and reigneth with thee and the Holy Ghost ever one God, world without end. *Amen.*

III.

BE pleased, O God, to accept of this our bounden duty and service, and command that the Prayers and supplications, together with the remembrance of Christs Passion, which we now offer up unto thee, may by the ministry of thy Holy Angels be brought up into thy Heavenly Tabernacle: and that thou not weighing our owne merits, but looking upon the blessed Sacrifice of our Saviour, which was once fully and perfectly made for

1 thy: the *6* 21 *om.* of *6*

22 command: vouchsafe *2 6*

24–25 by . . . brought up: bee received *2 3 6 8. The variant of 2 is the cancellans; the cancellandum, identical with 1, is also included (Q5[v]).*

us all, mayst pardon our offences, and replenish us with thy grace and heavenly benediction, through the same Jesus Christ our Lord.

HEAVENLY ASPIRATIONS

IMMEDIATELY BEFORE the receiving of the blessed Sacrament.

I.

I Will go unto the Altar of God: even unto the God of my joy and gladnesse.

II.

I Will offer thankesgiving unto my God: and pay my vowes unto the most Highest.

III.

O Lambe of God, that takest away the sinnes of the world: have mercy upon us.

IV.

O Lambe of God that takest away the sins of the world: grant us thy peace.

V.

GRant me gracious Lord, so to eate the flesh of thy deare Sonne, and to drinke his blood, that my sinfull body may bee made cleane by his Body, and my soule washed through his most precious Blood.

Add marginal notes 9 Psal. *2 3 6 8*: Psal. 43. 4. *4 5* 12 Psal. *2 3 6*: Psal. 50. 14. *4 5* 15 Ex Letan. *2 3 4 5 6* 18 Ex Letan. *2 3 4 5 6* 21 Ex Liturg. *2 3 4 5 6*

At the receiving of the Body.

LOrd, I am not worthy that thou shouldst come under my roofe, but speake the word, and my soule shall be healed.

Adding with the Priest.

THe body of our Lord Jesus Christ which was given for me, preserve my body and soule unto everlasting life.

And answere. Amen.

At the receiving of the Cup.

WHat reward shall I give unto the Lord for all the benefits that he hath done unto me? I will take the Cup of salvation, and call upon the Name of the Lord.

Adding with the Priest.

THe Blood of our Lord Jesus Christ which was shedde for me, preserve my body and soule unto everlasting life.

Answering againe. Amen.

THANKSGIVING

AFTER WE HAVE RECEIVED THE BLESSED SACRAMENT.

I.

OH my God, thou art true and holy: Oh my soule thou art blessed & happie.

Add marginal notes 2 Ex Evang. *2 3 4 5 6* 6 Ex Liturg. *2 3 4 5 6* 11 Ps. 116. *2 3 4 5 6* 16 Ex Liturg. *2 3 4 5 6*

II.

OH the depth of the wisedome and knowledge of God, how incomprehensible are his judgements, and his wayes past finding out!

III.

PRayse the Lord, O my soule, and all that is within mee prayse his holy Name, which saveth thy life from destruction, and feedeth thee with the bread of heaven.

IV.

GLory be to God on high, and in Earth peace, good will towards men. Wee worship thee O Lord, and wee magnifie thy Name for ever, who hast vouchsafed to fill our soules with gladnes, and to feed us with the heavenly mysteries of Christs sacred Body and Blood: humbly beseeching thee that from henceforth wee may walke in all good workes, and serve thee in holinesse and purenesse of living, to the honour of thy Name. *Amen.*

MEDITATIONS

WHILEST OTHERS ARE COMMUNICATED.

I.

HAppie are those servants, whom when their Lord commeth, Hee shall find thus doing.

Add marginal notes 2 Ro. 11. 33. *2 3 4 5 6* 6 Ps. 103. 1. 2. *2 3 4 5 6* 11 Ex Liturg. *2 3 4 5* 24 Ex Evang. *2 3 4 5 6*

II.

KNow yee not that yee are the Temple of God, and that the Spirit of God dwelleth in you? If any one defile the Temple of God, him will God destroy.

III.

BEhold, thou art made whole, sinne no more, least a worse thing happen unto thee.

IV.

THe houre commeth, and now it is, when the true worshippers shall worship the Father in spirit and in truth.

V.

BE wee followers of God, as deare children, and walke in love, even as Christ loved us, and gave himselfe an offering and a sacrifice of a sweet savour unto God for us.

At the end of the Communion.

THE DOXOLOGIE.

TO the King Eternall, the Immortall, Invisible and onely wise God, be all honour and glory, now and for evermore. *Amen.*

Add marginal notes 2 Ex S. Paulo *2 3 4 5 6* 6 Joh. 5. 14. *2 3 4 5*: Joh. 5. 13. *6* 9 Joh. 4. 23. *2 3 4 5 6* 13 Ephes. 5. *2 3 4 5 6*

DIVERS FORMES OF DEVOUT AND PENITENT CONFESSIONS OF OUR SINNES,

TO BEE USED, AS AT other times, so especially before the receiving of Christs blessed Sacrament.

According to the direction of the Church.

Exhortation before the Communion.

☞ If any require comfort and counsell for the quieting of his conscience, let him come to some discreet Minister of Gods Word, and opening his griefe, receive the benefit of Absolution.

I. JOHN I. 9.

☞ If we confesse our sinnes, He is faithfull and just to forgive us our sinnes, and to cleanse us from all unrighteousnesse.

THE PREPARATION.

I.

ALmightie God, unto whom all hearts bee open, all desires knowne, and from whom no secrets are hid, cleanse the thoughts of my heart, by the inspiration of thy holy Spirit, through Jesus Christ. *Amen.*

II.

ALmighty and everlasting God, which hatest nothing that thou hast made, and doest forgive the sins of all them that be penitent, create and make in me a

8 *Exhortation*: *Direction 6* 17 *om.* THE PREPARATION. *6* 26 be: are *7 8*

new and contrite heart, that I worthily lamenting my sinnes, and knowledging my wretchednesse, may obtaine of thee the God of all mercy, perfect remission and forgivenesse, through Jesus Christ. *Amen.*

THE CONFESSION.

I Confesse &c. those sins, which if I would, I cannot hide from him: my sinnes of pride & vaineglory, of hatred and envy, of gluttony and wantonnesse, &c. which I acknowledge through my fault, even through my owne fault, and my most grievous fault to have committed against his heavenly and awfull Majestie. I am an uncleane and a sinfull creature: *I accuse my selfe of my wicked thoughts and desires that I have had, &c. of my wanton and evill words, that &c. of my naughty and ungodly deeds, that &c. for all which I am truly penitent from the depth of my soule, and am stedfastly resolved to shew forth the fruits of repentance in my future course of life. And therefore in all lowlinesse and humilitie of a broken heart I beg my pardon, and crie unto God for mercy towards me a most sinfull and unworthy creature: that hee whose nature and propertie it is to forgive sinners, and ever to have mercy upon them that truly turne unto him, would vouchsafe of his great pitie and goodnesse, to give me the comfort of Absolution, and a perfect remission of all my sinnes: to strengthen me in all good workes, and to bring mee unto life everlasting, through Jesus Christ. *Amen.*

*Here may the Penitent have recourse to the severall breaches of Gods commandements, specified in the beginning of this Book.

---

12 *marginal note enclosed in brackets, italicized, and inserted within the text after* creature: *4 5*: *om. stars* (*) *4 5*

OTHER FORMES OF GENERALL CONFESSIONS.

I.

ALmighty and most mercifull Father, I have erred & strayed from thy wayes like a lost sheepe, I have followed too much the devices and desires of my own heart: I have offended against thy holy Lawes: I have left undone those things which I ought to have done, and I have done those things which I ought not to have done, and there is no health in me: but thou, O Lord, have mercy upon me, miserable offender. Spare thou mee O God, which confesse my faults, restore thou me that am penitent, according to thy promises declared unto mankind in Christ Jesus our Lord: and grant O most mercifull Father for his sake, that I may hereafter live a godly, righteous and sober life, to the glory of thy holy Name. *Amen.*

II.

ALmighty God, Father of our Lord Jesus Christ, Maker of all things, Judge of all men, I knowledge and bewaile my manifold sinnes and wickednesse, which I from time to time most grievously have committed by thought, word and deed, against thy divine Majestie: provoking most justly thy wrath and indignation against mee: I doe earnestly repent, and am heartily sorie for these my misdoings, the remembrance of them is grievous unto me, the burden of them is intolerable. Have mercy upon me, have mercy upon me most mercifull Father, for thy Sonne our Lord Jesus Christs sake,

20 knowledge: acknowledg *7 8*

forgive me al that is past, and grant that I may ever hereafter serve and please thee in newnesse of life, to the honour and glory of thy Name, through Jesus Christ our Lord. *Amen.*

III.

FOrgive me my sins, O Lord, forgive mee the sinnes of my youth, and the sins of mine age, the sinnes of my soule, and the sinnes of my body, my secret and my whispering sinnes, my presumptuous and my crying sins, the sinnes that I have done to please my selfe, and the sinnes that I have done to please others. Forgive me my wanton and idle sinnes. Forgive me my serious and deliberated sinnes. Forgive me those sinnes which I know, and those sinnes which I know not: the sinnes which I have striven so long to hide from others, that now I have even hid them from mine owne memory. Forgive them, O Lord, forgive them all, and of thy great goodnesse let me be absolved from mine offences.

A DEVOUT MANNER OF PREPARING OUR SELVES, TO RECEIVE ABSOLUTION.

I That am a wretched sinner, here personally appearing and prostrate before the presence of the everlasting God, having in remembrance the exceeding mercie of his great goodnesse towards me, whom hee hath created of nothing, preserved, sustained, and loved, when I was most unworthy of any thing: whom hee hath of his incomprehensible clemency so often invited to repentance, and whose conversion and amendment hee hath so patiently expected: as also having in memorie, that at the day of my Christning I was so happily and holily vowed and dedicated unto my God, to be his child, and to live in his continuall service: yet that contrary to the profession which was then made in my name, I have so many and sundry times, so execrably and detestably violated my vowes, profained my sacred promises, and imployed my soule to the service of the World, the Flesh, and the Devill: thereby despising the graces, and contemning the goodnes of Gods divine Majestie: at length recalling my selfe, and in all lowly and devout wise heere casting my soule and body prostrate before the dreadfull Throne of his Justice, I acknowledge and confesse, and I yeeld my selfe a most miserable wretched sinner, guiltie of that Death and Passion which Christ once suffered for mee upon the tormenting Crosse. But turning my selfe to the Throne of his infinite Mercy, and with all my might and force from the very bowels of my hart, detesting the iniquities of my forepassed life: I most humbly beg and crave pardon for the same, with an entire absolution from all my sinnes, even for the precious death and passions sake of my Lord and Saviour: upon whom, as upon the only foundation of my hope, I repose all my confidence, and unto whom I promise and confirme againe, I advow, and solemnely renew the sacred profession of loyall service and fidelitie, which was made in my name, and in my behalfe unto him at my holy Baptisme: renouncing unfainedly the vanities of this wicked World, the lusts of all sinfull Flesh, and the suggestions of the Divell: and converting my selfe unto my most gracious & mercifull God, I desire, deliberate, purpose, and fully resolve to honour him, serve him, love him, and obey him now and for ever hereafter.

Giving and dedicating unto him, for this end, the powers of my soule, the affections of my heart, and the faculties of my body, to bee his faithfull, loyall and obedient servants for ever, without unsaying, revoking, or repenting me of this my holy and sacred promise, or any part thereof. And I most humbly beseech Almighty God the Father, Son and Holy Ghost to confirme me in this constant resolution, and to accept of this my broken and contrite heart, which he hath promised not to despise: entirely desiring his fatherly goodnesse, that as he hath given me a desire and will to purpose, so hee would give mee strength and grace to performe all holy actions, thorow Jesus Christ.

THE PRAYER.

O God, whose nature and propertie is ever to have mercy and to forgive, that hast compassion upon all men, and hatest nothing that thou hast made, nor wouldest the death of a sinner, but rather that hee should turne from sinne, and bee saved: mercifully heare the devout and lowly prayers of thy servant, and spare all those which confesse their sinnes unto thee: that they whose consciences by sinne are accused, by thy merciful and gracious pardon may be absolved, through Jesus Christ our Lord. *Amen.*

AFTER ABSOLUTION.

BLessed is he whose unrighteousnesse is forgiven, and whose sin is covered.

Blessed is the man, unto whom the Lord imputeth no sinne.

---

21 which: who *7 8*

PRAYERS
FOR
THE KING
AND
QUEENE.

PRAYERS FOR THE KING AND QUEENE.

OUr Father which art in heaven. Hallowed be thy Name. Thy kingdom come. Thy will be done in earth as it is in heaven. Give us this day our daily bread. And forgive us our trespasses, as we forgive them that trespasse against us. And leade us not into temptation: but deliver us from evill. *Amen.*

Vers. O God make speed to save me.
Resp. O Lord make haste to help me.

Glory bee to the Father, and to the Sonne : and to the holy Ghost.
As it was in the beginning, is now, and ever shall bee : world without end. *Amen.*

ALLELUIA. *Prayse the Lord.*

THE HYMNE.

GReat God of Kings,
whose gracious hand hath led
our sacred Soveraigne Head
Unto the Throne
from whence our blisse is bred:
Oh send thine Angels
to his blessed side,
and bid them there abide,
To be at once
his Guardian and his Guide.

8 evill. *Amen.*: evill, &c. *2 3 6*: evil. For thine is the Kingdom, and the Power, and the Glory, for ever and ever. *Amen. 7 8*
13–14 bee: . . . *Amen.*: be, &c. *4 5*   15 *add The Lord's Name be praised. 7 8*

Deare be his life,
    all glorious be his dayes,
    and prospering all his wayes:
Late adde thy last Crowne
    to his peace and prayse.
And when he hath
    outliv'd the Worlds long date,
    let thy last Change translate
His earthly Throne
    to thy celestiall state.

Amen.

THE ANTIPHONA.

BEhold, O God, our Defender, and looke upon the face of thine Anointed.

PSAL. 21.

THe King shall reigne in thy strength, O Lord : exceeding glad shall hee bee of thy salvation.

2 Thou hast given him his hearts desire : and hast not denied him the request of his lips.

3 For thou hast prevented him with the blessings of goodnesse : and hast set a crowne of pure gold upon his head.

4 He shall aske life of thee, and thou shalt give him a long life : even for ever and ever.

5 His honour is great in thy salvation, glory and great worship shalt thou lay upon him.

6 For thou shalt give him everlasting felicitie : and make him glad with the joy of thy countenance.

7 And why ? Because the King putteth his trust in the Lord, and in the mercy of the most Highest, he shall not miscarry.

16 reigne: rejoice *7 8*

Glory bee to the Father, and to the Sonne : and to the Holy Ghost.

As it was in the beginning, is now, and ever shall be : world without end. *Amen.*

PSAL. 61.

HEare my prayer, O God : give eare unto my calling.

2 Thou shalt grant the King a long life : that his yeeres may endure throughout all generations.

3 Hee shall dwell before God for ever : O prepare thy loving mercy and faithfulnesse, that they may preserve him.

4 So will I alwayes sing prayses unto thy Name : that I may daily performe my vowes.

Glory bee to the Father, and to the Sonne : and to the holy Ghost.

As it was in the beginning, is now, and ever shall be : world without end. *Amen.*

PSAL. 89.

THou hast made a Covenant, O Lord, with thy chosen : and with thy holy oyle thou hast anointed him.

2 Let thy hand hold him fast : and thy arme strengthen him.

3 Let not the enemie bee able to doe him violence : and let not the sonne of wickednesse hurt him.

4 Smite down his foes before his face : and plague them that hate him.

1–2 Father, and . . . Ghost.: Father, &c. *4 5*   3–4 is . . . *Amen.*: &c. *4 5*
6 prayer: crying *7 8*   7 calling: prayer *7 8*
13 prayses: praise *7 8*   15–16 Father, and . . . Ghost.: Father, &c. *4 5*
17–18 is . . . *Amen.*: &c. *4 5*   21 thou hast: hast thou *6*

5 Let thy truth also and thy mercy bee with him : and in thy Name let his horne be exalted.

6 Let him say, Thou art his Father, his God, and his strong salvation.

7 Let thy mercy be kept for him evermore : and let thy Covenant stand fast with him.

Glory bee to the Father, and to the Sonne : and to the holy Ghost.

As it was in the beginning, is now and ever shall bee : world without end. *Amen.*

The Antiphona.

BEhold, O God our Defender, and looke upon the face of thine Anoynted.

THE LESSON.

1. Tim. 2. 1.

I Will therefore that Prayers and Supplications with giving of thanks bee made for all men: for Kings, and for all that are in authority, that we may live a quiet and a peaceable life in all godlinesse and honestie. For this is good and acceptable in the sight of God our Saviour.

Vers. O Lord save the King.
Resp. And mercifully heare us when we call upon thee.

THE PRAYERS.

I.

ALmightie GOD, whose Kingdome is everlasting, and power infinite, have mercy upon the whole Congregation, and so rule the heart of thy chosen servant

7–8 Father, and . . . Ghost.: Father, &c. *4 5*   9–10 is . . . *Amen.*: &c. *4 5*
28 Congregation: Church *7 8*

Charles our King and Governour, that hee (knowing whose Minister hee is) may above all things seeke thy honour and glory, and that we his subjects (duely considering whose authoritie he hath) may faithfully serve, honour, and humbly obey him, in thee and for thee, according to thy blessed Word and Ordinance, through Jesus Christ our Lord, who with thee and the holy Ghost, liveth and reigneth ever one God, world without end. *Amen.*

II.

ALmighty and everlasting God, we be taught by thy holy Word, that the harts of Kings are in thy rule and governance, and that thou doest dispose and turne them as it seemeth best to thy godly wisedome: we humbly beseech thee, so to dispose and governe the heart of *Charles* thy servant our King and Governor, that in all his thoughts, words, & works, he may ever seeke thy honour and glory, and study to preserve thy people committed to his charge, in wealth, peace, and godlinesse. Grant this, O mercifull Father, for thy deare Sonnes sake, Jesu Christ our Lord. *Amen.*

III.

WE beseech thee, O Lord, to save and defend all Christian Kings, Princes and Governours, and specially thy servant *Charles* our King, that under him we may be godly and quietly governed: and grant unto his whole Counsell, and to all that be put in authoritie under him, that they may truly and indifferently minister justice, to the punishment of wickednes and vice, and to the maintenance of Gods true Religion and vertue. *Amen.*

3 we his: we and all his *7 8*

IV.

O Lord our heavenly Father, high & mighty, King of kings, Lord of Lords, the only Ruler of Princes, which dost from thy Throne behold al the dwellers upon earth, most hartily we beseech thee, with thy favour to behold our most gracious Soveraigne Lord King *Charles*, and so replenish him with the grace of thy holy Spirit, that he may alway encline to thy wil, and walke in thy way: endue him plenteously with heavenly gifts, grant him in health and wealth long to live, strengthen him that he may vanquish and overcome all his enemies, and finally after this life, hee may attaine everlasting joy and felicitie, through Jesus Christ our Lord. *Amen.*

V.

Ex libro Regali.

O Almightie and everlasting God, Creator and Lord of all things, give eare we beseech thee, unto our humble prayers, and multiply thy blessings upon thy Servant, our Soveraigne King *Charles*, whom in all lowly devotion we commend unto thy high Majestie: that Hee being strengthened with the faith of *Abraham*, endued with the mildnes of *Moses*, armed with the magnanimitie of *Joshua*, exalted with the humilitie of *David*, beautified with the wisedome of *Salomon*, and replenished with the goodnes and holinesse of them all, He may walke uprightly before thee, in the way of righteousnesse, and like a mightie King, may be powerfull over his enemies, governing his people with equitie, and preserving thy Church with Truth and Peace, through Jesus Christ our Lord. *Amen.*

VI.

GOd, the unspeakeable Author of the world, Creator of men, Governour of Empires, and Establisher of all Kingdomes, who out of the loynes of our Father *Abraham* didst choose a King that became the Saviour of all Kings and Nations of the earth: Blesse, we beseech thee, thy faithfull Servant, and our dread Soveraigne Lord King *Charles* with the richest blessings of thy Grace. Establish him in the Throne of his Kingdome by thy mightie aide and protection: visit him as Thou didst visit *Moses* in the Bush, *Joshua* in the Battell, *Gideon* in the field, and *Samuel* in the Temple. Let the Deaw of thine abundant mercies fall upon his head, and give unto him the blessing of *David* and *Salomon*. Be unto him an Helmet of salvation against the face of his enemies, and a strong Towre of defence in the time of adversitie. Let his Reigne bee prosperous, and his dayes many. Let peace, and love, and holinesse: let justice and truth, and all Christian vertues flourish in his time: let his people serve him with honour and obedience: and let him so duly serve thee here on earth, that he may heereafter everlastingly reigne with thee in Heaven, thorow Jesu Christ our Lord. *Amen.* Lib. Reg.

VII.

LOoke downe Almightie God with thy favourable Countenance upon thine Anoynted, and our glorious King. Blesse him as thou didst blesse *Abraham*, *Isaac*, and *Jacob*, and powre upon him the fulnesse of thy Mercy and Grace. Give unto him of the Deaw of Heaven, and of the fatnesse of the earth, abundance of Corne, and Wine, and Oyle, and plentie of all things Lib. Reg.

1 VI: *appears incorrectly as* IV *in all but* 6 7 8

long to continue: that in his time there may be health in our Countrie, and peace throughout all his Kingdomes: that the glorie of his Royall Court may shine forth farre and neere in the eyes of all Nations, even through Him who is the King of Kings, and Lord of all things, our Saviour Jesus Christ. *Amen.*

VIII.

Lib. Reg. GRant, we beseech thee Almightie God, that our Soveraigne Lord the King may bee a most mightie Protector of his People, a religious Defender of thy sacred Faith, a bountifull Comforter of thy holy Church, a glorious Triumpher over all his enemies, a gracious Governor unto all his Subjects, and a happie Father of many children, to rule this Nation by succession in all ages, thorough Jesus Christ our Lord. *Amen.*

PRAYERS FOR THE QUEENE.

I.

ALmightie God, the Fountaine of all mercy, we humbly beseech thee to powre downe the Riches of thine abundant goodnesse upon the Head of thine Handmaid, our most gracious Q. *Marie*, that shee being continually beautified with the Royall ornaments of thy heavenly Grace, may be holy and devout as *Hester*, loving to the King as *Rachel*, fruitfull as *Leah*, wise as *Rebecca*, faithfull and obedient as *Sarah*: and with long life and glory continuing in her High & Princely estate here, shee may at last be brought to the great happinesse of thine everlasting estate hereafter, through Jesus Christ our Lord. *Amen.*

21 Q. *Marie*: Queen CATHERINE *7 8*

II.

ALmightie God our Heavenly Father, we be taught by thy holy Word, that the bringing forth of children, and the fruitfulnesse of the wombe is in thy rule and governance, an heritage and blessing that commeth from the Lord: we humbly beseech thee so to dispose, comfort, and blesse thine humble Handmaid, our most gracious Queene *Marie*, that she may grow up as a fruitfull Vine upon the walls of the Kings house, and become a joyfull Mother of many children, to the joy and welfare of this Kingdome, and to the glory of thy holy Name, through Jesus Christ our Lord. *Amen.*

III.

O God from whom all good graces do proceed, we beseech thee to multiply upon thy devoted Handmaid, our gracious Queene, the manifold gifts of thy holy Spirit, the Spirit of Wisdome and Understanding, the Spirit of Counsell and Ghostly strength, the Spirit of Knowledge and true Godlinesse, and fulfill her, O Lord, with the Spirit of thy holy feare, for Jesus Christ his sake. *Amen.*

IV.

ALmighty God, blesse her with the blessings of Heaven above, and the blessings of the earth beneath. Let peace and plentie dwell about her: let Holinesse and Honour be her Guard, and let all the fulnesse of thy blessings be upon her, through Jesus Christ our Lord. *Amen.*

---

8 *Marie*: CATHERINE *7 8*

28 *add* V. Almighty God, the fountaine of all goodnesse, we humbly beseech thee to blesse our most gracious Queen *Marie*, Prince *Charles*, and the

A PRAYER FOR THE PR. PALAT. WITH THE LADY ELIZAB. &c.

ALmighty GOD, the Fountaine of all goodnesse, heare our humble supplications which wee make unto thee for thy blessings and favours upon *Frederick* Prince Elector Palatine, and the Lady *Elizabeth* his wife, with their Princely issue: endue them with thy holy Spirit, enrich them with thy heavenly Grace, prosper them with all happines, and bring them to thine everlasting Kingdome, through Jesus Christ our Lord. *Amen.*

The Lords Name be praysed.

rest of the royall Progenie: endue them with thy holy Spirit, enrich them with thy heavenly grace, prosper them with all happinesse, and bring them to thine everlasting kingdome, through Jesus Christ our Lord. *Amen.* *4 5*

1–3 A PRAYER . . . &c.: *A Prayer for the Lady Elizabeth, and her issue. 4 5*: A PRAIER for *The Royal Family. 7 8*

5–8 heare . . . issue: we humbly beseech thee to bless our gracious Queen CATHERINE, MARY the Queen-Mother, JAMES Duke of *Tork*, and all the Royal Family *7*: *as in 7 but om.* MARY the Queen-Mother, *8*

6–8 *Frederick* . . . their: the Lady *Elizabeth*, his Majesties only Sister, with her *4 5*

PRAYERS
FOR
THE FOURE EMBER WEEKES.

PRAYERS FOR THE FOURE EMBER WEEKES.

AMong all the Set-Fasts of the yeare, LENT hath the first, & These EMBER Daies the second place: Dayes of Devotion and Fasting, which were instituted of old, and observed at the foure seasons of the yeare, as for many other, so chiefly for these reasons. First, *That *Christians* in these religious duties towards God might let the world know they were as devout and forward as formerly the *Jewes* had been, whose custome it was to observe foure severall and solemne Times of Fast in the yeare, though for other ends and upon other occasions, than now the use of the Church is to do. 2. For that these Times are as the *first fruits* of everie Season, which wee rightly dedicate to the service and the honour of God. 3. *That by *beginning* these severall parts of the yeare with an holy, righteous and sober life, we might the better learne how to spend the *remainder* of every season accordingly. 4. That we might obtain the continuance of Gods favour towards us for the *fruits* of the earth, which at these *Times* are for the most part eyther *sowne*, or *sprung up*, or comming to their *ripenesse*, or *gathered* into the Barne. 5. That we might recall, bewaile and repent us the more seriously of those sinnes which all the *season* before wee have through our frailtie and wilfulnesse committed. 6. That our *bodies* might by the imploring of Gods mercies, bee freed from those common *distemperatures*, which usually these *foure seasons* of the yeer through the *predominant humours* then reigning, doe bring along with them. 7. And lastly, for that at these

**Leo* de jejun. decimi mensis, Serm. 4. S. *Hieron.* in *Zach 8. Gratian.* dist *76 c.* jejun.

**Leo* de jejun. Sept. mens. Serm. 9.

Const. & Canons, cap. 31. *Luc. 6. 12* *Acts 13. 3*

Times it was the ordinarie custome of the Church, *and is so still, by the Imposition of her Bishops hands, to give holy and *sacred Orders*; which Orders were ever given aswel by *Christ and his *Apostles, as their Successors, with solemne *Prayer* and *Fasting* before hand.

Vers. Our helpe standeth in the Name of the Lord.
Resp. Who hath made Heaven and Earth.
Vers. Blessed bee the Name of the Lord.
Resp. From henceforth world without end. *Amen.*

THE PSALMES.

PSAL. 119.

Beati immaculati.

BLessed are those that are undefiled in the way : and walke in the Law of the Lord.

2 Blessed are they that keepe his testimonies : and seeke him with their whole heart.

3 For they which doe no wickednesse : walke in his wayes.

4 Thou hast charged : that we shall diligently keepe thy Commandements.

5 O that my wayes were made so direct : that I might keepe thy Statutes.

6 So shall I not bee confounded : while I have respect unto all thy Commandements.

7 I will thanke thee with an unfained heart : when I shall have learned the Judgements of thy righteousnesse.

6 standeth: is *7 8*   9 From henceforth: Henceforth *7 8*

8 I will keep thy ceremonies : O forsake me not utterly.

Glory be to the Father, and to the Sonne : and to the holy Ghost.
As it was in the beginning, is now, and ever shall be : world without end. *Amen.*

Legem pone.

TEach me, O Lord, the way of thy statutes : and I shall keepe it unto the end.

2 Give me understanding, and I shall keepe thy Law : yea, I shall keepe it with my whole heart.

3 Make me to goe in the path of thy Commandements : for therein is my desire.

4 Incline my heart unto thy Testimonies : and not to covetousnesse.

5 O turne away mine eyes lest they behold vanitie : and quicken thou me in thy way.

6 O stablish thy Word in thy servant : that I may feare thee.

7 Take away the rebuke that I am afraid of : for thy Judgements are good.

8 Behold, my delight is in thy Commandements : O quicken me in thy righteousnesse.

Glory bee to the Father, and to the Sonne : and to the holy Ghost.
As it was in the beginning, is now, and ever shall be : world without end. *Amen.*

3–4 Father, and . . . Ghost: Father, &c. *4 5*
5–6 is . . . *Amen.*: &c. *4 5*
24–25 Father, and . . . Ghost: Father, &c. *4 5*
26–27 is . . . *Amen.*: &c. *4 5*

Appropinquet.

LEt my complaint come before thee, O Lord : give me understanding according to thy Word.

2 Let my supplication come before thee : deliver me according to thy Word.

3 My lips shall speake of thy praise : when thou hast taught me thy Statutes.

4 Yea, my tongue shall sing of thy Word : for all thy Commandements are righteous.

5 Let thine hand helpe me : for I have chosen thy Commandements.

6 I have longed for thy saving health, O Lord : and in thy Law is my delight.

7 O let my soule live, and it shall praise thee : and thy Judgements shall helpe me.

8 I have gone astray like a sheepe that is lost : Oh seeke thy servant, for I doe not forget thy Commandements.

Glory be to the Father, and to the Sonne : and to the holy Ghost.
As it was in the beginning, is now and ever shall bee : world without end. *Amen.*

After these Psalmes, the LETANY may be said.

O God the Father of Heaven, have &c. *as before.*

---

1 *Appropinquet*: *Appropinquavit 6*
19–20 Father, and . . . Ghost: Father, &c. *4 5*
21–22 is . . . *Amen.*: &c. *4 5* 24 have &c.: have mercie upon us, &c. *6*

THE PRAYERS COMMON TO ALL THE EMBER DAYES,

DISPOSED ACCORDING TO THE SEVEN REASONS BEFORE SPECIFIED.

I.

For Gods acceptance of our humiliation.

ALmighty God, who didst command thy people Israel to afflict their soules before thee on the day of attonement, and by whose divine inspiration the succeeding Ages of that Church appointed other set times of publike Fasting and Humiliation: Grant we beseech thee, that as our knowledge of thee, and of thy truth farre exceeds theirs, so in this, and al other duties of Religion, our Righteousnesse may exceed their Righteousnesse, that men seeing our good works, may glorifie thee our heavenly Father, through Jesus Christ thy Sonne our Saviour. *Amen.*

II.

For consecrating the beginning of every Season unto God.

ALmightie God, from whom we have the beginning and continuance of our life: Grant we beseech thee, that we thy humble servants may so consecrate unto thy divine Majestie the first fruits of this Time and Season of the yeere, that the good purposes which thou puttest into our hearts, may have full effect in our lives, to thy glory, and our soules health, through Jesus Christ our Lord. *Amen.*

III.

For Grace to spend the whole Season aright.

ALmighty God our heavenly Father, we most humbly beseech thee, that wee thy servants who do begin this Time and season of the yeere with fasting and sober living, may find thereby such ghostly strength and comfort, that we may bee the more able and willing to spend both the remainder of this season, and the rest of our dayes accordingly, using this world as it becommeth those who are pilgrims and strangers here, and doe looke for an abiding Citie in the Heavens, through the merits of Jesus Christ our Saviour. *Amen.*

IV.

For the fruits of the Earth.

ALmightie God, Lord of heaven and earth, in whom wee live, move, and have our being, who doest good unto all men, making thy Sunne to rise on the evill and on the good, and sending Raine on the just & on the unjust: favourably behold us thy people, who doe call upon thy Name: and send us thy blessing from heaven, in giving us fruitefull Seasons, and filling our hearts with food and gladnesse: that both our hearts and mouthes may be continually filled with thy prayses, giving thanks to thee in thy holy Church, through Jesus Christ our Lord. *Amen.*

V.

For pardon of sinnes past.

ALmightie and most mercifull Father, who for our many and grievous sinnes, those especially which we have committed against thee since the last solemne

22 food: joy *4 5*

Time of our Humiliation and Repentance, mightest most justly have cut us off in the midst of our dayes, but in the multitude of thy mercies hast hitherto spared us: Accept we most heartily beseech thee, our unfeigned sorrow for all our former transgressions, and grant that wee may never so presume of thy mercy, as to despise the Riches of thy goodnesse, but that thy forbearance, and long suffering may leade us to repentance, and amendment of our sinfull lives, to thy honour and glory, and our finall acquittance and absolution at the last day, through Jesus Christ our Lord. *Amen.*

VI.

For the health of our Bodies.

O God the Father of Lights, from whom commeth downe every good and perfect gift, mercifully looke upon our frailtie and infirmitie, and grant us such health of Body, as thou knowest to be needfull for us: that both in our Bodies and Soules we may evermore serve thee with all our strength and might, through Jesus Christ our Lord. *Amen.*

VII.

For the ordination of Priests and Deacons.

ALmighty God our heavenly Father, who hast purchased to thy selfe an universall Church by the precious blood of thy deare Sonne: mercifully looke upon thy whole Congregation, and at this time so rule and governe the harts and minds of thy servants, the Bishops and Pastors of thy Flocke, that they may lay hands

26 thy . . . Congregation: the same *7 8* 26 rule: guide *7 8*
27 *om.* harts and *7 8*

suddenly on no man, but faithfully and wisely make choyce of fit men to serve thee in the sacred Ministery of thy Church: and to those that shall be ordained to that holy Function, give thy Grace and heavenly benediction, that both by their life and doctrine they may set forth thy glory, and set forward the salvation of all men. Grant this O Lord for his sake, who is the great Shepheard, and Bishop of our soules, Jesus Christ our Lord. *Amen.*

THE PRAYERS PROPER TO THE FOURE SEVERALL EMBER WEEKES.

I.

In the time of Advent.

GRant we most humbly beseech thee, O heavenly Father, that with holy *Simeon*, and *Anna*, and all thy devout servants, who waited for the consolation of Israel, we may at this time so serve thee with fasting and prayer: that by the celebration of the Advent and Birth of our blessed Redeemer, we may with them be filled with true joy and consolation, through the same Jesus Christ our Lord. *Amen.*

II.

For the Ember weeke in Lent.

O Lord Jesus Christ, the Son of God, and Saviour of the World, who didst foretell to thine Apostles, that at the Time of thy sufferings, they should weepe

2 men: persons *7 8* 2 *om.* thee *7 8*
3 that: which *7 8* 3 to that holy: to holy *6*: to any holy *7 8*

and lament, while the world rejoyced, and that they should be sorrowfull, but their sorrow should be turned into joy, Grant that during this time wherein thou didst suffer, and wast afflicted with extreme sorrow and anguish for the sinnes of the whole world, we thy unworthy servants may so weepe and lament, and be sorrowfull for our sinnes, the cause of all those thy sorrowes and sufferings, that on the day of thy triumphant Resurrection, we may rejoyce with that joy, which no man can take from us. Grant this O blessed Lord and Saviour, who didst die for our sinnes, and rise againe for our justification, and now livest and reignest with the Father, in the Unitie of the Holy Ghost, world without end. *Amen.*

III.

For the Ember weeke after Pentecost.

O Lord Jesus Christ, the Eternall Son of the Eternall Father, who at the time of thy glorious Ascension diddest command thine Apostles to tarry in Jerusalem, untill they were endued with Power from on high: and when in obedience to this thy commandement they had there continued with one accord in praier and supplication, didst according to thy promise send downe upon them the Holy Ghost the Comforter: Grant we beseech thee, that we thy most humble servants abiding in the unitie of thy Holy Catholike Church, the Mother of us all, and continually serving thee as thou hast commanded, may bee evermore replenished with the heavenly grace of the Holy Ghost, through thy precious merits and most powerfull intercession, who livest and reignest with the Father in the Unitie of the same Spirit, ever world without end. *Amen.*

IV.

For the Ember Weeke in September.

ALmightie God, who givest to all life and breath, and all things, and bringest forth food out of the Earth for the use of Man: keepe us ever in mind, that this world, with all the glory of it, fadeth, and the fashion thereof passeth away: and grant that wee may so use the fruites of the ground which thou hast now given us, and all other thy temporall Blessings wherewith thou crownest the yeere, as we abuse them not to the satisfying of our wanton and inordinate appetites: but may evermore serve thee in Christian temperance and sobriety, as it becommeth those, who living on earth, have their conversation in heaven, that at the last wee may be admitted into thy heavenly Kingdome, where we shall never hunger or thirst againe, being satisfied with the plenteousnesse of thy House, and filled with the abundance of thy pleasures for evermore. Grant this O heavenly Father, for Jesus Christs sake our Lord. *Amen.*

ASsist me mercifully, O Lord, in these my supplications and prayers, and dispose the way of thy servants toward the attainement of everlasting salvation, that among all the changes and chances of this mortall life, they may ever bee defended by thy most gracious and ready helpe, through Christ our Lord. *Amen.*

PRAYERS
FOR
THE SICKE.

PRAYERS FOR THE SICKE.

OUr Father which art in heaven, hallowed be thy, &c.

Vers. Our helpe standeth in the Name of the Lord.
Resp. Which hath made heaven and earth.
Vers. Blessed bee the Name of the Lord.
Resp. Henceforth world without end. *Amen.*

Glory be to the Father, &c.
As it was in the beginning, &c.

THE ANTIPHONA.

BLessed are they whom Thou chastenest, O Lord, and teachest them in thy Law.

PSAL. 25.

UNto thee, O Lord, doe I lift up my soule, &c.
as before pag. 112.

PSAL. 27.

HEarken unto my voyce O Lord, when I cry unto thee : have mercy upon me, and heare me.

2 O hide not thy face from me : nor cast thy servant away in displeasure.

3 Thou hast been my succour : leave me not, neither forsake mee O God of my salvation.

4 I should utterly have fainted : but that I believe verily to see the goodnesse of the Lord in the land of the living.

4 standeth: is *7 8*
5 Which: Who *7 8*

5 O tarry thou the Lords leisure : be strong, and he shall comfort thine heart, and put thou thy trust in the Lord.

Glory be to the Father, &c.
As it was in the beginning, &c.

Psal. 31. 34.

IN thee O Lord have I put my trust : let me never be put to confusion: deliver me in thy righteousnesse.

2 Bow downe thine eare unto me : make haste to deliver me.

3 And bee thou my strong Rocke, and the house of my defence, that thou mayst save me.

4 My time is in thy hand : deliver me from the hand of mine enemies.

5 Shew thy servant the light of thy countenance : and save me for thy mercies sake.

6 The eyes of the Lord are over the righteous : and his eares are open unto their prayers.

7 The Righteous crie, and the Lord heareth them : and delivereth them out of all their troubles.

8 The Lord is nigh unto them that are of a contrite heart : and will save such as be of an humble spirit.

9 Great are the troubles of the righteous : but the Lord delivereth them out of all.

10 The Lord delivereth the soules of his servants : and all they that put their trust in him, shall not be destitute.

Glory be to the Father, &c.
As it was in the beginning, &c.

THE ANTIPHONA.

BLessed are they whom thou chastenest, O Lord, and teachest them in thy Law.

The seven Penitentiall Psalmes.

REmember not Lord our offences, nor the offences of our Forefathers, &c.

as before, pag. 161.

The Letany.

O God the Father of Heaven, have mercy, &c.

as before, pag. 172.

The Confession.

I Confesse unto Almightie God, &c.

as before, pag. 236.

An humble Protestation of free forgivenesse to others.

I Doe further most humbly desire all and every one whom I have offended, that they would vouchsafe to forgive me. And I doe freely and heartily forgive all the world, whereinsoever any one hath offended me, or done mee any manner of injurie whatsoever; even as I desire to be forgiven of God, and to be absolved from my sinnes for the merits of my blessed Redeemer. *Amen.*

THE CREED.

I Beleeve in God, the Father Almightie, &c.

as before.

After the Creed.

IN this Faith, which I doe unfainedly and wholly believe as a true member of Christs Catholike Church, doe I purpose to finish my life: and if ought shall happen by the violence of my sicknesse, or the suggestions of my ghostly enemies, whereby I shall come to thinke, say, or doe any thing contrary to this holy Faith and purpose, I doe here revoke it before hand, and protest from my soule, even before Christ and his holy Angels, that I give no consent thereunto; giving most humble and hearty thanks unto my loving Creator and Redeemer, that by the wonderfull goodnesse of his bountie, he hath vouchsafed to bring me to the knowledge of this Faith in him, which with my soule and body I commend into his most holy and mercifull hands, now and at the houre of my death. *Amen.*

THE PRAYERS.

Lord have mercy upon me.
Christ have mercy upon me.
Lord have mercy upon me.

OUr Father which art in heaven, hallowed, &c.

Vers. O Lord save thy servant.
Resp. Which putteth his (or *her*) trust in thee.
Vers. Send me helpe from thy holy place.
Resp. And evermore mightily defend me.
Vers. Let the enemie have no advantage over me.
Resp. Nor the wicked one approch to hurt me.

19 me: us *8* 27 *om.* one *7 8*

Vers. Be unto me, O Lord, a strong tower.
Resp. From the face of mine enemies.
Vers. O Lord heare my prayer.
Resp. And let my cry come unto thee.

I.

GOd who declarest thy almightie power most chiefely in shewing mercy and pitie, of thy goodnesse and favour, vouchsafe to heare these my humble and devout prayers, that being now justly punished for mine offences, I may be mercifully delivered by thy aboundant pitie, for the merits of Jesus Christ our Lord. *Amen.*

II.

O God who seest that I put not my trust in any thing which I can doe, mercifully grant, that by thy power I may be delivered from all adversitie, and be healed both in body and soule, through Jesus Christ our Lord. *Amen.*

III.

O Lord looke downe from heaven, behold, visit, and relieve me thy sicke servant, looke upon me with the eyes of thy mercy, give me comfort and sure confidence in thee, defend me from the danger of my deadly enemie, and keepe me in perpetuall peace and safetie, through Jesus Christ our Lord. *Amen.*

IV.

HEare me, Almighty and most mercifull God and Saviour: extend thine accustomed goodnes unto me thy humble servant, who am now grieved with

2 enemies: enemy *7 8* 29 thy: thine *7 8*

sicknesse. Visit me, O Lord, as thou didst visit *Peters* wives mother, and the *Captaines* servant: so visit and restore unto mee my former health (if it bee thy blessed will,) or else give me grace so to take thy visitation, that after this painfull life is ended, I may dwell with thee in life everlasting. *Amen.*

V.

O Sweete Jesus, I desire neither life, nor death, but thy most holy will: Thou art the thing O Lord that I looke for, be it unto me, according to thy good pleasure. If it be thy will to have me die, receive my soule, and grant that in thee, and with thee I may receive everlasting rest. If it be thy will, to have me live any longer upon earth, give me grace to amend the rest of my life, and with good works to glorifie thy holy Name, who with the Father and the holy Ghost livest & reignest ever one God, world without end.

VI.

O God whose nature and propertie is ever to have mercie and to forgive, receive my humble petitions: & though I be tyed and bound with the chaine of my sins, yet let the pittifulnes of thy great mercy loose me, for the honour of Jesus Christs sake our onely Mediator and Advocate. *Amen.*

1–3 Visit . . . will,): Sanctifie, I beseech thee, this thy Fatherly Correction to me, that the sense of my weakness may adde strength to my Faith, and seriousness to my Repentance; that if it shall be thy good pleasure to restore me to my former health, I may lead the residue of my life in thy fear, and to thy glory: *7 8*

17 *add Amen. 2 3 4 5 6 7 8*

23–24 Christs . . . Mediator: Christ our Mediator *7 8*

The blessing.

THe Almightie Lord, who is a most strong Towre to them that put their trust in him, to whom all things in heaven and in earth, and under the earth doe bow, and obey, bee now and evermore my defence, and make me know and feele, that there is no other Name under heaven given to man, in whom and through whom I may receive health, or salvation, but onely the Name of our Lord Jesus Christ. *Amen.*

PRAYERS AT THE HOURE OF DEATH.

OUr Father which art in Heaven, hallowed be thy &c.

Vers. O Lord save thy servant.
Resp. Which putteth his (or *her*) trust in thee.

PSAL. 13. and 16.

COnsider and heare mee O Lord my God : lighten mine eyes that I sleepe not in death : lest mine enemie say, I have prevailed against him.

2 My trust is in thy mercy : and my heart shall bee joyfull in thy salvation.

3 All my delight is upon the Saints : and upon such as excell in vertue.

4 The Lord himselfe is the portion of mine inheritance, and of my cup : yea, I have a goodly heritage.

2–3 to them: to all them *7 8*
4 heaven and: heaven, *7 8*
6 no: none *7 8*
8 health, or: health and *7 8*

5 I have set God before mine eyes : for he is on my right hand, and therefore I shall not fall.

6 Wherefore my heart was glad, and my glory rejoyced : my flesh also shall rest in hope.

7 For why? Thou shalt not leave my soule in hel, neither shalt thou suffer me to see corruption.

8 Thou shalt shew me the path of life : in thy presence is the fulnesse of joy, and at thy right hand there is pleasure for evermore.

Glory be to the Father, &c.
As it was in the beginning, &c.

PSAL. 23.

THe Lord is my Shepheard : therefore can I lacke nothing.

2 He shall feed me in a greene Pasture : and leade me forth besides the waters of comfort.

3 He shall convert my soule : and bring me forth in the paths of righteousnesse for his Names sake.

4 Yea, though I walk through the valley of the shadow of death, I will feare no evill : for thou art with me, thy Rod and thy Staffe doe comfort me.

5 Thy loving kindnesse and mercy shall follow me : and I will dwel in the house of the Lord for ever.

Glory be to the Father, &c.
As it was in the beginning, &c.

PSAL. 38. and 39.

PUt me not to rebuke, O Lord, in thine anger : neither chasten me in thy heavy displeasure.

2 For thine arrowes stick fast in me : and thy hand presseth mee sore.

3 There is no health in my flesh, because of thy displeasure : neither is there any rest in my bones, by reason of my sinne.

4 For my wickednesses are gone over my head : and are like a sore burthen too heavy for me to beare.

5 My wounds stinke, and are corrupt through my foolishnesse.

6 I am brought into so great trouble and miserie : that I goe mourning all the day long.

7 My Loynes are filled with a sore disease : and there is no whole part in my body.

8 I am feeble and sore smitten : I have roared for the very disquietnesse of my heart.

9 Lord thou knowest all my life : and my groaning is not hid from thee.

10 Forsake me not, O Lord my God : be not thou farre from me.

11 Lord let mee know mine end, and the number of my daies : for thou hast made them as a span long, and verily every man living is altogether vanitie.

12 For man walketh in a vaine shadow, he disquieteth himself in vaine : he heapeth up riches, and cannot tell who shall gather them.

13 And now Lord what is my hope? Truly my hope is even in thee.

Glory be to the Father, &c.
As it was in the beginning, &c.

10 My: For my *7 8*   14 life: desire *7 8*

PSAL. 102.

HEare my prayer, O Lord : and let my crying come unto thee.

2 Hide not thy face from mee in the time of my trouble : encline thine eares unto me when I call : O heare me, and that right soone.

3 For my dayes are consumed away like smoke : and my bones are burnt up as it were a firebrand.

4 My heart is smitten downe and withered like grasse : so that I forget to eate my bread.

5 For the voyce of my groaning, my bones will scarce cleave to my flesh.

6 My dayes are gone like a shadow : and I am withered like grasse.

7 O Lord let it be thy pleasure to deliver me : make haste O Lord to helpe me.

8 Thou art my Helper and Redeemer : make no long tarrying, O my God.

Glory be to the Father, &c.

As it was in the beginning, &c.

JOB 14.

MAn that is borne of a Woman, hath but a short time to live, and is full of miserie. Hee commeth up, and is cut downe like a Flowre : he fleeth away like a shadow, and never continueth in one stay.

Vers. O Lord heare our prayer.

Resp. And let our cry come unto thee.

25 in: at *6* 26 our: my *6* 27 our: my *6*

THE LETANIE.

O God the Father of heaven: have mercy upon us miserable sinners, and upon the soule of this thy servant.

O God the Father, &c.

O God the Sonne, Redeemer of the World, have mercy upon us miserable sinners, and upon the soule of this thy servant.

O God the Sonne, &c.

O God the holy Ghost, proceeding from the Father and the Sonne, have mercy upon us miserable sinners, & upon the soule of this thy servant.

O God the holy Ghost, &c.

O Holy, Blessed, and Glorious Trinitie, three persons and one God, have mercy upon us miserable sinners, and upon the soule of this thy servant.

O holy, blessed, and glorious Trinitie, &c.

Remember not Lord our iniquities, nor the iniquities of our forefathers, neither take thou vengeance of our sins: Spare us good Lord, and spare this thy servant, whom thou hast redeemed with thy most precious blood: and be not angry with us for ever.

Spare us good Lord.

From all evill and mischiefe, from the crafts and assaults of the devill.

Good Lord deliver him (or *her.*)

From thy wrath, and from everlasting damnation.

Good Lord deliver, &c.

From the feare of death, from the burden of his (or *her*) sinnes, and from the power of Hell.

Good Lord deliver, &c.

5 *Father, &c.: Father of Heaven &c.* 6

By the multitude of thy mercies, and by thy goodnesse which hath been ever of old.

Good Lord deliver, &c.

By the mystery of thy holy Incarnation, by thy Holy Nativitie and Circumcision, by thy Baptisme, Fasting and Temptation.

Good Lord deliver, &c.

By thine Agony and bloody Sweat, by thy Crosse and Passion.

Good Lord deliver, &c.

By thy precious Death and Buriall: and by thy glorious Triumph over Death and Hell.

Good Lord deliver, &c.

By thy most wonderfull Resurrection and Ascension, and by the miraculous comming downe of the Holy Ghost.

Good Lord deliver, &c.

In this time of his (or *her*) tribulation, in this houre of death, and in the day of Judgement.

Good Lord deliver, &c.

We Sinners doe beseech thee to heare us O Lord God: that it may please thee to deliver the soule of this thy servant from the power of his (or *her*) enemies.

Wee beseech thee to heare us good Lord.

That *he* may evermore have a sure affiance and trust in thy mercie.

We beseech, &c.

That it may please thee to bee *his* Defender and Keeper, giving *him* the victory over Death, Hell, and Sinne.

We beseech, &c.

That it may please thee to succour, helpe, and comfort *him* in this *his* danger, necessitie, and tribulation.

We beseech, &c.

That it may please thee of thy goodnesse to forgive *him* all *his* offences.

We beseech, &c.

That it may please thee to asswage *his* paine, and to give *him* a quiet and joyfull departure.

We beseech, &c.

That it may please thee to guard *him* with thy holy Angels, and to take *him* unto thy favour, through the merits of Christ our Saviour.

We beseech, &c.

That it may please thee to shew *him* the path of everlasting life, and the fulnesse of joy at thy right hand, where there is pleasure for evermore.

We beseech, &c.

Sonne of God we beseech thee to heare us.

Sonne of God, &c.

O Lambe of God, that takest away the sinnes of the world.

Grant him *thy peace.*

O Lambe of God, that &c.

Have mercy upon him.

O Christ heare us.

O Christ &c.

Lord have mercy upon *him.*

Christ have, &c.

Lord have mercy upon *him.*

THe peace of God the Father, the Sonne, and the Holy Ghost bee with *him* evermore.

THE MANNER OF COMMENDING THE SOULE INTO THE

hands of God, at the very point of time when it is departing from the body.

WE brought nothing into this world, neither may we carry any thing out of this world. The Lord giveth, and the Lord taketh away. Even as the Lord pleaseth, so commeth every thing to passe. Blessed be the Name of the Lord.

INto thy mercifull hands, O Lord, wee commend the soule of this thy servant now departing from the body: acknowledge, we meekely beseech thee, a work of thine own hands, a Sheepe of thine owne fold, a Lambe of thine owne Flocke, a Sinner of thine own redeeming. Receive *him* into the blessed armes of thy unspeakeable mercy, into the sacred rest of everlasting peace, and into the glorious estate of thy chosen Saints in heaven.

God the Father who hath created thee, God the Sonne who hath redeemed thee, God the holy Ghost who hath infused his Grace into thee, be now & evermore thy defence, assist thee in this thy last triall, and bring thee into the way of everlasting life. *Amen.*

Christ that redeemed thee with his Agonie & bloody Death, have mercy upon thee, and strengthen thee in this agonie of death. *Amen.*

Christ Jesus that rose the third day from death, raise up thy body againe in the resurrection of the just. *Amen.*

Christ that ascended into Heaven, and now sitteth at the right hand of God, bring thee unto the place of eternall happinesse and joy. *Amen.*

God the Father preserve and keepe thee. God the Sonne assist and strengthen thee. God the Holy Spirit defend and aide thee. God the Holy Trinitie be ever with thee, that thy death may bee precious in the sight of the Lord, with whom thou shalt live for evermore. *Amen.*

Then let be said plainely, distinctly, and with some pauses, these ejaculatorie Meditations and Prayers.

GOe to thy rest, O my soule, for the Lord hath upholden thee.

From death to life: from sorrow to joy: from a Vale of miserie, to a Paradise of mercie.

I know that my Redeemer liveth, and that I shall bee raised againe in the last day.

I shall walke before the Lord in the land of the living.

In thee, O Lord, have I trusted, let mee never bee confounded.

Make me to be numbred with thy Saints in glory everlasting.

Into thy hands I commend my spirit, for thou hast redeemed me, O Lord, thou God of Truth.

I am poore and needy, but the Lord careth for me.

I desire to be dissolved, and to be with Christ.

Thou art my Helper and Redeemer, make no long tarrying, O my God.

Come Lord Jesu, Come quickly.

O Lord, let it be thy pleasure to deliver me: make hast, O Lord, to helpe me.

Lord Jesus receive my spirit.

And these to bee repeated untill the soule be departed.

Then

O Thou Lambe of God, that takest away the sinnes of the world, grant *him* thy peace.

With this Prayer.

O Lord, with whom doe live the spirits of them that die: and by whom the soules of thy servants after they be delivered from the burthen of this flesh, be in perpetuall joy and felicitie: We most meekely beseech thee for this thy servant, that having now received the Absolution from all *his* sinnes which *hee* hath committed in this world, *hee* may escape the gates of Hell, and the paines of eternall darkenesse: that *he* may for ever dwell with *Abraham*, *Isaac*, and *Jacob* in the Region of light, and thy blessed presence, where there is neither weeping nor heavinesse. And that when the dreadfull day of the generall Judgement shall come, *hee* may rise againe with the just, and receive this dead body, which must now be buried in the earth, to be joined with *his* soule, and be made pure and incorruptible for ever after in thy glorious Kingdome, for the merits of thy deare Sonne our Saviour Jesus Christ. *Amen.*

---

1 *these to*: *these (with the Prayers following) to 2 3 6*: *these (with the Prayers next following) to 8*

1 *repeated untill*: *repeated (with these prayers following) untill 4 5*

2 *om. Then 2 3 4 5 6 8* 5 *om. With this Prayer. 2 3 4 5 6 8*

14 Region: reigne *5*

18–20 and receive . . . in thy: his body being reunited to his soule, pure and incorruptible, and be received into thy *2 3 6 8*: his bodie being reunited to his soule, and be made pure and incorruptible for ever after in thy *4 5*

PRAYERS
AND
THANKSGIVINGS
FOR
SUNDRY PURPOSES.

A PRAYER AND THANKSGIVING FOR THE WHOLE ESTATE OF CHRISTS CATHOLIKE CHURCH.

☞ With a *Commemoration* of the Saints before us.

Ex Liturg. Eccl.

ALmighty God, who by thy holy Apostle hast taught us to make Prayers & Supplications for all men: we humbly beseech thee most mercifully to receive these our prayers, which wee offer unto thy divine Majestie for all men in generall: and more especially for thine owne people, the holy Catholik Church, the Mother of us all that beare the Name of Christ: beseeching thee to inspire it continually with the Spirit of truth, unitie, and concord: and grant that all they who doe confesse thy holy Name, may agree in the truth of thy holy Word, and live in unitie and godly love, being one Fold, under one Shepheard, Jesus Christ our Lord. And here forasmuch as we be not onely taught to pray, but to give Thanks also for all men, we doe offer up unto thee most high laud, and heartie thanks for all thy wonderfull Graces and Vertues, which thou hast declared in all thy Saints, and by them bestowed upon thy holy Church from the beginning of the world: and chiefely in the glorious and most *blessed Virgin MARIE, the Mother of thy Sonne Jesus Christ our Lord: as also in the blessed Angels of Heaven: & in all other holy persons upon earth, who by their Lives and Labours have shined forth as Lights in the severall generations of the World: such as were the holy

*Luk. 1. 48.

5 om. marginal reference 4 5 8   *23 om. marginal reference 4 5*

Patriarchs, Prophets, Apostles, and Martyrs, whom we remember with honour, and commemorate with joy: and for whom, as also for all other thy happie Servants our Fathers and Brethren, who have *departed this life with the seale of Faith, and doe now rest in the sleepe of peace, wee prayse and magnifie thy glorious Name: most humbly desiring, that wee may still continue in their holy Communion, and enjoy the comfort thereof while we are on earth, following with a glad will and mind their holy examples of godly living and stedfastnes in thy Faith: and that at the last day we with them, and they with us may attaine to the Resurrection of the just, and have our perfect consummation both of soule and body in the Kingdome of heaven. For these, and for all other things that Thou, O God, wouldst have us to pray, and to praise thy great Name, we are bold to call upon thee, and say as Christ our Lord hath taught us. *Our Father, &c.*

*Injunct. cap. ult. & Can. 55.

For our Parents.

ALmightie God, Father of our Lord Jesus Christ, of whom the whole family in heaven and in earth is named: I give thee most humble thanks, for that thou didst of thy divine providence vouchsafe to let me bee borne of Christian Parents, by whose care I was first brought unto thy holy Baptisme, and afterwards brought up in thy holy Religion. I beseech, O blessed God, who art the Rewarder of every good worke, to recompense them their full reward, even out of the riches of thy bountie and goodnesse. Give them peace and plentie: defend them from all dangers both of body and soule: keepe them in the stedfastnesse of thy faith,

4 *om. marginal reference* 4 5

and in the obedience of thy holy commandements: that so having thee their mercifull and gentle Father, after many happy daies here in this life, they may at last be brought unto life everlasting, through Jesus Christ. *Amen.*

Another for our Parents.

ALmightie God, who hast streightly commanded us to honour our Father & our Mother next unto thee: Grant me of thy goodnes and grace so to love, and to honour my parents, to feare and to obey them, to helpe, and to pray for them, as Thou in thy holy Word hast directed and charged me to doe: that both in their life and at their death, their soules may blesse me, and by thy Fatherly mercie I may obtaine that blessing, which thou hast promised to those that honour their father and their mother: and that thou seeing my unfeigned heart and reverence towards them, mayst become my loving heavenly Father, and number me among those thy children, who are heyres of thy glorious Kingdome, thorough thy welbeloved and deare Sonne Jesus Christ our Lord. *Amen.*

For our children.

ALmightie God, the Father and Maker of us all, who of thy blessing and goodnesse hast vouchsafed to make me a Father (or *Mother*) of children: be pleased also to accept my heartie thanksgiving and devout praise for the same. And grant me thy heavenly grace & assistance so to traine them up in thy godly nourture, vertue, religion, and discipline, that they may continually serve, honour, and obey thee their heavenly Father: and that thou acknowledging & blessing them as thy children here, mayst bring them to the blessing prepared for thy children hereafter, through Jesus Christ our Lord. *Amen.*

A Prayer to be used by women that travell with Child.

ALmightie God, the Father of all mercie and comfort, of whose onely gift it is, that the wombe becommeth fruitfull, graciously behold me thine humble and unworthie Handmaid: that as by thy good providence I have conceived a Child within my wombe, into which thou hast breathed a spirit of life: so by thy continuall aide I may be preserved with it from all perils, and at the fulnesse of my time may safely bring it forth into the world, to the joy and comfort of my owne soule, and to the glorie of thy holy Name, through Jesus Christ our Lord. *Amen.*

Another.

MErcifull Lord, who, when thou tookest upon thee to deliver Man, didst not abhorre the Virgins wombe, but when the fulnesse of time came, wast thy selfe made of a woman, I beseech thee for thy tender pitie and goodnesse to protect and strengthen me against all the dangers and paines of my Labour and Travell: that through thy most mightie aide I may be safely delivered of this happy fruit which thou hast created in my wombe: and when it is borne and brought forth into the world, vouchsafe also that it may bee borne againe by Baptisme, and brought up in thy holy Religion, till it be finally brought to thine everlasting Kingdome, where with the Father and the holy Ghost thou livest and reignest ever one God world without end. *Amen.*

A Thanksgiving after childbirth.

GRacious God, by whose providence wee are all fearefully and wonderfully made, who beholdest us when wee are yet unperfit, and in whose Booke are all our members written: I humbly beseech thee to accept this my reverence of thy power, and to receive this my most heartie praise and thanksgiving, which I now offer up unto thy divine Majesty, for thy blessed favour and goodnes towards me, in vouchsafing to assist me during the time of this my dangerous Travell, and to blesse me with a joyfull Benediction, even the fruit of mine owne wombe. Behold, O Lord, what thine owne hands alone have fashioned, and grant that this little Infant which thou hast made by thy power, may be preserved by thy goodnesse, and forthwith enjoying the benefit of thy holy Baptisme: may be made a lively member of thy Church, and bee carefully brought up to serve thee in all godlinesse and honestie, through the merits of thy welbeloved Sonne Jesus Christ our Lord. *Amen.*

A Thanksgiving for Recoverie from sicknesse.

PRaise the Lord, O my soule, & all that is within me praise his holy Name: who hath saved thy life from destruction, and crowned thee with mercy and loving kindnesse. O Lord my God I cryed unto thee, and thou hast healed me. Therefore will I sing of thy praise without ceasing, and I will pay my vowes, and give thankes unto thee for ever. *Amen.*

A Prayer in the time of Warre.

O Almightie God, King of all Kings, and Governour of all things, whose power no creature is able to resist, to whom it belongeth justly to punish sinners, and to bee mercifull unto them that truly repent: save and deliver us, we humbly beseech thee, from the hands of our enemies, abate their pride, asswage their malice, and confound their devices: that wee being armed with thy defence, may be preserved evermore from all perils to glorifie thee, who art the giver of all victorie, through the merits of thy onely Sonne Jesus Christ our Lord. *Amen.*

A Thanksgiving for Peace and Victorie.

O Almightie God, who art a strong Towre of defence unto thy servants: we give unto thee most heartie praise & thanks for that thou hast delivered us from our enemies, & from those many & fearefull dangers wherewith we were lately compassed: acknowledging thy goodnes, that we were not consumed by them, and beseeching thee for thy mercies to establish us in this happie Peace, and to continue on thy loving kindnesse to us (who art our onely Saviour and mightie Deliverer) through Jesus Christ our Lord. *Amen.*

12 the giver: the only giver *7 8*

26 '*A Thanksgiving for restoring publick Peace at home*' *is added here by 7 8* (*see Appendix, p. 312*)

A Prayer in the time of any common Plague.

ALmighty God, who in thy wrath in the time of king *David*, didst slay with the plague of Pestilence threescore and ten thousand, and yet remembring thy mercy didst save the rest: have pitie upon us miserable sinners, who are now visited with great sicknesse and mortalitie, that like as thou didst then command thine Angell to cease from punishing, so it may now please thee to withdraw from us this plague and grievous sicknesse, through Jesus Christ our Lord. *Amen.*

A Thanksgiving for deliverance from any Plague.

O Lord, who hast wounded us for our sinnes, and consumed us for our transgressions, by thy late, heavie, and dreadfull visitation: and now in the midst of judgement remembring mercy, hast redeemed our soules from the jawes of death, we offer unto thee our selves, our soules and our bodies, which thou hast delivered, to be a living sacrifice unto thee, alwaies praising and magnifying thy mercies, through Jesus Christ our Lord. *Amen.*

3 ALmighty: O Almighty *7 8*

3 wrath . . . time: wrath didst send a Plague upon thine own people in the wilderness for their obstinate rebellion against *Moses* and *Aaron*, and also in the time *7 8*

7 are now: now are *7 8*

8–9 command . . . cease: accept of an atonement, and didst command the destroying Angel to cease *7 8*

14 Lord, who: Lord God, who *7 8*

18 thee . . . selves: thy fatherly goodness our selves *7 8*

19 and our bodies: and bodies *7 8*

21 mercies, through: mercies in the midst of thy Church, through *7 8*

A Prayer and Thanksgiving for every true Subject to use upon the Anniversary Day of the Kings Reigne.

LOrd, by whom Kings doe reigne, and Princes are set up to beare rule over their people: and by whose gracious Providence thy Servant and our dread Soveraign King CHARLES was as this day placed in the Royall Throne of his Kingdome: Accept, we beseech thee, the gratefull Commemoration which wee now make before Heaven and before Thee, of this thy great goodnesse and blessing towards us: that while we offer up our vowes and sacrifices of Thanksgiving to the praise of thy glorious Name, thou maist blesse the King with thy favours, and crowne him with continuall honour: granting him a long, prosperous, and religious Reigne over his people: and granting us a true, quiet, humble, and obedient subjection under Him: that He ruling us prudently with all his power, we may obey him loyally with all lowlinesse and chearefulnesse of mind: and that both Hee and we evermore endevouring to set forth the beautie of thy Church Militant here on earth, may be at last exalted to the glorie of thy Church triumphant in the Heavens, through Jesus Christ our Lord. *Amen.*

A Prayer and Thanksgiving upon the Anniversarie day of our Birth.

ALmightie God, the Father and Maker of all things, by whose blessed goodnesse I was fearefully and wonderfully made in my mothers wombe, and unto whose blessed providence I have beene left ever since I was borne, and hung upon my mothers breasts: I

18 prudently: providently *4 5*

praise and magnifie thy glorious Name for this thy great goodnesse towards mee: most humbly beseeching thee, that I may be taught to number my daies, and to apply my heart unto wisedome: that I may know to what end I was borne, and had both body and life given me, even to serve thee the living God: that I may bewaile my sinfull yeeres past, and spend the rest of my time here in a godly, righteous, and sober life: that as I have now finished *ooo.* yeeres of my life here in thy favour, so I may continue and finish up the remainder of my daies in thy feare: and, that as thou didst upon this day take mee out of my mothers wombe to live here a little time: so thou maist at the last day take mee out of my mothers wombe againe, even the grave and the wombe of the earth, to live with thee for ever, through Jesus Christ our Lord. *Amen.*

A Prayer and Thanksgiving upon the Anniversarie day of our Baptisme.

O Lord heavenly Father, Almightie & everlasting God, who of thine infinite goodnesse towards me, when I was borne in sinne, and was no other then an heire of everlasting wrath, didst vouchsafe that I should as upon this day bee borne againe of water and the Holy Ghost in the blessed Laver of Baptisme, being therby made a member of Christ, and an heire of eternall life: for this thine inestimable favour I doe here gratefully commemorate that happie day, and in most humble and heartie wise I do extoll the abundant riches of thy glorious grace: in thy sight, and in the sight of thy holy Angels, with all the company of Heaven, renewing that sacred vow which was then made in my Name, to

31 my: thy *45*

forsake this wicked World, and to live as a Christian ought to do, in obedience to thy holy Faith and Commandements: most humbly beseeching thee of thy great mercy to pardon me all former breaches of my solemne promise, and to endue me so with the assistance of thy holy Spirit, that henceforth I may walke in newnesse of life, worthy of that blessed estate whereunto thou hast called me: and keeping my selfe unspotted of the World, the flesh, and the divell, I may daily die unto sinne, for which cause I was baptized into the death of Christ: and as I have had my part this day in the first regeneration, so I may at the last day have my part in the second and great regeneration of the world, to live and reigne with thee for ever, through the merits of Jesus Christ our Lord. *Amen.*

A PRAYER WHEREWITH S. AUGUSTINE BEGAN HIS DEVOTIONS:

Admiring the unspeakable Majestie and Attributes of God.

Confess. l. 1. c. 4.

WHat art Thou, O my God? What art thou I beseech thee, but the Lord my God? For who is Lord besides our Lord, or who is God besides our God? O thou supreme, most powerfull, most mercifull, most just, most secret, most present, most beautiful, most mightie, most incomprehensible, most constant, and yet changing all things: immutable, never new and

21 *om. marginal reference* 4 5 7 8

never old, and yet renewing all things: ever in action, and yet ever quiet: heaping up, yet needing nothing, creating, upholding, filling, protecting, nourishing, and perfecting all things.

Thou lovest, and yet thou art not transported: Thou art jealous, yet thou art voyd of feare: Thou doest repent, yet thou art free from sorrow: Thou art angrie, and yet never art unquiet: Thou takest what thou findest, yet didst thou never loose any thing: Thou art never poore, and yet thou art glad of gaine: never covetous, and yet thou exactest profit at our hands. We bestow largely upon thee, that thou mayst become our debtor: yet who hath any thing but of thy gift? Thou payest debts, when thou owest nothing: Thou forgivest debts, and yet thou loosest nothing. And what shal I say, O my God, my life, my joy, my holy deare delight? Or what can any man say, when he speaketh of thee? And woe bee to them that speake not of thee, but are silent in thy praise: for even they who speake most of thee, may bee accounted to be but dumbe. Have mercy upon me, O Lord, that I may speake unto thee, and praise thy Name. *Amen.*

A Praier wherewith to conclude all our Devotions.

ALmightie God, who hast promised to heare the petitions of them that aske in thy Sonnes Name, I beseech thee mercifully to encline thine eares unto me, who have now made my prayers and supplications unto thee: and grant that those things which I have faithfully asked according to thy will, may bee effectually obtained,

27 *om.* to *4 5*

to the reliefe of my necessitie, and to the setting forth of thy glory, through Jesus Christ our Lord. *Amen.*

THE BLESSING.

THe Peace of God which passeth all understanding: the blessing of God Almightie, the Father, the Sonne, and the Holy Ghost: the vertue of Christs blessed Crosse and Passion; the succour of all holy Angels, and the suffrages of all the chosen of God, be with me, now, and at the houre of death; of thy mercy Lord I beg it. *Amen.*

FINIS.

7–9 Passion . . . beg it: Passion be with me, now, and at the houre of death *2 3 4 5 6 7 8*

APPENDIX

THE PRINCIPAL VARIANTS OF THE EDITIONS OF 1664 (*7*) AND 1672 (*8*)[1]

[1] The variants of *8* as against *7* are insignificant and are ignored throughout this Appendix, which reproduces the text of *7*.

TABLES & RULES

Pages 33–37.

FOR

The Moveable and Immoveable FEASTS:

Together with
The Daies of *Fasting* and *Abstinence*,
through the whole year.

Easter-day, from 1665 to 1742.

1665	M. 26	1691	A. 12	1717	A. 21
1666	A. 15	1692	M. 27	1718	A. 13
1667	A. 7	1693	A. 16	1719	M. 29
1668	M. 22	1694	A. 8	1720	A. 17
1669	A. 11	1695	M. 24	1721	A. 9
1670	A. 3	1696	A. 12	1722	M. 25
1671	A. 23	1697	A. 4	1723	A. 14
1672	A. 7	1698	A. 24	1724	A. 5
1673	M. 30	1699	A. 9	1725	M. 28
1674	A. 19	1700	M. 31	1726	A. 10
1675	A. 4	1701	A. 20	1727	A. 2
1676	M. 26	1702	A. 5	1728	A. 21
1677	A. 15	1703	M. 28	1729	A. 6
1678	M. 31	1704	A. 16	1730	M. 29
1679	A. 20	1705	A. 8	1731	A. 18
1680	A. 11	1706	M. 24	1732	A. 9
1681	A. 3	1707	A. 13	1733	M. 25
1682	A. 16	1708	A. 4	1734	A. 14
1683	A. 8	1709	A. 24	1735	A. 6
1684	M. 30	1710	A. 9	1736	A. 25
1685	A. 19	1711	A. 1	1737	A. 10
1686	A. 4	1712	A. 20	1738	A. 2
1687	M. 27	1713	A. 5	1739	A. 22
1688	A. 15	1714	M. 28	1740	A. 6
1689	M. 31	1715	A. 17	1741	M. 29
1690	A. 20	1716	A. 1	1742	A. 18

Golden Number	Easter Limit.
1	April 5
2	Mar. 25
3	April 13
4	April 2
5	Mar. 22
6	April 10
7	Mar. 30
8	April 18
9	April 7
10	Mar. 27
11	April 15
12	April 4
13	Mar. 24
14	April 12
15	April 1
16	Mar. 21
17	April 9
18	Mar. 29
19	April 17

RULES to know when the moveable *Feasts* and *Holy-daies* begin.

ADvent Sunday is alwaies the Sunday after the six and twentieth of *November*.

Easter-day is alwaies the Sunday after the day which is called *The Easter-limit*, which is found for any year by the help of its Golden Number in the Table before.

All the other moveable Feasts depend upon *Easter*; for

Septuagesima	*Sunday* is	9	weeks before *Easter*.
Sexagesima		8	
Quinquagesima		7	
Quadragesima		6	

Rogation Sun.	is	5. weeks	after *Easter*.
Ascension-day		40. daies	
Whitsunday		7. weeks	
Trinity Sund.		8. weeks	

A Table of all the *Feasts* that are to be observed in the Church of *England* through the year.

ALL Sundaies in the year.

The daies of the Feasts of

The Circumcision of our Lord JESUS CHRIST.
The Epiphany.
The Conversion of S. *Paul.*
The Purification of the B. Virg.
S. *Matthias* the Apostle.
The Annunciation of the B. Vir.
S. *Mark* the Evangelist.
S. *Philip* & S. *Jacob* the Apost.
The Ascension of our Lord JESUS CHRIST.
S. *Barnabas.*
The Nativity of S. *John Baptist.*
S. *Peter* the Apostle.
S. *James* the Apostle.
S. *Bartholomew* the Apostle.
S. *Matthew* the Apostle.
S. *Michael*, and all Angels.
S. *Luke* the Evangelist.
S. *Simon* & S. *Jude* the Apostles.
All Saints.
S. *Andrew* the Apostle.
S. *Thomas* the Apostle.
The Nativity of our LORD.
S. *Stephen* the Martyr.
S. *John* the Evangelist.
The Holy Innocents.

Munday and Tuesday in *Easter*-week. Mund. and Tuesd. in *Whitsun*-week.

A Table of the *Vigils*, *Fasts*, and *daies of Abstinence*, to be observed in the year.

The Evens or Vigils before

- The Nativity of our LORD.
- The Purification of the Blessed Virgin *Mary*.
- The Annunciation of the B. Vir.
- *Easter*-day.
- *Ascension-day*.
- *Pentecost*.
- S. *Matthias*.
- S. *John Baptist*.
- S. *Peter*.
- S. *James*.
- S. *Bartholomew*.
- S. *Matthew*.
- S. *Simon* and S. *Jude*.
- S. *Andrew*.
- S. *Thomas*.
- All Saints.

Note, that if any of these Feast-daies fall upon a Monday, then the Vigil or Fast-day shall be kept upon the Saturday, and not upon the Sunday next before it.

Daies of *Fasting* or *Abstinence*.

1. THe Fourty daies of *Lent*.

2. The *Ember-daies* at the four seasons, being the *Wednesday*, *Friday* and *Saturday*

after
- the 1. Sunday in *Lent*.
- the Feast of *Pentecost*.
- *September* 14.
- *December* 13.

3. The three *Rogation-daies*, which be the *Munday*, *Tuesday*, and *Wednesday* before *Holy-Thursday*, or the *Ascension* of our Lord.

4. All the *Fridays* in the year except *Christmas day*.

Certain solemn daies, for which particular Services are appointed.

THE Fifth day of *November*, being the day of the Papists Conspiracy.

2. The Thirtieth day of *January*, being the day of the Martyrdom of King *Charles* the First.

3. The Nine and twentieth day of *May*, being the day of the Birth and Return of King *Charles* the Second.

Note, that the Supputation of the year of our Lord in the Church of England *beginneth the Five and twentieth day of* March.

The times wherein Marriages *are not solemnized.*

From	*Advent* Sunday,	until	8. daies after the *Epiphany*.
	Septuag. Sunday,		8. daies after *Easter*.
	Rogation Sunday,		*Trinity* Sunday.

Some of these being Times of solemn Fasting and Abstinence, some of Holy Festivity and Joy, both fit to be spent in such sacred Exercises, without other Avocations.

The Collect for the third Sunday in Advent.

Page 184.

O Lord *Jesu* Christ, who at thy first coming didst send thy messenger to prepare thy way before thee; grant that the ministers and stewards of thy mysteries may likewise so prepare and make ready thy way, by turning the hearts of the disobedient to the wisedom of the just, that at thy second coming to judge the world we may be found an acceptable people in thy sight, who livest and reignest with the Father and the holy Spirit, ever one God, world without end. *Amen.*

The Collect for Saint Stevens day.

Page 185.

GRant, O Lord, that in all our sufferings here upon earth for the testimony of thy truth, we may stedfastly look up to heaven, and by faith behold the glory that shall be revealed; and being filled with the holy Ghost, may learn to love and bless our persecutors, by the example of thy first Martyr Saint *Stephen*, who praied for his murtherers to thee, O blessed *Jesus*, who standest at the right hand of God to succour all those that suffer for thee, our onely Mediator and Advocate. *Amen.*

The Collect for S. John the Evangelists day.

MErcifull Lord, we beseech thee to cast thy bright beams of light upon thy Church, that it being enlightned by the doctrine of thy blessed Apostle and Evangelist Saint *John*, may so walk in the light of thy truth, that it may at length attain to the light of everlasting life, through *Jesus* Christ our Lord. *Amen.*

Page 186.

The Collect for Innocents day.

O Almighty God, who out of the mouths of babes and sucklings hast ordained strength, & madest Infants to glorifie thee by their deaths; mortifie and kill all vices in us, and so strengthen us by thy grace, that by the innocency of our lives, and constancy of our faith even unto death, we may glorifie thy holy Name, through *Jesus* Christ our Lord. *Amen.*

Pages 187–8.

The Collect for the fourth Sunday after the Epiphany.

O God, who knowest us to be set in the midst of so many and great dangers, that by reason of the frailty of our nature we cannot alwaies stand upright; grant to us such strength and protection as may support us in all dangers, and carry us through all temptations, through *Jesus* Christ our Lord. *Amen.*

Page 188.

The Collect for the sixth Sunday after the Epiphany.

O God, whose blessed Son was manifested that he might destroy the works of the Devil, and make us the Sons of God and heirs of eternal life; grant us, we beseech thee, that having this hope, we may purifie our selves even as he is pure; that when he shall appear again with power and great glory, we may be made like unto him in his eternal and glorious kingdom, where with thee, O Father, and thee, O holy Ghost, he liveth and reigneth ever one God world without end. *Amen.*

The Collect *for Easter Even.*

Page 201.

GRant, O Lord, that as we are baptized into the death of thy blessed Son our Saviour *Jesus* Christ; so by continual mortifying our corrupt affections, we may be buried with him, and that through the grave and gate of death we may pass to our joyfull resurrection, for his merits who died, and was buried, and rose again for us, thy son *Jesus* Christ our Lord. *Amen.*

THE ANTHEMES UPON EASTER DAY.

Pages 202–3.

CHrist our passeover is sacrificed for us: therefore let us keep the Feast. Not with the old leven, neither with the leven of malice and wickedness: but with the unlevened bread of sincerity and truth.

CHrist being raised from the dead dieth no more: death hath no more dominion over him. For in that he died, he died unto sin once: but in that he liveth, he liveth unto God. Likewise reckon ye also your selves to be dead indeed unto sin: but alive unto God, through *Jesus* Christ our Lord.

CHrist is risen from the dead: and become the first-fruits of them that slept. For since by man came death: by man came also the resurrection of the dead. For as in Adam all die: even so in Christ shall all be made alive.

Gloria Patri follows.

Page 205.

THE COLLECT FOR THE FIRST SUNDAY AFTER EASTER.

ALmighty Father, who hast given thine onely Son to die for our sins, and to rise again for our justification; grant us so to put away the leven of malice and wickedness, that we may alwaies serve thee in pureness of living and truth, through the merits of the same thy Son *Jesus* Christ our Lord. *Amen.*

Page 210.

The Collect for the second Sunday after Trinity.

O Lord, who never failest to help and govern them whom thou dost bring up in thy stedfast fear and love; keep us, we beseech thee, under the protection of thy good providence, and make us to have a perpetual fear and love of thy holy Name, through *Jesus* Christ our Lord. *Amen.*

The Collect for the third Sunday after Trinity.

O Lord, we beseech thee mercifully to hear us; and grant that we, to whom thou hast given an hearty desire to pray, may by thy mighty aid be defended and comforted in all dangers and adversities, through *Jesus* Christ our Lord. *Amen.*

Page 212.

The Collect for the eight Sunday after Trinity.

O God, whose never-failing providence ordereth all things both in heaven and earth; we humbly beseech thee to put away from us all hurtfull things, and to give us those things which be profitable for us, through *Jesus* Christ, our Lord. *Amen.*

The Collect for the eighteenth Sunday after Trinity.

Page 215.

LOrd, we beseech thee, grant thy people grace to withstand the temptations of the World, the Flesh and the Devil, and with pure hearts and minds to follow thee the only God, through *Jesus* Christ our Lord. *Amen.*

The Collect on the Conversion of Saint Paul.

Page 219.

O God, who through the preaching of the blessed Apostle S. *Paul*, hast caused the light of the Gospel to shine throughout the world; grant, we beseech thee, that we having his wonderful conversion in remembrance, may shew forth our thankfulness unto thee for the same, by following the holy doctrine which he taught, through *Jesus* Christ our Lord. *Amen.*

The Collect for S Lukes day.

Page 223.

ALmighty God, who calledst *Luke* the Physician, whose praise is in the Gospel, to be an Evangelist and Physician of the soul; may it please thee, that by the wholesome medicines of the doctrine delivered by him all the diseases of our Souls may be healed, through the merits of thy Son *Jesus* Christ our Lord. *Amen.*

Page 289.

A Thanksgiving for restoring publick Peace at home.

O Eternal God our heavenly Father, who alone makest men to be of one mind in a house, and stillest the outrage of a violent and unruly people; We bless thy holy Name that it hath pleased thee to appease the seditious tumults which have been lately raised up amongst us; most humbly beseeching thee to grant to all of us grace, that we may henceforth obediently walk in thy holy commandments, and leading a quiet and peaceable life in all godliness and honesty, may continually offer unto thee our sacrifice of praise and thanksgiving for these thy mercies towards us, through *Jesus* Christ our Lord. *Amen.*

COMMENTARY

COMMENTARY

THE principal intention of these notes is to give information about Cosin's sources, wherever they can be identified, and about the chief influences upon subsequent revisions of the Book of Common Prayer. The notes are generally of two sorts—notes which point out items, comparable to those in the *Devotions*, in various Primers and other devotional books which Cosin may have used as sources, and notes which clarify his many references (some 130 in all) to the Fathers and early Councils of the Church.

With regard to the former, the most obvious sources are those acknowledged by Cosin himself, the Book of Common Prayer (the 1549 edition in particular), the two Elizabethan Primers, of 1560 and 1564, and so on; in addition, however, it is clear that Cosin used various other Primers, at least one of the unreformed devotional books cited by Prynne—*A Manual of Prayers* (1583)—and, to a small extent, the *Breviarium Romanum*.

With regard to the latter, it would not have been necessary for Cosin to explore in detail all his patristic and conciliar sources, since the quotations and references he gives had been assembled in the works of several liturgical commentators. Prynne charges Cosin with plagiarizing three Roman Catholic works in particular, and discovering in them, and not in the primary texts, most of his defence of the canonical hours. Cosin does not mention anywhere in the *Devotions* an indebtedness to these authorities, but he must have been aware of them: the annotated Rheims (Douay) Bible (1582); St. Robert Cardinal Bellarmine (1542–1621), 'De operibus bonis in particulari', a part of the *Disputationum de Controversiis Christianae Fidei adversus hujus temporis Haereticos* . . . (Ingolstadt, 1586–93); Azorius (Juan Azor, a Spanish Jesuit, 1533–1603), *Institutionum Moralium* (Rome, 1600). All of these include (with some repetition) most of the patristic and scriptural authorities for the observance of the canonical hours and the other liturgical practices noticed by Cosin, and they often give the particular passage which Cosin translates. Prynne, however, fails to draw attention to another important collection of liturgical observations, and it is one which Cosin himself refers to (at The Third Hour): Joannes Stephanus Durantus (d. 1589), *De Ritibus Ecclesiae Catholicae* (Rome, 1591; a 5th ed., London, 1606).[1] Durantus cites all the familiar authorities,

[1] Durantus (Jean-Étienne Duranti) was a French liturgiologist whose

not only in his defence of the use of canonical hours in general, but in separate chapters about each hour. There were, of course, only a certain number of such references and they would naturally have been known to any liturgical commentator. Although Cosin very likely knew the original sources from which these references were drawn, it was clearly unnecessary for him to turn to them, and most unlikely that he did so. There is no reason to doubt, as Prynne apparently does, Cosin's first-hand knowledge of patristic writings, but the *Devotions* was a hurried work, and Cosin would certainly have been grateful for any obvious help so efficient and encyclopedic as Durantus.

The translations from the Fathers, etc., are for the most part probably Cosin's own, few of these authorities being available then in English translations. Cosin presumably made direct use of Bellarmine, Azorius, and Durantus (the annotated Rheims Bible does not give careful or extended patristic quotations but summarizes from the sources); he perhaps then turned to editions of the works cited in them. We cannot be sure how independently Cosin worked nor how much he was translating from quotations and how much from the texts themselves, or even how much he may have ignored the commentators altogether. We have therefore quoted Cosin's texts so far as possible from contemporary editions which he could have used, or later texts based upon them. For the Greek Fathers, we have used Latin translations, generally in Greek–Latin editions.

For references to the Primers, we have given the name of the Primer and, wherever it is described in Hoskins, the number and usually the page of its entry. Prayers which Cosin has taken from the Book of Common Prayer, unless altered to some extent, are not referred to.

References most frequently cited in the Commentary are based upon the following texts, but we have silently corrected the few passages which contained errors:

Ambrose. Opera . . . Parisiis . . . 1549.

Athanasius. Athanasii Magni Alexandrini Episcopi . . . Opera [4 vols. bound in one] . . . Basileae, Anno M.D.LVI.

Augustine. D. Aurelii Augustini . . . Opera [10 vols.] Basileae, M.D.LXIX.

work depended largely on the *Rationale Divinorum Officiorum* by Gulielmus Durandus (1230–96), Bishop of Mende and a well-known writer on canon law. Cosin used the Third Book of Durantus's work, especially capp. ii (De certarum horarum ad orationem antiquitate), vii (De Prima), viii (De Tertia), ix (De Sexta), x (De Nona), xi (De Vesperis), xii (De hora Completorii). For the similarly relevant sections in Bellarmine, cf. *Opera*, III, Lib. i of 'De operibus bonis', 'De Oratione'; in Azorius, cf. Lib. X, 'De Horis Canonicis'.

Basil. Sancti Patris Nostri Basilii Magni . . . Opera [3 vols. in Greek and Latin] Parisiis M.DC.XXXVIII.

Bibliotheca Veterum Patrum . . . Parisiis M.DC.LIII. [This collection, in 16 vols., appeared in earlier editions, such as Cologne, 1608, Paris, 1624.]

Binius, Severinus, ed. Concilia Generalia, et Provincialia . . . [4 vols.] Coloniae Agrippinae . . ., Anno M.DC.VI.

Chrysostom. D. Joannis Chrysostomi . . . Opera Omnia [12 vols. bound in 4, in Greek and Latin] Moguntiae Sumptibus Joannis Davidis Zunneri, Bibliopolae Francofurt . . . M.DC.XCIIX. (i.e. M.DC.XCVIII.) [the version by F. Ducaeus, Paris, 1609.]

Cosin, J. Works. In 'The Library of Anglo-Catholic Theology', 5 vols. Oxford, 1843–55.

Cyprian. Opera D. Caecilii Cypriani . . . Antwerpiae . . . 1568.

Cyril. Cyrilli Hierosolymorum Archiepiscopi Catecheses . . . Parisiis . . . 1608.

Durham Book, The. Being the First Draft of the Revision of the Book of Common Prayer in 1661. Ed. G. J. Cuming. London, 1961.

Erasmus, Desiderius. Opera Omnia [9 vols.] Basileae 1540. [Vol. V contains 'Precationes Aliquot Novae'.]

Eusebius. Eusebii Pamphili, Ruffini, Socratis, Theodoriti, Sozomeni, Theodori, Evagrij, & Dorothei Ecclesiastica Historia. Basileae 1611.

Hooker, Richard. Of the Lawes of Ecclesiasticall Politie. The fift Booke. London, 1597 [bound with the first four books which are imprinted 1594].

Hoskins, E. Horae Beatae Mariae Virginis, or Sarum and York Primers, with Kindred Books and Primers of the Reformed Roman Use. London, 1901.

Isidore. Sancti Isidori Hispalensis . . . Opera Omnia . . . Coloniae Agrippinae, Anno M.DC.XVII.

Jerome. Sancti Hieronymi Stridoniensis Opera Omnia . . . Coloniae Agrippinae . . . Anno M.DC.XVI [9 vols. bound in three].

Manual of Prayers newly gathered out of many and divers famous authours aswell auncient as of the tyme present, A. [ed. G. F.] ?Douai, 1583.

Nazianzen. Sancti Gregorii Nazianzeni . . . Opera . . . Lutetiae Parisiorum . . . M.DCIX.

Nyssen. Gregorii episcopi Nysseni . . . Opera omnia . . . Parisiis . . . [1615].

Private Prayers put forth by authority during the Reign of Queen Elizabeth. Ed. W. K. Clay. Cambridge: The Parker Society, 1851.

Ruffinus. Cf. Eusebius.

Tertullian. Q. Septimii Florentis Tertulliani . . . Opera . . . Omnia . . . Antwerpiae . . . M.D.LXXXIIII.

THE APPROBATION

GEO: LONDON. The Bishop of London, George Montaigne or Mountain (1569–1628).

THE PRINTER TO THE READER

This first appeared in the second edition at the end of the text, in the third following The Approbation, and in the sixth after the preface to The Calendar. The Huntington Library copy of the second edition, however, binds it after 'Of the Calendar', and its copy of the third edition places it after the Calendar itself. Since there is considerable variety about the position of this 'apology', which has occurred anyway in only three editions, we have decided on the present arrangement as one which seems to place it in normal order. Cosin probably wrote it, as both Prynne and Burton declare in the concluding pages of their respective pamphlets.

THE PREFACE

This is based, to a considerable extent, on Richard Hooker's remarks on prayer, *Of the Lawes of Ecclesiasticall Politie* (1594, 1597), v. 23, 25, 26, 33, 35, several passages being verbatim.

FOr the good . . . *Prayer* and *Devotion*. Cf. Hooker, v. 35 (p. 72): 'for the good of whose soules there is not in Christian Religion any thing of like continuall use and force throughout every hower and moment of their whole lives'; and v. 23 (p. 52): 'these two ghostly exercises, the one *Doctrine*, the other *Prayer*'.

And therefore they . . . Disciples. Cf. Hooker, v. 35 (p. 72): 'And ot this the Apostles having taken notice, they request that as John had taught his, so Christ would likewise teach them to pray.'

And though men . . . his Patterne. Cf. Hooker, v. 35 (p. 72): 'Though men should speake with the toongs of Angels, yet words so pleasing to the eares of God as those which the Sonne of God himselfe hath composed were not possible for men to frame.'

the Fathers. This is the first of many such references to patristic authority. Cosin appears to refer, in the marginal notes, to St. Augustine's sermons *De Tempore*, the 186th in the series, second for 'Feria secunda Pentecostes de missione spiritus sancti'. But nothing in that is quite the same as the idea expressed in Cosin's text. Cf. rather Augustine's sermons specifically on the Lord's Prayer. 'In orationem Dominicam tractatus': 'Verba ergo quae Dominus noster Jesus Christus in Oratione docuit, forma est desideriorum. Non tibi licet petere aliud, quam ibi scriptum est' (x. 1524D. This text also appears in *Patrologia Latina*, ed. J.-P. Migne, as Sermon 56 in 'Sermones de Scripturis', v. 378.).

Cf. also Tertullian, *De Oratione* (p. 213), cap. 9 called 'Legitima Oratio': 'Ab ipso igitur ordinata religio orationis, & de spiritu ipsius iam tunc cum ex ore divino ferretur, animata suo privilegio ascendit in coelum commendans patri quae filius docuit. Quoniam tamen Dominus prospector humanarum necessitatum seorsum post traditam orandi disciplinam, Petite, inquit, & accipietis, & sunt quae petantur pro circumstantia cujusque, praemissa legitima & ordinaria oratione quasi fundamento, accidentium jus est desideriorum, jus est superstruendi extrinsecus petitiones.' Cosin alludes again to this passage in the next paragraph and there gives a partial translation of it. Cf. Hooker, v. 35 (p. 72): 'Tertullian and S. Augustine do for that cause terme it *orationem legitimam. . . .*'

the Patterne wherby . . . superfluitie of words. Cf. Hooker, v. 26 (p. 56): 'or as if our Lord . . . had not left us of his owne framing one, which might . . . serve as a paterne whereby to frame all other prayers with efficacie, yet without superfluitie of words.'

Thus we begin . . . *fundamento accidentium &c.* Cf. Hooker, v. 35 (p. 72): 'For which cause also our custome is both to place it[a] in the front of our prayers as a guide, and to adde it in the ende of some principall limmes or parts as a complement which fully perfecteth whatsoever may be defective in the rest.' Hooker's note *a* refers to the quotation from Tertullian, 'Praemissa legitima . . .', which appears in the margin of his text.

Horarium Regiâ authoritate editum. Complete reprints of these Elizabethan Primers appear in *Private Prayers.* The proper title of the 1560 Primer is *Orarium seu Libellus Precationum Per Regiam Majestatem Latine Aeditus.* The Primer of 1573 is largely a revised reprint of the 1564 Primer, but both are markedly different from 1560; the Primer of 1564 is titled, *Preces Privatae, in Studiosorum Gratiam collecte & Regia authoritate approbate.*

1. The first . . . when they list. Cf. Hooker, v. 25 (p. 56): 'To him which considereth the grievous and scandalous inconveniences whereunto they make themselves dayly subject, with whome any blinde and secret corner is judged a fit house of common prayer; the manifold

confusions which they fall into where every mans privat spirit and gift (as they terme it) is the only Bishop that ordeyneth him to this ministerie; the irkesome deformities whereby through endlesse and senselesse effusions of indigested prayers they oftentimes disgrace in most unsufferable manner the worthyest part of Christian dutie towards God, who herein are subject to no certaine order, but pray both what and how they list . . . .'

CAROL. MAG. IN LEGIB. Carolus Magnus in Legibus, i.e. the Laws set out by Charlemagne. Cf. *Corpus Juris Germanici Antiqui . . . Capitularium ab Ansegiso Abbate et Benedicto Levita Collectis* (Magdeburg, 1738), v. 25: 'Cum excommunicatis non licere communicare. Nec cum his qui per domos conveniunt, devitantes orationes Ecclesiae, simul orandum est. Ab alia Ecclesia non suscipiendus est qui in alia minime congregatur.'

MICR. *de eccles. obser. cap.* 5. Micrologus *De Ecclesiasticis Observationibus*. This chapter, from which Cosin quotes, is called 'De authenticis orationibus'. Cf. the edition by J. Pamelius, Antwerp, 1560 (reprinted by J.-P. Migne in *Patrologia Latina*, Paris 1881, CLI. 973–1022).

CONC. CARTHAG., i.e. Concilium Carthaginense III (A.D. 397), Canon 23: 'Ut nemo in precibus vel patrem pro filio, vel filium pro patre nominet. Et cum altari assistitur, semper ad patrem dirigatur oratio. Et quicunque sibi preces alicunde describit, non eis utatur, nisi prius eas cum instructioribus fratribus contulerit.' Cf. Binius, I. 544.

MILEVITAN COUNCEL. Cosin quotes from the twelfth canon of the Second Milevitan Council, held in 416. Cf. Binius, I. 600. The seventieth canon of the Council of Africa, under Celestine and Boniface of *c.* 397, looks forward to the canon of the Milevitan Council: 'Placuit etiam hoc, ut preces, quae probatae fuerint in Concilio, sive praefationes, sive commendationes seu manus impositiones, ab omnibus celebrentur: nec aliae omnino contra fidem proferantur, sed quaecunque cum prudentioribus fuerint collatae, dicantur.' Cf. Binius, I. 641.

COUNCELL of CARTHAGE. Cf. above.

By which passages . . . Ghosts of our owne. Cf. Hooker, V. 33 (p. 69): 'The brethren in Ægypt (saith S. Augustine, epist. 121.) are reported to have many prayers, but every [one] of them very short, as if they were darts throwne out with a kinde of suddaine quicknes. . . . But that which S. Augustine doth allow they condemne', and V.

25 (pp. 55–56): 'But of all helps for due performance of this service the greatest is that very set and standing order it selfe, which framed with common advise, hath both for matter and forme prescribed whatsoever is herein publiquely done', and V. 26 (p. 57): 'Hymnes and Psalmes are such kindes of prayer as are not woont to be conceived upon a suddaine, but are framed by meditation before hand', and cf. the passage from V. 25 (p. 56) quoted above, on pp. 319–20.

Councel at VENICE. The Council referred to was actually held at Vannes in Bretagne, about 465. Canon 14 reads: 'Clericus, quem intra muros civitatis suae manere constiterit, & matutinis hymnis sine probabili excusatione aegritudinis inventus fuerit defuisse, septem diebus a communione habeatur extraneus: quia ministrum sacrorum, eo tempore, quo non potest ab officio suo ulla honesta necessitas occupare, fas non est a salubri cessare.' Cf. Binius, II. 192.

Councel of MENTZ. Held in 1549. Canon 57 has the heading: 'Missae, sub concione aut solemni sacra, non celebrentur.' Cf. Binius, IV. 778: 'Et cum Apostolus jubeat, omnia honeste & secundum ordinem fieri in ecclesia, citraque tumultum: statuimus & ordinamus, ne deinceps Concionis tempore, aut sub solemne Missa, aliae speciales Missae celebrentur: sed aut Concionem & solemne Sacrum praecedant, aut in aliud tempus differantur, ne populus in diversa distractus, nulli Sacro aut Concioni satis intendat. Quam rem, pro opportunitate cuiusuis loci & temporis, Praelatorum discretioni relinquimus curandam.'

Injunctions. Cf. *Injunctions Given by . . . Edward VI* (1547), 'The Form of Bidding the Common Prayers' (pp. 8–9). The familiar words begin, 'you shall pray for the whole Congregation of Christs Church . . .'. Cf. also *Constitutiones sive Canones Ecclesiastici* . . . (1604), canon 55: 'Precationis formula, a Concionatoribus in concionum suarum ingressu imitanda': '. . . Precamini pro Christi sancta Ecclesia Catholica, id est, pro universo coetu Christiani populi per orbem terrarum diffusi ac disseminati. . . .'

*SANDERS. Cosin refers to several recusant authorities: Nicholas Sander[s] (d. 1581) was the author of *De Origine ac Progressu Schismatis Anglicani* (Ingolstadt, 1588), a work divided into three books, one each on Henry, Edward and Mary, and Elizabeth. William Rainolds (d. 1594) wrote *Calvino-Turcismus*, completed and published by his friend William Gifford in 1597; it sets out to prove that the religion of 'the Turk' is more satisfactory than Calvinism. Richard Bristow (1538–81) wrote, among other polemic books, *Demaundes to be proponed of Catholiques to the heretikes* (1576). 'Demon.' probably signifies *A demonstration: by English Protestant pretended bishops, and ministers, and by the cheife growndes of their religion, against these their owne pretended bishops and mynistery* . . . (1616), although it could refer to *Protestants demonstrations, for Catholiks recusance* (1615). Both works appeared anonymously, but they have been attributed to Richard Broughton by A. F. Allison and D. M. Rogers, 'A Catalogue of Catholic Books in English Printed Abroad or Secretly in England 1558–1640', in *Biographical Studies*, 3 (1955–6). Allison and Rogers identify *Certaine articles or forcible reasons. Discovering the palpable absurdities, and most notorious errors of the Protestants religion* as a work by Thomas Wright, falsely imprinted 'Anwerpe', but secretly printed in England with the initials 'H. T.' Three editions of *Certaine articles* appeared, all in 1600.

*S. AUG. *Veniunt*. . . We have so far been unable to locate this statement by St. Augustine.

In so doing . . . *Prayer* and *Devotion*. Cf. Hooker, v. 23 (p. 53): 'And therefore prayer being a worke common to the Church as well triumphant as militant, a worke common unto men with Angels, what should we thinke but that so much of our lives is celestiall and divine as we spend in the exercise of prayer.'

Of the CALENDAR. Cosin again borrows from Hooker, v. 69–71, quoting from the same places in Ecclesiasticus and St. Augustine.

S. [b]AUSTIN. Cosin's reference is evidently in error. Cf. instead *De Civitate Dei*, X. 4 (3): 'ei beneficiorum ejus solemnitatibus festis & diebus statutis dicamus sacramusque memoriam. . . . (V. 540D).' Hooker quotes this passage in v. 70 (p. 195): '*By Festivall solemnities and set dayes we dedicate and sanctifie to God the memorie of his benefites.* . . .'

And this Faith of ours . . . God *in heaven*. Cf. Hooker, v. 71 (p. 204): '. . . well to celebrate these Religious and sacred daies is to spend the flower of our time happily. They are the splendour and outward dignitie of our Religion, forcible witnesses of ancient truth, provocations to the exercise of all pietie, shadowes of our endlesse felicitie in heaven, on earth everlasting recordes and memorials, wherein they which cannot be drawne to hearken unto that we teach, may onely by looking upon that we doe, in a maner reade whatsoever we believe.'

l Tertul. *de Cor. mil.* Cf. Tertullian, *De Corona militis* (p. 346), c. xiii: 'Habes tuos census, tuos Fastos: nihil tibi cum gaudiis seculi; immo contrarium debes.'

S. Cypr. Cf. Cyprian, *Epistola xxxvii*: 'Denique & dies eorum quibus excedunt annotate, ut commemorationes eorum inter memorias martyrum celebrare possimus.' In the Antwerp edition by J. Pamelius (1568) a note refers to Tertullian and Eusebius, the same instances recorded here by Cosin.

Pont. Diac. Cf. Pontius, who was Deacon under Cyprian, Bishop of Carthage and Martyr (258), and wrote *De vita et passione sancti Cypriani.* Pontius's *Life* of Cyprian typically formed a prolegomenon to Cyprian's *Works*. At the beginning of his *Life*, Pontius tells of his determination to record the acts of Cyprian for the edification of succeeding generations.

m Euseb. *Hist. eccl.* Cf. Eusebius, *Ecclesiastica Historia*, IV. 15, which records the martyrdom of Polycarp; Eusebius observes: 'Nam hunc quidem tanquam filium Dei adoramus; martyres vero tanquam discipulos & imitatores Domini digne propter insuperabilem in regem ipsorum ac praeceptorem benevolentiam diligimus, quorum & nos consortes & discipulos fieri optamus' (p. 46E).

S. Basil *in Ascet. c. 40.* Cf. *Regularum Fusius Disputatarum*, Interrogatio [in *Ascetica*] 40: 'De nundinis illis, quae in sanctorum celebritatibus fiunt, quid?' (II. 589).

Calendar. With a few slight alterations, this is the Calendar which was compiled by a Commission of 1561, and appeared in the later issues of the Elizabethan Book of Common Prayer. Cosin has added St. Enurchus, after the Prayer Book of 1604, and commemorations of the inauguration of Charles I (black letter) and 'Powder Treason Day' (red letter), the latter being authorized by Act of Parliament, 3 Jac. I. c. 1. In the cases of St. Valentine, St. Cyprian, and St. Denys, there appears to be some confusion about the identity of the saint commemorated (see V. Staley, *The Liturgical Year*, London, 1907, pp. 48–49).

An interesting feature of this Calendar is the explanatory matter which Cosin has appended to many of these commemorations. Cosin's friend Richard Mountague may have helped in drawing up this version. He wrote to Cosin (21 Dec. 1626): 'I have sent you halfe the *Calendar* and all the *Saints* whose dayes I found there briefly related . . .' (Birch MS. [British Museum] 4274, f. 101). Another letter (12 Jan. 1627) in Cosin's *Correspondence* (I. 105), refers again to the Calendar, perhaps this time to proof-sheets of the *Devotions*. Mountague writes: 'Your calendar sheets I will dispatch *quantâ potero brevitate.*' Many of the small descriptive details of this Calendar passed into the Prayer Book at the revision of 1661, as follows (such details are not in parentheses):

(Circumc.) of our Ld. . . . (Epiphanie) of our Ld. . . . (Lucian) Pr. & Mart. . . . (Hilarie) B. (& Conf.) . . . (Prisca) Rom. Virg. & Mart. . . . (Fabian) B. of Rome & Mart. . . . (Agnes) Rom. Virg. & Mart. . . . (Vincent) Span. Deac. & M. . . . (Convers:) of S. (Paul). (restored to red-letter status) . . . (Purif. of Marie) ye (B) Virg. . . . (Blasius) an Armen. B. & M. . . . (Agatha) a Sicilian V. & M. . . . (Valentine Bish.) & M. . . . (Matthias) Apost. & M. . . . (David Arch-) B. of (Menevia) . . . (Cedde,) or Chad B. of Litchf. . . . (Perpetua Mauritan.) M. . . . (Gregorius M.) B. of Rome (, & C.) . . . (Edward) K. of ye. West Saxons . . . (Benedict) Abbot . . . (Richard) B. of Chichester . . . (Ambrose) B. of Millan. . . . (Alphege) Arch-B. of Cant. . . . (S. George) M. . . . S. (Mark Evang.) & Mart. . . . S. (Phil & S. Iac.) Ap. & M. . . . S. (Iohn Evang. ante) port. latin. . . . (Dunstan) Arch. B. of Cant. . . . (Aug:) ye. first Arch B. of Cant . . . (Nicomede) Rom. Pr. & M. . . . (Boniface) B. of Mentz & M. . . . S. (Barnab, Apost.) & M. (restored to red-letter status) . . . Transl: of (Edwd.) K. of ye. W. Sax. . . . (Nativ.) of S. (Iohn Bapt:) . . . (S. Pet. Apost.) & M. . . . Transl: of S. (Martin) B. (& C.) . . . (Swithun) B. of Winch. (Transl.) . . . (Margaret) V. & M. at Antioch. . . . S. Marie (Magdalen.) . . . S. (Iames Apost.) & M. . . . S. (Anne,) mother to ye. Bl. V. M. . . . (Lammas) day. . . . (Transfigur.) of our Lord. . . . (S. Laur.) Arch D. of Rom. & M. . . . S. (Barth. Apost.) & M. . . . S. (Aug.) B. of Hippo. (C.D.) . . . (Behead: of) S. (Iohn) Bapt. . . . (Giles) Abbot (& Conf.) . . . (Enurchus B.) of Orleans . . . (Holy crosse) day . . . (Lambert) B. & M. . . . (S. Mat.) Ap. Evang. & M. . . . S. (Cypr: Ar.) B. of Carth & M. . . . (S. Mich.) & all Angels . . . S. (Hierome) Pr. Conf. & Doct. . . . (Remigius) B. of Rhemes . . . (Faith) Virg. & M. . . . (S. Denys) Areop. B. & M. . . . Transl. of K. (Edward) Conf. . . . S. (Luke Evang.) . . . (Crispine) Mart. . . . S. (Sim. &) S. (Iud.) Ap. & M. . . . (All Saints) day . . . (Leonard) Confess. . . . (S. Martin) B. (& Conf:) . . . (Hugh) B. of Lincoln. . . . (Edmund) K. & M. . . . (Cecilia) Virg. & M. . . . (S. Clemt.) 1. B. of Rom. & M. . . . (Catherine) Virg. & M. . . . S. (Andr. Apost.) & M. . . . (Nicholas) B. of Myra in Lycia . . . (Concep:) of (ye. Bl. V. Mary.) . . . (Lucie) Virg. & M. . . . S. (Thomas Apost.) & M. . . . (S. Steph.) ye. first Mart. . . . (S. Iohn) Apost. & (Evang.) . . . (Innocents) day. . . . (Silvester) B. of Rome.

The name given to Christmas Day, 'The Nativitie of our Lord', is the one commonly found in the Sarum texts. It was introduced in the

1662 Prayer Book, as the heading for the Collect, Epistle, and Gospe for that day, as 'The Nativity of our Lord, or the Birth-day of Christ, commonly called *Christmas-day*'.

The tendency to add descriptive details to commemorations is carried further in some of the twentieth-century revisions of the Book of Common Prayer throughout the Anglican Communion, starting with the English Deposited Book of 1928. Certain of these details are similar to some of those in the *Devotions* which were not included in the 1662 book. Thus, the 1928 book and, following it, the revised Prayer Books of Scotland (1929), South Africa (1954), Canada (1959), and India, Pakistan, Burma, and Ceylon (1960) give, in many instances, the year of a saint's death or of whatever event is commemorated; many of these are identical with the year Cosin gives, although in other cases a revised dating is given. Other modifications of the Calendar which could derive from the *Devotions*, are as follows:

Hilary	Bishop of Poitiers (1928, South Africa).
	Bishop of Poitiers, France (Canada).
Benedict	Italy (Canada).
	in Italy (India, Pakistan, Burma, and Ceylon).
Peter	and Paul (South Africa, Canada).
Giles	southern France (Canada).
Denys	of Paris (Scotland, Canada).
Etheldred	Abbess of Ely (1928, South Africa).
	or Audrey, . . . Abbess of Ely (Canada).
Martin	of Tours (1928, Scotland).
	of Tours, France (Canada).
	of Tours in France (India, Pakistan, Burma, and Ceylon).
Catherine	at Alexandria (1928).
O Sapientia	the first Advent Anthem (South Africa).
	an ancient Advent Anthem (Canada).

A TABLE OF THE moveable Feasts. The Book of Common Prayer gave the dates for Easter Day only at this time.

RULES TO KNOW. This table, in this form, would appear to be of Cosin's own devising. It was introduced in the 1662 Prayer Book, by way of *The Durham Book*, at which stage it was slightly altered, the rule for determining Easter Day being restated. Cf. the Restoration variations of the *Devotions* in the Appendix, p. 303.

THE FASTING DAIES. This table also would appear to be Cosin's own work. It is based upon Acts of Parliament of the reign of

Edward VI. It was introduced in the 1662 Prayer Book, by way of *The Durham Book*, at which stage a number of additions and omissions were made. Cf. the Appendix, pp. 305–6.

THE SUMME OF THE CATHOLIKE FAITH. Such a full arrangement of catechetical material is unusual in the Primer, although briefer versions, usually known as the 'A.B.C.' or the 'Articles of the Faith', are to be found from the earliest editions. Cosin's arrangement is similar in outline to that given in *Catholicum Precationum Selectissimarum Enchiridion* (Antwerp, 1594); *A Manual of Prayers newly gathered out of many and divers famous authours aswell auncient as of the tyme present* (the 1st ed. of 1583 does not contain such catechetical material, but succeeding editions do: 1589, 1595, etc.); Bellarmine's *An Ample Declaration of the Christian Doctrine*, trans. from Italian into English by Richard Hadock (1st ed., Roane, n.d.; 2nd ed., Doway, 1604). Cf. also the Primers of 1571 (*Officium B. Mariae Virginis, nuper reformatum . . . Romae . . .*: Hoskins, no. 266, p. 349) and of 1599 (*The Primer or Office of the blessed Virgin Mary, in Latin and English, according to the reformed Latin . . .* Antwerp: Hoskins, no. 267, p. 357).

THE APOSTLES *CREED*: *Divided into Twelve Articles.* The division of the Creed into several articles represented the common belief that the twelve articles went back to the Apostles, each of whom made his individual contribution to the formula. It is so divided amongst the catechetical material in several of the earlier Primers (e.g. Hoskins, nos. 131, 143, 144, 147, 159, 239). For the summary of the Creed, pp. 38–39, cf. the Prayer Book Catechism.

THE LORDS PRAYER. Several of the earlier Primers divided the prayer in this way amongst their catechetical material (e.g. Hoskins, nos. 115, 117, 161, 194). For the exposition of the prayer, cf. the Prayer Book Catechism.

THE TEN COMMANDEMENTS. A similarly arranged exposition is to be found in Marshall's Primer (1534), Hoskins, no. 115, and cf. also the 'Exposition briefue des commandmens de Dieu' in a book in Cosin's Library (Durham), *Manuale Sacerdotii . . . Ecclesie Parisiensis* (Paris: Kerver, 1537), from either of which Cosin may have got the idea for his exposition.

The Precepts of the Church. A comparison with Bellarmine's version of these precepts in *Christian Doctrine* is instructive of Cosin's intention of providing a reformed and distinctively Anglican formulation: '1 To be present at Masse on commanded feastes. 2 To fast the Lent, the foure Imbre Weekes, and commanded Eves of Feastes. Also to abstayn from flesh upon fryday and saturday. 3 To confesse at the least once in the yeare. 4 To receive the B. Sacrament at the least at Easter. 5 To pay tithes to the Church. 6 Not to solemnise Marriages in times prohibited. . . .' (chap. 7. 'The declaration of the Precepts of the Church', p. 202). Cosin, it will be seen, has included the observance of the Prayer Book offices, and related confession to communion.

*Can. 6. and the Preface of Ceremonies. Cf. *Constitutiones sive Canones Ecclesiastici* . . . (1604). Can. 6 concerns 'Caeremoniarum in Ecclesia Anglicana obtinentium usus, Pius & licitus'. The 'Preface of Ceremonies' refers, of course, to the introductory material in the Prayer Book, 'Of ceremonies, why some be abolished, and some retained'.

*Bishop *Overals*, and Bishop *Andrewes* Articles in the Visitation of their Diocesse. Cf. Overall's 'Articles to be enquired of in the Diocese of Norwich in the Ordinarie Visitation' (1619), no. 21: 'Whether doth your Minister before the severall times of the administration of the Lords Supper, admonish and exhort his Parishioners, if they have their Consciences troubled and disquieted, to resort unto him, or some other learned Minister, and open his griefe, that hee may receive such ghostly counsell and comfort, as his Conscience may be relieved, and by the Minister hee may receive the benefit of Absolution, to the quiet of his conscience, and avoyding of scruple. . . .' Richard Mountague quotes this article approvingly (the text followed here) in *A Gagg for the new Gospell? No: A New Gagg for an Old Goose* (1624), p. 84, and he also copies it into his own visitation articles for Chichester (1628). Cf. also Andrewes's 'Articles to be enquired of by the Churchwardens and Sworne-men . . .' (1625), especially Article 16 under the section 'Touching Ministers, Service, and Sacraments', where he commends penitence and absolution through auricular confession. Andrewes's 'Articles' are included in 'The Anglo-Catholic Library' edition of his *Works*, in the volume called *Two Answers to Cardinal Perron and other Miscellaneous Works* (Oxford, 1854), p. 131.

As Archdeacon of the East Riding, Cosin had drawn up 'Articles to be inquired of by the Churchwardens and Swornmen . . . in the ordinary visitation' . . . (1627). Cosin, who actually prepared this document in 1626, recommends auricular confession and the receiving of 'ghostly counsel and comfort'. Cf. Article 26 (*Works*, II. 11). He also writes of 'the virtue and force of this sacred action' (i.e. Confession and

Absolution) concerning the Rubric which urges Confession in the Order for the Visitation of the Sick. Cf. 'The First Series of Notes on the Book of Common Prayer', *Works*, V. 163–4. Cosin reaffirms his belief in his answer to one of 'The Objections which some have been pleased to make against a Booke intituled the Houres of Praier', where he refers to this marginal note. Cf. Cosin's *Correspondence*, ed. G. Ornsby (Durham: The Surtees Society, 1869–72), I. 131. 'The Objections' reproduces S.P.D. [LXV. 72]—Charles I. 1627 [May?], a date evidently in error, for Cosin seems to be answering the attacks of Prynne and Burton whose pamphlets appeared in 1628 (cf. n. 42 of the Introduction).

aCatech. *of the Sacram.* Cf. the Catechism in the Prayer Book.

S. Aug ep. 118. In his 118th Epistle, Augustine writes to Januarius about the Sacraments, festal days, fasting, and the Eucharist. About the Sacraments he says: 'unde Sacramentis numero paucissimis, observatione facillimis, significatione praestantissimis, societatem novi populi colligavit, sicuti est baptismus trinitatis nomine consecratus, communicatio corporis & sanguinis ipsius, & si quid aliud in Scripturis canonicis commendatur . . .' (II. 556C).

Articles of Relig. Article 25 (of the 39 Articles), 'Of the Sacraments', declares that 'there are two Sacraments ordained of Christ our Lord in the Gospel . . . Baptism, and the Supper of the Lord'.

a S. *Basil.* Cf. *Regularum Fusius Disputatarum*, Interrogatio 37: 'Nunquid per simulationem orationum, psalmodiaeve negligi opera debeant: & quae sint adorationem apposita tempora: & primo an oporteat laborare' (II. 584).

b S. *Chrysost.* Cosin's reference is to the 21st and last sermon on the Statues (preached 'ad Populum Antiochenum' during the Lent of 387). It gets the number 59 from its position in the series of homilies; thus Savile's edition of 1612, VI. 604: 'Statuarum 21. Catechesis ad illuminandos . . . *oratio* lix.' Cosin may have had in mind the following passage: 'vidisti alium feliciter agentem, ne invideas, nam nec hic paupertas impedimentum est. Rursum cum orare convenit, sobria & vigili mente hoc effice, & nec hic ullum erit obstaculum. . . . Et hoc est virtutis maximum, quod non divitiis, non potentia, non gloria, non alia quapiam talium rerum opus habet, sed anima tantum sanctificata, & nil amplius inquirit' (I. 238E–239A). This quotation does not explicitly reflect Cosin's statement; but it has the general sense—that the Christian should serve God well though many of the unbaptized do not, an idea, indeed, which is one theme of Chrysostom's homily. Cf., for a further example, an earlier passage: '*Fidelis* enim propterea vocaris, quoniam & credis Deo, & ab eo creditam ipse justitiam habes, sanctitatem, munditiam animae, in filium adoptionem, regnum coelorum, & haec tibi commendavit. Tu vicissim ipsi alia credidisti, & commendasti, eleemosynam, preces, modestiam & omnem aliam virtutem' (234E).

c S. *Aug*. Cf. Augustine's *De Haeresibus ad Quodvultdeum*. The particular reference is to 'Psalliani, alias Massaliani, sive Euchitae', numbered 57 in the prefatory index of heresies: 'Psallianorum postremam ponit Epiphanius haeresim, quod nomen ex lingua Syra est, Graeci autem dicuntur *Εὐχῖται* ab orando sic appellati. Tantum enim orant, ut eis qui hoc de illis audiunt incredibile videatur. Nam cum Dominus dixerit, Oportet semper orare & non deficere. Et Apostolus: Sine intermissione orate: quod sanissime sic accipitur, ut nullo die intermittantur certa tempora orandi, isti ita nimis hoc faciunt, ut hinc judicentur inter haereticos nominandi' (VI. 26, § 57).

The Epistle to Proba (numbered 130 in the Benedictine edition of Augustine's Works) offers counsel on the subject of prayer (II. 617–30, esp. 622 f.).

Isid. de eccl. off. Cf. St. Isidore, *De Ecclesiasticis Officiis*, I. 22, 'De vigiliis': 'Est autem quoddam genus haereticorum, superfluas existimantium sacras vigilias, & spiritali opere infructuosas, dicentes Jura temerari divina, qui noctem fecit ad requiem, sicut diem ad laborem' (p. 396).

Isid. etym. Cf. Isidore's *Originum sive Etymologiarum*, VI. 19, 'De officiis': 'Sed & Danielem legimus haec tempora in oratione observasse: & utique ex Israelis disciplina, ut ne minus quam ter in die adoremus. Debitores enim sumus trium personarum, Patris & Filii & Spiritus sancti, exceptis utique & aliis legitimis orationibus, quae sine ulla admonitione debentur in ingressu lucis ac noctis sive vigiliarum: sed & cibum non prius sumere, quam interposita oratione debemus' (p. 52 [F]).

h S. *Sypr*. Cf. St. Cyprian, *De Oratione Dominica*, § 15: 'In orationibus vero celebrandis invenimus observasse cum Daniele tres pueros in fide fortes, & in captivitate victores, horam tertiam, sextam, nonam, sacramento, scilicet, trinitatis; quae in novissimis temporibus manifestari habebat' (p. 272).

S. *Ambr*. Cf. Ambrose, *De Virginibus III*: 'Oratio quoque nos Deo crebra commendet. Si enim Propheta dicit: Septies in die laudem dixi tibi: qui regni erat necessitatibus occupatus, quid nos facere oportet qui legimus: Vigilate & orate, ne intretis in tentationem? Certe solemnes orationes cum gratiarum actione sunt deferendae, cum e somno surgimus, cum prodimus, cum cibum paramus sumere, cum sumpserimus, & hora incensi, cum denique cubitum pergimus' (p. 95C).

i S. *Cypr*. Cf. above, p. 329.

S. GREG. NYSSEN. Cf. St. Gregory of Nyssa, *De Oratione I*: 'Oratio conversatio sermocinatioque cum Deo est, visum effugientium contemplatio, eorum quae concupiscuntur, certa fides: ejusdem cum Angelis honoris conditio, bonorum progressus & incrementum, malorum subversio, peccatorum emendatio, praesentium fructus, futurorum comprehensio' (I. 715).

S. CHRYSOST. *de orando Deum*. Cf. *De Precatione I* (I. 746D): 'Quando igitur aliquem video a precationis studio abesse, neque illius ardenti, ac vehementi amore teneri; jam mihi exploratum est, nihil ab eo magnificum, nihil praeclarum possideri.'

IDEM. *ibid.* As above (I. 743E): '. . . ut corpus Solis lumine, sic animus precationum radiis illustratur.'

IDEM. *ibid.* As above (I. 743A): 'Jam vero Dei benignitatem atque clementiam quis non admiretur; quis non suspiciat, quam nobis ostendit, cum tantum honorem hominibus deferat, ut eos precatione ac sua consuetudine dignetur?'

IDEM. *Homil. contra Pseudo-Proph.* Cf. *De Pseudoprophetis, & falsis Doctoribus: & de impiis haereticis* . . . (VI. 407E–C): 'Audi & Apostolum clamantem: *Sine intermissione orate*: hoc est, in omni tempore, & noctu, & die, & quacumque hora: & dum intentus es operi, & iter facis, & curas gregem, & agrum colis, & dormis. . . . Et tu igitur, frater, ne expectes diem, vel horam: sed etiam, cum dormies, ora; & in via, & dum cubas, & cum surgis, & in quocumque loco. Ora autem vigilanter, ac diligenter: . . . ora vero cum humilitate. . . .'

PIOUS EJACULATIONS. A collection of short prayers and sentences of this sort was included in many of the Primers. Cf. for example the Primer of 1536 (*This Prymer in english and in latin is newly translated after the Latin text* . . . Rouen: Hoskins, no. 124, p. 159), and the Primers of 1571 and 1599, noted at p. 326.

According to the direction of S. AMBROSE. Cf. the reference to *De Virginibus III*, pp. 329–30. The following quotation continues that one: 'Sed etiam in ipso cubili volo psalmos cum oratione dominica frequenti contexas vice, vel cum evigilaveris, vel antequam corpus sopor irriget, ut te in ipso quietis exordio rerum secularium cura liberam, divina meditantem somnus inveniat. Denique etiam ille philosophiae ipsius qui nomen invenit, quotidie priusquam cubitum iret, tibicinem jubebat molliora canere, ut anxia curis secularibus corda mulceret.'

When we first awake. A similar prayer occurs in all the editions of *A Manual of Prayers* (1583, etc.). After an exhortation to prayer based on Chrysostom's *De Orando Deum I* (similar to Cosin's, p. 64), there are various prayers suitable to one's daily course.

At our uprising. Cf. the Primer of 1536, and also the Primers of 1571 and 1599 (noted above).

Or this. Cf. *A Manual of Prayers*: 'When ye doo aryse . . . [say] In the name of oure Lorde Jesus Christe crucified, I doo ryse: [may] he blesse me, governe me, keepe me, save me, and bringe me unto everlasting lyfe' (p. 3). Cf. also the Primer of *c.* 1528: *Hortulus animae recenter diversis ac odoriferis flosculis decoratus, cum additionibus variis . . . adjectis secundum usum Sarum horis beatae Mariae virginis, septem psalmis, atque vigiliis* . . . (Hoskins, no. 86, p. 135).

At our Apparrelling. . . . S. BASIL . . . JULIT. Cf. St. Basil, *Homilia in Martyrem Julittam* (I. 318). Basil urges that we make all our daily actions conscious recollections of God's grace towards us; our devotion needs no words—we do all for the glory of God. Cosin particularly recalls, 'Tunicam indueris? gratias agito benigno datori.' Cf. the 'Oratio inter vestiendum' in the Elizabethan Primer of 1564 (*Private Prayers*, p. 244), although Cosin does not appear to have used it as his model.

At the washing of our hands. Cf. the Elizabethan Primer of 1564 (*Private Prayers*, pp. 244–5), the prayer 'Inter lavandum manus': 'Ablue, Domine Deus, aqua tuae divinae gratiae animum meum ab omnibus vitiorum sordibus et inquinamentis, quibus totus in conspectu tuo insordescit. Asperge illum hysopo verae poenitentiae et compunctionis, ut in limpidissimo gratiae tuae fonte lotus supra nivem dealbari, tibique exinde jugiter inservire, valeam, per Christum Dominum nostrum. Amen.' This may have been Cosin's model, but if so, he has used it very freely, interpolating a phrase from the Prayer for the Church at Holy Communion.

And then humbly.... *Amen.* A conflation of a prayer, 'Recommendatio ad Deum: In manus ineffabilis misericordiae tuae commendo animam meam . . . ', in the Primer of 1528, referred to above, and the Prayer Book collect at the end of the Order of Holy Communion, originally one of the Breviary collects for Prime: 'O Almighty Lord, and everlasting God, vouchsafe we beseech thee, to direct, sanctify, and govern both our hearts and bodies. . . .' Many of the prayers in the *Devotions* are made up like this one—out of two or more sources.

At our going abroad. Cf. the Primers of 1528, 1571, and 1599, noted before.

When wee heare . . . Cf. the Elizabethan Primer of 1564, 'Concede mihi, Domine Deus, felicem ac salutarem vivendi ac moriendi horam' (*Private Prayers*, p. 394).

At our entrance into the Church. Cf. the Primers of 1564, 1571, 1599, and also of 1494 (Wynkyn de Worde, Westminster: Hoskins, no. 7, p. 107), and of 1537 (*This Prymer in english and in latin is newly translated after the Latin text*, London: Hoskins, no. 128, p. 168).

RADUL. DE RIVO. Radulph de Rivo (d. 1403) compiled *De canonum observantia liber*. In Propositio 14 Radulph distinguishes the hours of prayer and gives liturgical history and comment as justification for doing so. There is a folio edition, Cologne, 1618; a modern text is that by P. Cunibert Mohlberg (Münster, 1915).

S. *Hieron.* in vit. Hil. S. Jerome writes in his *Vita Hilarionis Eremitae*: 'Et sanctus, Maledictus, ait, qui prius refectionem corporis, quam animae quaesierit. Oremus, psallamus, reddamus Domino officium, & sic ad vineam properabitis' (I. 95H).

CONST. APOST. Cosin quotes from Book 8, chapter 34 of the Clementine *Constitutiones Apostolicae* at each of the hours. The chapter is called 'Quibus horis, & quare in eis precandum est', with the relevant passage: 'Precationes facite mane, tertia hora, ac sexta, & nona, & vespere, atque ad gallicantum: Mane gratias agentes, quod illuminarit nos nocte sublata & reddito die: Tertia, quod ea hora Pilatus judicium adversus Dominum pronunciavit: Sexta, quod ea hora in crucem actus est: Nona, quod tum omnia mota, & tremefacta sunt Domino crucifixo: quia horrerent audaciam impiorum Judaeorum, & contumeliam Domini ferre non possent: Vespere quod noctem dederit ad requiescendum a diurnis laboribus: Ad gallicantum, quod ea hora nunciet adventum diei ad facienda opera lucis.' Cf. Binius, I. 95. The Greek text appears in J.-P. Migne, *Patrologia Graeca* (Paris, 1886), I. 1135.

TERTUL. APOLOGET. Cf. Tertullian, *Apologeticus adversus Gentes pro Christianis* (p. 27): 'Plinius enim Secundus cum provinciam regeret damnatis quibusdam Christianis, quibusdam gradu pulsis, ipsa tamen multitudine perturbatus, quid de caetero ageret, consuluit tunc Traianum imperatorem, allegans praeter obstinationem non sacrificandi, nihil aliud se de sacris eorum comperisse, quam coetus antelucanos ad canendum Christo & deo. . . .' Pliny the Younger does not of course assert these things about the Christians; he tells Trajan only what the Christians themselves have said for their own defence: 'Adfirmabant . . . , hanc fuisse summam vel culpae suae, vel erroris, quod essent soliti stato die ante lucem convenire, carmenque Christo quasi deo dicere secum invicem. . . .' Cf. Pliny, *Epp.* x. 96–97 and A. N. Sherwin-White, *The Letters of Pliny* (Oxford, 1966), pp. 691 ff.

S. CYPRIAN DE ORAT. DOM. St. Cyprian writes in the last part of *De Oratione Dominica*: 'Sed nobis, fratres dilectissimi, praeter horas antiquitus observatas, orandi nunc & spatia & sacramenta creverunt. Nam & mane orandum est, ut resurrectio domini matutina oratione celebretur . . .' (p. 272).

S. ATHANAS. DE MEDITAT. Cf. St. Athanasius, *De Virginitate sive de Meditatione* (p. 601): 'Meditare in sacris scripturis: habe Psalterium, & Psalmos disce. Oriens sol videat librum in manibus tuis.'

S. BASIL. . . . RUP. DE DIVIN. OFF. CAP. 2. St. Basil writes in *Regularum Fusius Disputatarum* (Interrogatio 37): '. . . Post intervertendum diluculum est, & ad orationem surgendum, cavendumque ne dies nos in lectulo dormientes opprimat: & ille imitandus, qui dixit, Praevenerunt oculi mei diluculum, ut meditarer eloquia tua' (II. 587). Rupertus (d. ?1135) wrote mainly about the ecclesiastical year in *De Divinis Officiis*; the first chapter distinguishes the canonical hours and the second discusses the first hour: 'Prima hora creatori nostro laudes referre debemus, ante omnem curam corporis . . .' (cf. *Bibliotheca Patrum*, x. 855).

ID. IBID. Cf. the quotation from St. Basil, above.

IDEM EPIST. 63. Cf. St. Basil's Epistola 63: '. . . hoc habeo quod dicam: quod videlicet qui iam obtinuerunt ritus omnibus Ecclesiis Dei concordes sunt & consoni. De nocte siquidem populus consurgens antelucano tempore domum precationis petit: inque labore & tribulatione ac lachrymis indesinentibus facta ad Deum confessione, tandem ab oratione surgentes ad psalmodiam traducuntur' (III. 96).

IDEM IN EPIST. I. AD NAZIANZEN. Cf. St. Basil's first letter to St. Gregory Nazianzen (III. 43): 'Ecquid igitur beatius, quam hominem in terra concentum Angelorum imitari? veniente statim die in orationes ire? in hymnis & canticis creatorem venerari?'

S. CHRYS. DE OR. DEUM. Cf. St. Chrysostom, *De Precatione I* (I. 747B–D): 'Quamobrem & cum lectulo surgimus, antevertere Solem oportet Dei cultu, & cum mensae accumbimus, & cum somni caussa cubamus: imo vero singulis horis precatio est ad Deum adhibenda, & in ea diei cursus conficiendus. . . . Age vero quomodo Solem aspicies, non illum ante veneratus, qui oculis tuis lucem Solis dulcissimam profert?'

S. AMBROS. IN EXAMER. LIB. 5. CAP. 12. Cf. St. Ambrose, *In Hexameron*: 'Quis enim sensum hominis gerens non erubescat sine Psalmorum celebritate diem claudere, cum etiam minutissimae aves solemni devotione & dulci carmine ortus dierum ac noctium prosequantur?' (p. 864C).

IDEM DE VIRG. The selection from *De Virginibus III* recalls the quotations given before, pp. 329–30, 331. In the same place, there follows: 'Symbolum quoque specialiter debemus tanquam nostri signaculum cordis antelucanis horis quotidie recensere' (p. 95D).

S. HIERON. AD LAETAM. Cf. *Ad Laetam de institutione filiae*, Epistola vii: 'Praeponatur ei probae fidei, ac morum & pudicitiae virgo veterana, quae illam doceat, & assuescat exemplo ad orationes & psalmos nocte consurgere mane hymnos canere, tertia, sexta, nona hora stare in acie quasi bellatricem Christi, accensaque lucerna reddere sacrificium vespertinum. Sic dies transeat, sic nox inveniat laborantem' (I. 16H).

IDEM AD EUSTOCHIUM. Cf. *Ad Eustochium de custodia virginitatis*, Epistola xxii: 'Horam tertiam, sextam, nonam, diluculum quoque, & vesperam, nemo est qui nesciat' (I. 55A).

RAB. MAUR. DE INST. CLER. Cf. Rabanus Maurus, *De Institutione clericorum* and the conclusion of the chapter called 'De Nocturna Vigiliarum celebratione': 'Iste autem est catholicus ordo divinarum celebrationum, qui ab universa Ecclesia Christi incommutabiliter servatur' (*Bibliotheca Patrum*, X. 589).

God be in . . . AMEN. Cf. the Primer of 1514 (Richard Pynson, London). The title-page has on it, 'God be in my head, and in mine understanding . . .' (cf. Hoskins, no. 44, p. 129). Cf. also the Primer of 1538: *Hereafter followeth the Prymer in english set out along after the use of Sarum* (Nicolas LeRoux, Rouen, for François Regnault [Paris]). On the reverse of the title-page is 'God be in my head, And in mine understanding . . .' (cf. Hoskins, no. 135, p. 174).

PRevent mee . . . *Amen.* The Primers of 1571 and 1599 have this prayer in a similar position, 'Before the beginning of any office'.

THE MATTINS. This office follows, with some variations, the arrangement of 'Preces Matutinae' and 'Laudes' in the Elizabethan Primers of 1560 and 1564, noted before on p. 319.

S. AMBROSE saith. Cf. *Ps.-Athanasius Sermo in Annuntiationem Deiparae 13* (in *Patrologia Graeca*, ed. J.-P. Migne, XXVIII. 936), a work which is probably a century later than the author to whom it was ascribed. The following passage fits Cosin's reference which is incorrect; there is nothing like this in the works of St. Ambrose: 'ὡς καὶ κατ' ἀρχὰς τῶν εὐχῶν συγκαλούμενοι ἀλλήλους, ἀνακράζουσι λέγοντες· Δεῦτε, προσκυνήσωμεν, καὶ προσπέσωμεν αὐτῷ Χριστῷ τῷ βασιλεῖ ἡμῶν.' (The translation is given in Migne, p. 935: 'Venite, adoremus et procidamus coram Christo Rege nostro. . . .') The quotation is not, of course, quite exact (the last few words are an obvious Christian adaptation of the original words of the Psalm). We do not know to what service it refers or the Church whose usage it reflects (possibly Constantinople). There is a story recorded by St. John Chrysostom and St. Augustine that the faithful used to wait for the Venite and then hastened into Church; of this tradition Cosin must have been aware. Professor Turner, who provided the information of this note, has failed to find any reference to St. Ambrose in books on the Prayer Book of Cosin's own date; the source of his mistake (if it is not a slip of memory), therefore, cannot be traced.

THE HYMNE. Assigned to Prime in the Breviary, and introduced into Matins in the first authorized Primer of 1545: *The Primer set forth by the King's majesty, and his clergy* . . . London . . . (Hoskins, no. 174, p. 237). This evidently is Cosin's translation. Cf. John Julian, *A Dictionary of Hymnology* (London, 1925), p. 577.

The Psalms. The choice of Psalms, both here and in Cosin's other offices, is largely traditional.

BENEDICTUS. The heading for this canticle has found its way into the Prayer Book of the Church of India, Pakistan, Burma, and Ceylon in the form 'the Hymn called Benedictus (or the Song of Zacharias)'.

THE CREED. The alteration of the name 'Ponce Pilate', the form in which it appeared in the earlier editions of the Prayer Book, to 'Pontius Pilate', was carried over into the Prayer Book of 1662 by way of *The Durham Book.*

A DEVOUT PRAYER . . . II. Cf. 'Of the unspeakable sweetnesse of God' in *Certaine Select Prayers gathered out of S. Augustines Meditations* (1574), 'My joy draw my hart unto thee, My sweete foode, let me feede upon thee. My head, direct Thou me, Thou light of myne eyes, inlighten me. My melodie, delight thou me. . . .'

III. Cf. St. Ignatius of Loyola's *Spiritual Exercises* (1548), the section 'Contemplation for obtaining love', at the end of the Fourth Week: 'Tomad, Señor, y recibid toda mi libertad, mi memoria, mi entendimiento, y toda mi voluntad, todo mi haber y mi posseer; vos me lo distes, a vos, Señor, lo torno; todo es vuestro, disponed a toda vestra voluntad, dadme vuestro amor y gracia, que ésta me basta' (quoted from a text, Barcelona, ?1959, based on the first edition). Cf. the Latin version which Cosin would probably have known, 'Contemplatio ad Amorem spiritualem in nobis excitandum': 'Suscipe Domine universam meam libertatem. Accipe Memoriam, Intellectum, atque Voluntatem omnem. Quicquid habeo, vel possideo, mihi largitus es: id tibi totum restituo, ac tuae prorsus voluntati trado gubernandum. Amorem tui solum cum gratia tua, mihi dones, & dives sum satis, nec aliud quicquam ultra posco' (ed. Rome, 1609).

VIII–X. Cf. the 'Precatio Aurea' of St. Thomas Aquinas, in the translation made by Queen Mary, and included in the Elizabethan Primer of 1559, *The Primer set forth at large with many godly and devout prayers*, London (Hoskins, no. 239, p. 250), included in *Private Prayers*, especially 'A fruitful prayer to be said at all times' (pp. 107–8). Cosin slightly rearranges, but otherwise follows closely, the translation of Queen Mary. A Latin adaptation of this prayer appeared in the Elizabethan Primer of 1560 (*Private Prayers*, p. 201); the original text may be found in *Opera Omnia* (Parma, 1869), 24. 242: 'Concede mihi, misericors Deus . . . .'

Sources for I and IV–VII have not been identified, but internal evidence suggests that all derive, however remotely, from the Latin.

THE THIRD HOURE OF PRAYERS. This, the other two mid-day offices, and Vespers, follow the pattern of the same offices in the Elizabethan Primer of 1560, with only slight variations. Much more than in earlier versions of the canonical hours, Cosin's Third Hour is an office of the Holy Spirit.

The THIRD HOURE . . . RUPERTUS. Stephanus Durantus in *De Ritibus Ecclesiae Catholicae* (Cologne, 1592) observes of the Third Hour: 'Hora diei tertia, vulgo apud Italos aurea hora appellatur, in jure vero hora sacra' (III. viii). Durantus next refers to the Decree Cosin notices and to Rupertus. Cf. *Decretum . . . Gratiani . . . Juris Canonici Compendium* . . . (London, 1560), under Distinctio XLIIII, the last canon: 'Nec oportet clericos vel laicos religiosos ante sacram horam diei tertiam inire convivia. . . .' Cf. Rupertus, *De Divinis Officiis*, I. iii, 'De Tertia', in *Bibliotheca Patrum*, X. 855.

For the general importance of Durantus, cf. the introduction to the Commentary. Durantus gives nearly every reference that appears among Cosin's authorities for the canonical hours, along with a Latin text from which Cosin might have worked without necessarily looking in a complete edition of each authority. Sometimes Cosin follows the same order of references as Durantus gives—so with the Third Hour: Cosin exactly follows Durantus except that Durantus gives Jerome on Dan. 6 where Cosin gives two different references, but still to Jerome. Of these, the first, *Ad Eustochium*, appears in an earlier chapter of Durantus (III. ii), and the second, *De Obitu Paulae*, is given by Bellarmine in 'De operibus bonis' (Book I), in the chapter (xiii) called 'Demonstratur antiqua, & rationabilis institutio canonicarum Horarum' (cf. *Opera*, III. 1358). Cosin's references at Vespers are likewise very close to Durantus; not only are they the same (only the Basil does not occur at this point in Durantus, but it is in his chap. ii); they appear also in the same order.

saith S. CYPRIAN *and* S. HIEROM. Cf. below at the quotations from these Fathers.

CONST. CLEM. Cf. the passage quoted at Matins, pp. 332–3.

TERTUL. DE JEJUN. Cf. Tertullian, *De Jejuniis Adversus Psychicos*, cap. X: 'Porro cum in eodem commentario Lucae, & tertia hora orationis demonstretur . . . et sexta . . . et nona . . . cur non intellegamus salva plane indifferentia semper et abique et omni tempore orandi tamen tres istas horas, ut insigniores in rebus humanis quae diem distribuunt, quae negotia distinguunt, quae publice resonant, ita & solemniores fuisse in orationibus divinis?' (p. 1179B).

S. CYPRIAN DE ORAT. DOM. St. Cyprian describes the canonical hours and defines their historical or special intention towards the end of his treatise on the Lord's Prayer (*De Oratione Dominica*). He writes: 'In orationibus vero celebrandis invenimus observasse cum Daniele tres pueros in fide fortes, & in captivitate victores, horam tertiam, sextam, nonam, sacramento, scilicet, trinitatis; quae in novissimis temporibus manifestari habebat. . . . Nam super discipulos hora tertia descendit Spiritus sanctus, qui gratiam dominicae repromissionis implevit' (II. 272. § 15).

S. BASIL. IN REG. FUS. DISP. Cf. *Regularum Fusius Disputatarum*, Interrogatio 37: 'Tertia vero hora, ut in ea ad orationem surgatur, fratresque omnes in unum congregentur, licet diversis in locis, alii in aliis operibus sint occupati: idque ea re, ut admoniti doni spiritus, quod circiter hanc ipsam horam Apostolis datum fuit, uno eodemque animo cuncti illum venerentur, ab eoque petant, ut & ipsi digni sint, qui sanctificationem suscipiant: simulque ut salutaris sibi doctrinae, & recti itineris dux esse, & autor velit . . .' (II. 586).

S. HIERON. AD EUSTOCH. Cf. the passage quoted from *Ad Eustochium* at 'The Ancient Use of Morning Prayer', p. 334, and also the commendations of 'Prayers for the Evening', p. 343.

IDEM DE OBITU PAULAE. Cf. St. Jerome's Epistola xxvii, c. 10, 'Ad Eustochium Virginem Epitaphium Paulae matris': 'Mane hora tertia, sexta, nona, vespere, noctis medio, per ordinem psalterium cantabant' (I. 66G).

ISID. DE ECCL. OFF. Chap. 19 of Book I of Isidore's *De Ecclesiasticis Officiis* is called 'De Tertiae, Sextae & Nonae horae officiis'. Cosin translates from the following: 'Tali enim sacramento legitimis ad precem temporibus per ternas horas, trinitatis perfectio aut laudatur celebritatibus, aut precibus impetratur . . .' (p. 395).

THE HYMNE. VENI CREATOR. This is a very defective translation, but nevertheless a pleasing version, of a hymn traditional at this hour. Cosin's version is to be found first written on a leaf of a copy of the order for the Coronation of Charles I (2 Feb. 1625/6), probably the copy which the King held in his hand on that occasion. Cf. Christopher Wordsworth, ed., *The Manner of the Coronation of King Charles the First of England* (London: Henry Bradshaw Liturgical Text Society, 1892), Appendix, p. 69. It was introduced into the Ordinal in 1662, probably by way of *The Durham Book*.

THE PRAYERS. I. A conflation, including parts from the Collects for Whitsunday and Epiphany I.

II. A considerably expanded version of the prayer of Invocation in the Order of Confirmation.

THE SIXTH HOURE OF PRAYER. An office of the Passion.

saith S. *CYPRIAN. Of the sixth hour St. Cyprian writes (in the same section quoted above): 'Item Petrus hora sexta in tectum superius ascendens, signo pariter & voce Dei monentis instructus est, ut omnes ad gratiam salutis admitteret, cum de emundandis gentilibus ante dubitaret. Et dominus hora sexta crucifixus. . . .'

CLEM. CONST. Cf. the passage quoted at Matins, pp. 332–3.

TERTUL. DE JEJUN. Cf. Tertullian, *De Jejuniis Adversus Psychicos* (p. 1179). This precedes the passage quoted at p. 337: 'Atqui facilius invenias Petrum hora sexta capiendi cibi causa prius in superiora ad orandum ascendisse, quo magis sexta diei finiri officio huic possit, quae illud absolutura post orationem videbatur.'

S. CYPRIAN DE ORAT. DOM. Cyprian does not write anything quite like this, but Cosin reflects his general sense. Cf. the quotations above.

S. BAS. IN REG. FUS. DISP. Cf. *Regularum Fusius Disputatarum*, Interrogatio 37: 'Porro sexta hora, sanctorum exemplo, necessariam esse orationem judicavimus, apud quos est: Vespere & mane, & meridie narrabo, & annunciabo, & exaudiet vocem meam. In qua quidem ut liberemur ab incursu & daemonio meridiano . . .' (II. 586).

S. ATHANAS. DE MEDITAT. Cf. *De Virginitate sive de Meditatione* (p. 601), and also the quotation at Matins, p. 333: 'Sexta hora absolves deprecationes cum Psalmis, ploratu, & supplicationibus: quoniam hac hora pependit Filius Dei in cruce.'

S. ISIDOR. LIB. 6. ETYM. CAP. ULT. Cf. *Originum sive Etymologiarum*, c. 19 (the last one of Book 6), 'De officiis' (p. 52): 'Nam est observatio quarundam horarum communium: quae diei interspatia signant, *tertia, sexta & nona*: Similiter & noctis, sed ideo orandi hae horae divisae sunt: ut si forte aliquo fuerimus opere detenti, ipsum nos ad officium tempus admoneat: . . . Debitores enim sumus trium personarum, Patris & Filii & Spiritus sancti, exceptis utique & aliis legitimis orationibus, quae sine ulla admonitione debentur in ingressu lucis ac noctis sive vigiliarum: sed & cibum non prius sumere, quam interposita oratione debemus.'

THE HYMNE. This is the earliest known version of part of Ben Jonson's 'A Hymne to God the Father', first printed in full in the Jonson folio of 1640–1 as part of 'The Underwood'. Cosin uses, in a different metre and with some rearrangement, lines 17–20 of Jonson's hymn, and he has borrowed a rhyme ('my losse/Crosse') from lines 29 and 32. Herford and Simpson, the editors of the Oxford Jonson, point out that the hymn was 'used as an anthem in one of the royal chapels in and after 1635 from a setting by William Crosse' (XI. 49), but they give no reference for the earlier existence of the hymn. It would seem more probable that Cosin is working from Jonson than Jonson from Cosin. There is no evidence that the two were acquainted, but it is likely that they would have met at Court, and Cosin might have learned of the hymn there. Cf. D. O'Connor, 'Jonson's "A Hymne to God the Father" ', *Notes & Queries*, N.S. XII (Oct. 1965), 379–80.

THE PRAYERS. I. A variation on the traditional Antiphon of the Cross.

II. A collect for the Compassion of our Lady regularly appears at the end of each office in the Sarum Enchiridion, the practice also of the Latin–English Primer of 1621 printed at St. Omer's by John Heigham, *The Primer, or Office of the Blessed Virgin Marie . . .* (Hoskins, no. 273), which follows closely the traditional pattern of the *Enchiridion . . . p̃clare de ecclesie Sarum . . .* (Paris: Kerver, 1528 [Hoskins, no. 83]). Cosin may be adapting such a collect here, or in a general way be recalling a section of the St. Omer Primer (again a traditional one), 'Planctus Beatae Mariae' (p. 456): 'Interveniat pro nobis, quaesumus Domine Jesu Christe, nunc & in hora mortis nostrae apud tuam clementiam, beata virgo Maria mater tua, cuius sacratissimam animam in hora tuae passionis doloris gladius pertransivit: Per te Jesu Christe salvator mundi. Qui cum Patre & Spiritu sancto, vivis & regnas in saecula saeculorum.' The translation is given on the opposite page: 'We beseech thee O Lord Jesu Christe, that the blessed virgin Mary thy mother, may be a meane for us with thy clemencie, now & at the houre of our death: through whose most sacred soule at the houre of thy passion, a sword of sorrow did passe: through thee o Jesu Christe saviour of the world: who with the Father & holy Ghost, livest and raignest world without end.'

THE NINTH HOURE. An office of the Passion, with a distinctive emphasis on the Passion as a revelation of the divine mercy and love.

CLEM. CONST. Cf. the passage quoted at Matins, pp. 332–3.

S. CYPR. DE ORAT. DOM. Cf. the selections from Cyprian above, pp. 338 and 339, at the third and the sixth hours. The last quotation continues: 'Et dominus hora sexta crucifixus, ad nonam peccata nostra sanguine suo abluit, & ut redimere & vivificare nos posset, tunc victoriam suam passione perfecit.'

S. BASIL. IN REG. Cf. the passages from *Regularum Fusius Disputatarum* quoted at the third and the sixth hours which this one continues: 'De nona vero, quod ea ad orationem nobis necessaria sit, id Apostoli ipsi declaraverunt in Actis, in quibus est, quod Petrus & Joannes ascendebant in templum ad horam orationis nonam.'

S. HIER. IN DAN. 6. Cf. *Commentariorum Hieronymi Liber I. In Danielem Cap. VI*: 'Orat autem secundum praeceptum Dei, dictaque Salomonis, qui contra templum orandum esse admonuit. Tria autem sunt tempora, quibus Deo flectenda sunt genua: tertiam horam, sextam, & nonam, Ecclesiastica traditio intelligit' (IV. 508D).

RAB. MAUR. L. 2. DE INST. CL. Cf. *De Institutione Clericorum* (included in *Bibliotheca Patrum*, X. 587), the second book, the sixth chapter, called 'De Officio nonae horae': 'Nona utique; hora inde consecratur, quia in ea Dominus pro inimicis postulans, in manus Patris spiritum commendavit, qua videlicet fideles quosque oportet ut se Deo commendent cum devota oratione, qua caput suum cognoscunt propriam animam patri suo commendasse, ut in ejus corpus coadunati, cum ipso regnum possint intrare perpetuum.'

RUP. LIB. I. DE DIV. OFF. Cosin uses the whole of the fifth chapter of the first book of Rupertus' *De Divinis Officiis* quite freely. Cf. especially: 'Nona quoque hora, jure in laudem Dei clamamus, quando clamans Dominus Jesu voce magna emisit spiritum, latrone admisso in Paradisum, & venia quamvis sero, veraciter poenitentibus & confitentibus dedicata, & rescisso velo legis & prophetarum coepimus revelata facie contemplari gloriam Domini. Tunc etiam latere ejus perforato, formandae Ecclesiae profluxerunt elementa sanguis, quo redimimur, aqua, qua abluimur' (cf. *Bibliotheca Patrum*, X. 855).

THE PRAYERS. I. An arrangement of the fourteenth of a series of medieval Passion prayers, known as 'The XV Oes of Saynt Brygitte', which had appeared in many of the Primers. Cosin's version is an adaptation of the translation in Bishop Hilsey's Primer of 1539 (Hoskins, no. 143, p. 225): 'The Manual of prayers, or the primer in english set out at length . . .' (included in *Three Primers Put Forth in the Reign of Henry VIII* . . . ed. Edward Burton [Oxford, 1834], pp. 376–8): 'O Jesu, the only begotten Son of Almighty God the Father, the brightness and figure of his godly substance, have mind of that entire commendation, in which thou didst commend thy spirit into the hands of thy Father; and with a torn body and broken heart shewing to us for our ransom the bowels of thy mercy, for the redeeming of us didst give up thy breath; for mind of that precious death, I beseech thee, King of saints, comfort me to withstand the fiend, the world, and my flesh, that I may be dead to the world, and living ghostly toward thee. And in the last hour of my departing from the world, receive my soul, coming to thee, which in this life is an outlaw, and a pilgrim. So be it.'

II. A variation on the Collect for Palm Sunday.

*PLA. 10. de legibus. Cf. Plato, *Opera Omnia*, in the edition by Marsilio Ficino (Frankfurt, 1602), II. 946. §§ E–F. Cosin's reference is to a passage in one of the speeches of the Athenian Stranger who must prove the existence of the gods to those who find the example of their elders insufficient, and 'who likewise see and hear the prostrations and invocations which are made by Hellenes and barbarians at the rising and setting of the sun and moon, in all the vicissitudes of life, not as if they thought that there were no Gods, but as if there could be no doubt of their existence, and no suspicion of their non-existence . . .' (cf. Jowett's translation in *The Dialogues of Plato* [4th ed., Oxford, 1953], IV. 455).

*ISID. *Etym. lib. 6.* Cf. the passage quoted at the sixth hour, p. 339.

CLEM. CONST. Cf. the passage quoted at Matins, pp. 332–3.

CONCIL.[ium] LAODIC.[enum]. The 18th canon of this Council, held in 364, declared: 'Idem precum ministerium omnino debere fieri in Nonis & vesperis.' Cf. Binius, I. 289.

S. BASIL. ORAT. IN S. JULIT. Cf. the note and quotation after p. [331], 'At our Apparrelling.' At the end of any day which we should devoutly have lived in memory of God's grace towards us, Basil counsels: 'Tibine dies expletus abiit? Illi referto gratiam, qui solem quidem nobis nihil tale commeritis indulsit in diurnae operationis ministerium: ignem vero contulit illustrandae nocti, utque subserviat reliquis vitae commoditatibus. Ipsa rursus nox alias ad orationem suggerere possit conciliareve occasiones' (I. 318).

S. AMBROS. Cosin refers to the beginning of the 11th letter of Ambrose (in Book III), this one written to Irenaeus. Ambrose says that while reading, he stopped to rest his mind and then began to meditate on 'that Versicle' (from Rom. 10. 15; Is. 52. 7)—'versiculum illum coepi mecum volvere, quo vesperi in vigiliis usi fueramus' (p. 526D).

S. HIER. AD EUSTOCH. Cosin has in mind the passage quoted also at Matins (p. 334) and at the third hour (p. 338).

ISID. . . . DE ECCL. OFF. The chapter Cosin cites is called 'De vespertinis': 'Proinde in honorem ac memoriam tantorum sacramentorum, in temporibus nos adesse decet Dei conspectibus, & personare in ejus cultibus, orationum nostrarum illi sacrificium offerentes, atque in ejus laudibus pariter exultantes' (p. 395).

THE HYMNE. A Compline hymn in the Sarum Breviary. The Elizabethan Primer of 1560 gives this hymn at Vespers, and that of 1564 includes it among some bedtime prayers. This would appear to be Cosin's own translation: cf. J. Julian, *Dictionary of Hymnology*, p. 988.

MAGNIFICAT AND NUNC DIMITTIS. The headings for these canticles (pp. 148, 153) were introduced into the Prayer Book of 1662, by way of *The Durham Book*, in the form 'Magnificat (or the song of the blessed virgin Mary)' and 'Nunc dimittis (or the song of Simeon)'.

THE PRAYERS. I. This is included among the evening prayers in the Elizabethan Primer of 1564.

III. An evening prayer by Erasmus in his 'Precationes Aliquot Novae . . .' (v. 998–1025), adapted in the Primer of 1545 (cited on p. 335), and, in a condensed form, in the Elizabethan Primers of 1560 and 1564. Cosin's is a new translation, based on the condensed form of the prayer, which he has used with great freedom, interpolating a phrase from the Collect for the Second Sunday in Lent. The prayer occurs in the Elizabethan Primers thus: 'Omnipotens Domine Deus, ex cuius ordine et voluntate iam nox et tenebrae appetunt, tuam clementiam deprecamur, ut nos misericorditer in tutelam tuam accipias, ne in nos principes tenebrarum aliquid potestatis habeant; et cum dormiendum pro corporis necessitate sit, nihilominus cor et animus noster ad te semper vigilent, et effice ne in conspectu tuo filii noctis et tenebrarum, sed diei et lucis perpetuo inveniamur. Qui vivis . . .' (*Private Prayers*, pp. 154, 271).

IV. A morning prayer by Erasmus in his 'Precationes'. This, too, had appeared in the three Primers just mentioned, and again, Cosin's is a new translation, keeping fairly close to the Latin original: 'Domine Jesu Christe, qui verus es mundi sol, semper oriens, nunquam occidens: qui tuo salutifero conspectu gignis, servas, alis, exhilaras, omnia, et quae in coelis, et quae in terris: illucesce, quaeso, propitius animo meo, ut, discussa nocte criminum ac nebulis errorum, te intus praelucente, citra offensionem per omnem vitam incedam, et tanquam in die decenter ambulem, purus ab operibus tenebrarum: qui vivis . . .' (*Private Prayers*, pp. 371–2).

THE COMPLINE. The general arrangement of this office is close to that of the Elizabethan Primers of 1560 and 1564.

S. CHRYS. LIB. I. DE ORANDO DEUM. Cf. St. Chrysostom, *De Precatione I* (I. 747D): 'Qua spe ad tempora nocturna pervenies? quae tibi visa secundum quietem objectum iri suspicaris, si nullus precibus praemunitus, nullo praesidio septus quieti te tradas? facillime te improbissimi daemones contemnent, & implicabunt, qui oberrant assidue, qui occasionem captant, observantes, ut, si quem precatione destitutum deprehenderint, sine mora corripiant. Quare, si quidem septos nos precibus viderint, continuo tanquam fures, ac scelesti resiliunt, qui gladium militis capiti appensum cernunt.'

PSAL. 91. . . . Saint BASIL, *in reg.* Basil, in *Regularum Fusius Disputatarum*, 37 (II. 587), says that at nightfall we must ask that our rest be sinless and untroubled: 'qua hora etiam necessario nonagesimus recitari psalmus debet.' Cosin gives Ps. 91, the same as the 90th in the Vulgate.

NUNC DIMITTIS. Cf. the note at p. 343.

THE PRAYERS. I. This derives from the same source as the third prayer at Vespers.

PRAYERS AT BED-TIME. This could hardly be described as an office, but it is some sort of provision for the observance of the seventh canonical hour.

WHEN WE ENTER INTO OUR BED. Cf. *A Manual of Prayers*, especially the prayer 'A prayer as thou entrest into thy bed' (p. 22): 'In the name of our Lorde Jesus Christe that was crucified for me, I goe into my bedde: let him blesse me, gouerne me, and defende me, and bringe me into lyfe everlastinge. Amen.'

III. The traditional Compline antiphon, included in the Elizabethan Primers of 1560 and 1564.

THE SEVEN PENITENTIALL PSALMES. The Penitential Psalms form a standard feature of the Primer along with the Litany.

THE LETANY . . . Devotion. The explanation that the Litany is to be used on Sundays, Wednesdays, and Fridays follows the earlier editions of the Book of Common Prayer. Cosin's direction that it should be used 'after the Morning Prayers' was introduced into the rubric before the Litany in the 1662 Prayer Book, by way of *The Durham Book.*

SUch miseries . . . prayers. Cf. Richard Hooker, *Lawes of Ecclesiasticall Politie*, V. 41 (p. 82): 'What dangers at any time are imminent, what evils hang over our heads, God doth know and not we.'

the **Primitive Church*. The marginal notes refer to a variety of early references (two of which are as in Hooker, V. 41) to the use of litanies in the ancient liturgy, but some refer only in passing, as Irenaeus in *Adversus Haereses Valentini et Similium*, II. 57 (cf. *Opus . . . Irenaei . . . in Quinque Libros* . . . Apud Inclytam Basilaeam . . . Anno M.D.XXVIII, p. 126), and also Prosper of Aquitaine, *De Vocatione Omnium Gentium*, II. 4 (in J.-P. Migne, *Patrologiae Cursus Completus* [Paris, 1846], LI. 690).

Tertullian, *Ad Uxorem*, II. 4 (p. 332): 'Domino certe non potest pro disciplina satisfacere habens in latere diaboli servum, procuratorem domini sui ad impedienda fidelium studia & officia. Ut si statio facienda est, maritus de die condicat ad balneas: si jejunia observanda sunt, maritus eadem die convivium exerceat: si procedendum erit, nunquam magis familiae occupatio adveniat.'

S. Jerome, *Ad Eustochium* (*De custodia virginitatis*, Epistola xxii): 'Martyres tibi quaerantur in cubiculo tuo. Nunquam causa deerit procedendi, si semper, quando necesse est processura sis' (I. 50E). Hooker quotes this in a note to V. 41 (p. 81).

S. Basil, Epistola lxiii (III. 96–97) probably does not in fact refer to a Litany with procession: 'De nocte siquidem populus consurgens antelucano tempore domum precationis petit: inque labore & tribulatione ac lachrymis indesinentibus facta ad Deum confessione, tandem ab oratione surgentes ad psalmodiam traducuntur. Et nunc quidem in duas partes divisi alternis succinentes psallunt: atque ex eo simul eloquiorum Dei exercitationem ac meditationem corroborant: & cordibus suis attentionem, & rejectis vanis cogitationibus mentis soliditatem suppeditant: deinde uni ex ipsis hoc muneris dato, ut quod canendum est prior ordiatur: reliqui succinunt: atque ita psalmodiae varietate precibusque subinde intersertis noctem superant. Illucescente jam die pariter omnes velut ore uno ac corde uno confessionis psalmum Domino offerunt, ac suis quisque verbis poenitentiam profitentur.'

Ruffinus, *Historia Ecclesiastica*, II. 33 (Cosin's reference is in error), tells of Theodosius in his war against Eugenius, in 397. The enemy is joined by a great number of barbarians. Theodosius falls down and prays to God: 'Tu, inquit, omnipotens Deus, nosti quia in nomine Christi filii tui ultionis justae, ut puto, praelia ista suscepi: si secus, in me vindica' (p. 203).

Sidonius Apollinaris, in a letter to Aper (472–3), says that he is sure Aper will return for the Rogations, 'Quarum nobis solemnitatem primus Mamertus pater & pontifex, reverentissimo exemplo, utilissimo experimento, invenit, instituit, invexit. Erant quidem prius . . . in his autem quas suprafatus summus sacerdos nobis & protulit pariter & contulit, jejunatur, oratur, psallitur, fletur.' In a letter to Mamertus (474), Sidonius recalls the great ills that beset him and his people before the institution of the Rogations; and now that the Goths threaten Auvergne, the principal help lies in that form of prayer: 'solo tamen invectarum te autore rogationum palpamur auxilio . . .' (cf. Sidonius Apollinaris, *Epp.* V. xiv and VII. i).

S. GREGORIE the Great. Cf. the Life of Gregory by John the Deacon in *Opera Gregorii* (Paris, 1605), I. 16.

*Wal. Strabo *de reb. Eccl. cap.* de Letaniis. Cf. *De Rebus Ecclesiasticis*, c. xxviii, 'De Litaniis agendis' (in *Bibliotheca Patrum*, X. 694): Strabo (d. 849) recalls that early litanies (as in the time of Mamertus) did not mention the names of saints. 'Litania autem sanctorum nominum, postea creditur in usum assumpta. . . .'

*R.H. *l.* 5. This refers, of course, to Richard Hooker, whose discussion of the litany Cosin has closely followed. Compare this paragraph: 'But this iron began at the length to gather rust. . . . For remedie whereof it was then thought better, that these and all other supplications or processions should be no where used but only within the walles of the house of God, the place sanctified unto prayer. And by us not only such inconveniences being remedied, but also whatsoever was otherwise amisse in forme or matter, it now remayneth a worke, the absolute perfection whereof upbraydeth with error or somewhat worse them whome in all parts it doth not satisfie' (§ 41, p. 82).

THE COLLECTS FOR THE SUNDAYES AND HOLIDAYES. Cf. Primers of 1540, no title-page (Hoskins, no. 156, p. 176); 1553, *A Primmer or book of private prayer, needful to be used of all faithful christians.* ... London, William Seres (Hoskins, no. 200, p. 289); 1560, *A Primer or Book of private prayer, needful to be used of all faithful christians* . . . London, William Seres (Hoskins, no. 243, p. 299). A novel feature of this section is Cosin's inclusion of a series of explanatory passages on the liturgical year.

It is the peculiar Computation ... spirituall darkenesse. Cosin bases this paragraph upon a passage from Joannes Ferus (d. 1554), Domin. xxvi post Pentecost. Sermo I in *Postillae sive Conciones*, vol. II (Cologne, 1559), p. 376[b]: 'Ea enim neque solis, neque lunae rationem habet, neque dies, neque menses numerat, neque solares neque lunares computat annos. Christus unicus illius sol, lumen & sydus est, cuius ductum sequitur. Cum illo annum orditur, cum illo finit. Cum hic sol oritur, hoc est, cum nobis Christianis iterum adventus & incarnatio Christi proponitur, tum orditur Ecclesia suum annum, id quod proxima Dominica fiet. Si itaque illa prima Dominica erit juxta Ecclesiae calculum ultima haec sit necesse est.' An English version of this same passage occurs in the First Series of Notes on the Book of Common Prayer, 'Of the First Sunday in Advent', in Cosin's *Works*, V. 70.

**Serm. 1. in Septua.* Cf. St. Bernard's sermon 'In Septuagesima': 'Sic & Christum audio mensuram sine mensura promittentem. Mensuram, inquit, confertam & coagitatam, & superfluentem. Sed quando venient ista? Profecto in fine praesentis septuagesimae: quod est tempus captivitatis nostrae. . . . Unde & reticetur interim: Alleluia solemne, & humanae transgressionis historia miserabilis ab exordio recensetur' (*Opera Omnia* . . . Antwerpiae . . . M.D.LXXVI, p. 25).

Councell of *AUXERRE. Held in 578. The second canon declared: 'Ut omnes presbyteri ante Epiphaniam missos suos dirigant, qui eis de principio quadragesimae nuncient, & in ipsa Epiphania ad populum indicent.' Cf. Binius, II. 954.

Not as if she thought ... desires. Cf. Hooker, V. 72 (p. 206): '. . . his [i.e. the Apostle Paul's] purpose [expressed in Rom. 14. 17] . . . was farre from any intent to derogate from that fasting which is no such scrupulous abstinence as onely refuseth some kinds of meates and drinkes least they make him uncleane that tasteth them, but an abstinence whereby we either interrupt or otherwise abridge the care of our bodily sustenance, to show by this kinde of outward exercise the serious intention of our minds fixed on heavenlier and better desires, the earnest hunger and thirst whereof depriveth the body of those usuall contentmentes, which otherwise are not denied unto it.' And also, in writing of the different kinds of fasting, Hooker refers to those who deprive themselves of food altogether as well as those who fast 'by abating both the quantitie and kind of diet'.

The final two paragraphs of THE FIRST DAY OF LENT follow the pattern suggested by Bellarmine, *De bonis operibus*, II. xiv, 'De origine, & institutione jejunii Quadragesimalis'. Cf. *Disputationes* (discussed in the introductory note to this Commentary), III. 1453. Most, but not all, of Cosin's references appear also in Bellarmine, and in the same order. He begins, like Cosin, 'Ex Graecis, S. Ignatius in epist. ad Philippenses', then turns later to the Latin authorities, beginning first with Tertullian.

IGNATIUS. Cf. 'Epistola ad Philippenses . . . de Baptismate': 'Festivitates ne dehonestetis. Quadragesimale jejunium ne spernatis: continet enim imitationem conversationis Dominicae' (*Bibliotheca Patrum*, XI. 20).

IRENAEUS. Cf. Eusebius, V. xxiii (pp. 63–64). This section concerns the dispute over the tradition of the Paschal season and how it should be observed. Irenaeus counsels a wideness and generosity in interpreting what should be the custom. According to Eusebius, he advises: '. . . id quidem approbavit, sola Dominica die resurrectionis Domini celebrandum esse mysterium: Victorem vero ne cunctas ecclesias Dei antiquae consuetudinis traditionem retinentes alienaret, competenter ac multis admonet, & ad verbum ista dicit. Non enim de die tantum discrepatio est, sed & de ipsa specie jejunii.'

ORIGEN. Cf. *Origenis . . . Opera . . . omnia* (Apud Basileam ex officina Frobeniana, 1536), p. 179: 'Habemus enim quadragesimae dies jejuniis consecratos. Habemus quartam & sextam septimanae dies, quibus soleniter jejunamus.'

Generall Councell of *NICE. Canon 5 of this council (325) mentions the Lent fast in passing. The excommunication of either a clergyman or a layman by the sentence of a single bishop shall be valid everywhere until it be reviewed by a provincial council which shall be held twice a year, once in the autumn, and also in the spring: 'Synodi . . . fiant, una quidem ante Quadragesimam . . . .' Cf. Binius, I. 306.

S. CYRILL. There are several references to the Lent fast in St. Cyril of Jerusalem. Cf. esp. § xiv (*Catecheses*, p. 502): 'De tradita namque vobis ad profitendum sancta & Apostolica fide, quantum catechesis capere potuit, per Dei gratiam diximus, praeteritis hisce quadragesimae diebus.'

S. CHRYSOSTOME. Cf. *In caput Geneseos primum Homilia prima*: '. . . per omne tempus sanctae Quadragesimae, spirituales merces negociati fuerimus . . .' (II. 70.) Cf. also *Ad Populum Antiochenum*, Homilia xviii: 'Multos etenim video se ita pusillanimiter habentes, ut in praesenti de futura soliciti sint quadragesima, multosque dicentes audivi, quod post jejunii liberationem non sentiunt voluptatem ex remissione propter futuri anni solicitudinem' (I. 202B).

S. BASIL. Basil writes: 'Ita jejunium per omne quidem tempus utile est iis qui illud sponte suscipiunt. . . . Nec ulla est insula, nec ulla terra continens, non civitas, non gens ulla, non extremus mundi angulus, ubi non sit auditum jejunii edictum' (I. 287).

ATHANASIUS. Cf. *Ad Orthodoxos in Persecutione* (p. 336): 'Vidisses enim presbyteros & Laicos in jus trahi, virgines a coetu suo divulsas, ad tribunal praesidis raptari, & in carcerem connici, alios fisco addici, alios flagellis caedi, panes sacrificiorum, ministris & virginibus interdici. Haec autem sub Pascha, in sacra quadragesima acta sunt, per quod tempus jejuniis dediti erant.'

S. GR. NYSSEN . . . NAZIANZEN. Cosin has inverted the proper order. It is Gregory Nazianzen who wrote *Oratio in Sanctum Baptisma* (Oratio Quadragesima), and Gregory Nyssen who wrote *De Pauperibus Amandis et Benignitate Complectendis*. For the first, cf. I. 659: 'Christus paulo ante tentationem jejunavit: nos ante Pascha . . .', and for the second, I. 970: 'Jejunium virtutis fundamentum est', but the Nyssen's commendation of fasting is more general since he does not treat the Lenten fast particularly.

TERTULLIAN. Cf., for example, *De Jejuniis Adversus Psychicos*, (p. 1175B): 'Certe in Evangelio illos dies jejuniis determinatos putant, in quibus ablatus est sponsus: & hos esse iam solos legitimos jejuniorum Christianorum abolitis legalibus & propheticis vetustatibus.'

S. CYPRIAN. Cf. 'De Bono Patientiae', in *Opera*, p. 316: 'Diebus quadraginta jejunat, per quem ceteri saginantur. . . .' Cf. also 'De Jejunio, et Tentationibus Christi' (pp. 460–6).

S. AMBROSE, S. HIEROM, and S. AUGUSTINE. Cf. *Liber de Noe & arca,* p. 965B: 'Unde nunc iam non pœnae praescripti sunt dies quadraginta, sed vitae, ut hoc numero jejuniis & orationibus crebrioribus nostrorum levemus supplicia peccatorum, atque ad decreta legis intenti devotione ac fide nostrum corrigamus errorem.' Cf. also the sermons of Ambrose on Quadragesima (23–26) and on fasting (27), pp. 714–20. Cosin also cites Jerome later in this paragraph. The passage occurs in Epistola LIIII, 'ad Marcellam, adversus Montanum'. Cosin quotes exactly although he omits one phrase: 'Nos unam quadragesimam secundum traditionem apostolorum, toto anno, tempore nobis congruo, jejunamus' (I. 162B). Cosin also cites Augustine's letter to Januarius: 'Quadragesima sane jejuniorum habet autoritatem, & in veteribus libris ex jejunio Moysi & Heliae: & ex Evangelio, quia totidem diebus dominus jejunavit . . .' (II. 572–3, § XV).

CHRYSOLOGUS. Cf. *Petri Chrysologi . . . insigne & pervetustum opus Homiliarum*... (Paris, 1543), 'De jejunio & tentationibus Christi', p. 16: 'Videtis fratres, quia quod Quadragesimam jejunamus, non est humana inventio, authoritas est divina, & est mysticum, non praesumptum: nec est de terreno usu, sed de caelestibus est secretis.'

*Clem. *Const. lib. 8.* Cf. the Clementine *Constitutiones Apostolicae*, in Binius, I. 94. Chap. 33 to which Cosin apparently refers is called 'Quibus diebus feriandum sit famulis'.

*S. Aug. *ep.* 86. *ad Cas.* Cf. the letter to Casulanus, 'de jejunio sabbati . . .': 'Cur autem quarta & sexta maxime jejunet ecclesia, illa ratio reddi videtur, quod considerato Evangelio, ipsa quarta sabbati quam vulgo quartam feriam vocant, consilium reperiuntur ad occidendum Dominum fecisse Judaei. Intermisso autem uno die cuius vespera Dominus pascha cum discipulis manducavit, qui finis fuit ejus diei quem vocamus quintam sabbati, deinde traditus est ea nocte quae iam ad sextam sabbati, qui dies passionis ejus manifestus est, pertinebat. Hic dies primus azymorum fuit a vespera incipiens. . . . Prima autem azymorum accesserunt discipuli ad Jesum dicentes: Ubi vis paremus tibi comedere pascha? Hoc ergo die intermisso passus est Dominus, quod nullus ambigit, sexta sabbati, quapropter & ipsa sexta recte jejunio deputatur. Jejunia quippe humilitatem significant. Unde dictum est: Et humiliabam in jejunio animam meam' (II. 391D–2C).

EPIPHANIUS, HAERES. 75. Cf. *Epiphanii . . . Opera . . . Coloniae Agrippinae* . . . Anno M.DC.XVII, 'Contra Aerium, haeresim LXXV', (in *Contra Haereses* III. i), pp. 215–17. Cosin quotes from a passage on

p. 216A: 'In diebus autem paschatis quando apud nos fiunt humi dormitiones, castitates, afflictiones, siccorum esus, preces, vigiliae, ac jejunia, & omnes animarum salutes per sanctas afflictiones: ipsi a summo mane obsonantur, carneque ac vino venas suas explentes cachinnantur, ridentes, ac subsannantes eos qui sanctum hunc cultum hebdomadis paschatis perficiunt.' Hooker had given a translation of this (v. 72, p. 211), and Cosin follows his version almost word for word.

**Ep. 119.* Cf. the epistle to Januarius, noted before on p. 350, with the authorities for Lent. Cosin probably is referring here to § xiii: 'Dies tamen Dominicus non Judaeis, sed Christianis resurrectione Domini declaratus est, & ex illo habere coepit festivitatem suam.'

*Nazianz. *Orat.* I. *in Pasch.* The reference is actually to 'Oratio Secunda in Pascha'. Cf. Gregory Nazianzen, I. 676: 'Pascha Domini, Pascha, iterumque Pascha dicam, in honorem Trinitatis Haec nobis festivitatum festivitas, & celebritatum celebritas, tanto caeteris omnibus, non solum humanis & humi defixis, sed iis etiam, quae ipsius Christi sunt, ac propter ipsum celebrantur, superior, quanto sol stellas antecellit.'

*S. Aug. *Epist* 118. Addressed to Januarius. Cosin refers to this epistle also in listing 'The Sacraments of the Church', p. 54. Having commended the sacraments, Augustine further notes certain observances to be kept, too: 'Illa autem quae non scripta sed tradita custodimus, quae quidem toto terrarum orbe observantur . . . sicuti quod Domini passio & resurrectio & ascensio in coelum, & adventus de coelo Spiritus sancti, anniversaria solemnitate celebrantur. . . .' (II. 556C).

*Const. *in ep. ad om. Eccl.* Cf. Constantine's letters to all churches in Eusebius's *Life.* The reference is to chap. xvii of Book III: 'Unum enim libertatis nostrae diem festum, hoc est, sanctissimae passionis, Servator noster nobis tradidit, unamque Ecclesiam catholicam esse voluit' (cf. Eusebius, p. 147).

MUNDAY AND TUESDAY IN EASTER WEEKE. The following discussion is, to some extent, based upon Hooker's 'The manner of celebrating Festival daies' (v. 70, p. 195). Hooker has reviewed all the principal feasts: 'Over and besides which number not great, the rest bee but foure other daies heretofore annexed to the feast of Easter and Pentecost by reason of generall Baptisme usuall at those two feastes, which also is the cause why they had not as other dayes any proper name given them. Their first institution was therefore through necessitie, and their present continuance is now for the greater honour of the principals whereupon they still attend.'

S. Aug. *de civit. Dei. l. 22. c. 8.* Cosin seems to be referring to a passage in the story of Paulus and Palladia, with which Augustine concludes this chapter: 'Sequenti itaque die post sermonem redditum, narrationis ejus libellum in crastinum populo recitandum promisi. Quod cum ex Dominico paschae die tertio fieret in gradibus exedrae, in qua de superiore loquebar loco, feci stare ambos fratres, cum eorum legeretur libellus' (cf. v. 1350c). There is nothing so precise here as Cosin's 'In tertium Diem festi', but the reference to the preaching of a sermon on the Tuesday in Easter Week makes the liturgical observance of that day a reasonable inference.

Hom. 1 *in Pasch.* Cf. the full title of St. Gregory Nyssen's Homily: '. . . in Sanctum Pascha, et de Triduano festo Resurrectionis Christi' (II. 814–31).

**Ep. 118. ad* Januar. Cf. above, and also p. 328.

*Cyril. *in Catech.* In exhorting the Catechumens to make themselves ready for baptism, St. Cyril reminds them of the greatness of the new life that awaits them: 'captivitatis liberatio, peccatorum remissio, mors peccati, animae regeneratio, vestimentum candidum, signaculum sanctum, indelebile. . . .' Cf. *Catecheses*, p. 16. The quotation is from the Procatechesis. Cf. the passage from Hooker quoted above on MUNDAY AND TUESDAY IN EASTER WEEKE.

DEVOUT PRAYERS. Many of the Primers had included Eucharistic devotions, but few of them are as full as these.

At the Consecration. In editions of the Prayer Book prior to the *Devotions*, the title 'The Prayer of Consecration' was not used. It is first found in the Scottish Liturgy of 1637 (and subsequently in the 1662 Prayer Book). Cosin's phrase, 'At the Consecration', could conceivably be the origin of this.

THE HYMNE. This is a translation and adaptation of the second, fifth, and sixth verses of the Corpus Christi Hymn, 'Lauda Sion Salvatorem' by St. Thomas Aquinas, written about 1260, at the same time as the first prayer which follows, for the Mass of the Festival of

Corpus Christi. They were included in the new office for the Festival which he prepared in 1263, at the request of Urban IV, for the *Breviarium Romanum*. Both hymn and prayer probably found their way into the Missale at the same time, and the hymn appears in a Sarum Missal of 1370.

The verses Cosin uses proceed thus:

(2) Laudis thema specialis,
  panis vivus et vitalis
  hodie proponitur;
Quem in sacrae mensa coenae
  turbae fratrum duodenae
  datum non ambigitur.

(5) Quod in coena Christus gessit,
  faciendum hoc expressit
  in sui memoriam.
Docti sacris institutis,
  panem, vinum, in salutis
  consecramus hostiam.

(6) Dogma datur Christianis,
  quod in carnem transit panis,
  et vinum in sanguinem.
Quod non capis, quod non vides,
  animosa firmat fides,
  praeter rerum ordinem.

Cosin has avoided the word 'hostiam' (although he contributes 'our Altars' at this point), and has modified the lines 'quod in carnem transit panis, / et vinum in sanguinem' to 'Christians are by Faith assured / That by Faith Christ is received' in keeping with the doctrine expressed in the 28th and 29th Articles of the Church of England.

THE PRAYER. I. This is a paraphrase of the Corpus Christi prayer by St. Thomas Aquinas, with phrases from the Eucharistic canon in the 1549 Prayer Book, and the Prayer for the Church in the 1552 edition: 'Deus, qui nobis sub sacramento mirabili passionis tuae memoriam reliquisti; tribue, quaesumus, ita nos corporis et sanguinis tui sacra mysteria venerari, ut redemptionis tuae fructum in nobis jugiter sentiamus' (cf. *Missale ad Usum . . . Sarum*, ed. F. H. Dickinson [the Burntisland edition, Oxford: J. Parker, 1861–83], p. 455). The Hymn, quoted above, appears on p. 457.

II. III. Many phrases are from the Prayer of Oblation in the 1549 Prayer Book. Cosin's notes on the Book of Common Prayer show that he wished to see the Prayer of Oblation restored to its 1549 position before the Communion. Cf. *Works*, v. 114, 347. He also wished to see the Agnus Dei (see below) restored, cf. *Correspondence*, II. 60, and the Prayer of Humble Access (see below) immediately before the Communion: cf. *Works*, v. 105, 470, *Correspondence*, II. 59.

And answere. Amen. Cf. Cosin's First Series of Notes on the Book of Common Prayer, *Works*, v. 112: 'Here are the people to answer Amen, according to all ancient and modern liturgies. From whence we gather, that the priest did not deliver the Sacrament to any, or say, 'Take and eat', before the communicants had professed their faith of Christ's Body to be exhibited unto them. *Dicit tibi sacerdos, Corpus Christi, et tu dicis Amen, hoc est, Verum; non otiose dicis Amen, sed jam confitens, quod accipias Corpus Christi.* Ambr. *de Sacr*. lib. iv. cap. 5.', etc.

THANKSGIVING AFTER WE HAVE RECEIVED.... I. 'OH my God ...'. Cf. Hooker, v. 67 (p. 181): '... why should any cogitation possesse the minde of a faithful communicant but this, *O my God thou art true, O my soule thou art happie*'.

IV. Glory be to God on high ... *Amen.* A conflation, with phrases from the Gloria in Excelsis, the Te Deum, the Prayer of Thanksgiving after the Communion, and the Collect for the second Communion on Easter Day.

MEDITATIONS. ... These sentences were included at a similar the Prayer Book of 1549, although the fifth is an adaptation.

DIVERS FORMES .... A frequent feature of the Primer.

1. JOHN 1. 9. The verse used here as a penitential sentence before confession was added to the verse 1 John 1. 8 among the penitential sentences at Morning Prayer in the 1662 Prayer Book, by way of *The Durham Book.*

THE CONFESSION. *Marginal note.* Cf. the second Exhortation in the 1552 Prayer Book: 'First to examine your lives and conversacion by the rules of goddes commaundements'.

OTHER FORMES OF GENERAL CONFESSIONS. III. Cf. John Donne's sermon 'Preached to the King, at White-Hall, the first Sunday in Lent' [probably 11 February 1626/7], in *The Sermons of John Donne*, ed. E. M.

Simpson and G. R. Potter (Berkeley, 1954), VII. 361: 'Forgive me *O Lord, O Lord* forgive me my sinnes, the sinnes of my youth, and my present sinnes, the sinne that my Parents cast upon me, Originall sinne, and the sinnes that I cast upon my children, in an ill example; Actuall sinnes, sinnes which are manifest to all the world, and sinnes which I have so laboured to hide from the world, as that now they are hid from mine own conscience, and mine own memory; Forgive me my crying sins, and my whispering sins, sins of uncharitable hate, and sinnes of unchaste love. . . .'

Since Donne's sermon and Cosin's *Devotions* are almost exactly contemporary, one can only speculate about who influenced whom. Cosin might have heard Donne give the sermon (it was not printed until long afterwards), but Donne could have seen the *Devotions* in manuscript or proof-sheets (it appeared about three weeks after the sermon). Or Donne and Cosin might have been working from a common source, an idea which E. Milner-White would support. He includes Donne's version (in modified form) as a prayer of confession in his *My God, my glory* (London, ed. 1961), p. 25, and he says in a note (p. 166) that 'Donne himself was quoting it from a 16th century source which I once stumbled across and since have been unable to trace.' Milner-White, however, makes no reference to the *Devotions*, and it is possible that by the '16th century source' he may have been recalling, inaccurately, Cosin's book.

THE PRAYER. A conflation, with phrases from a prayer included after the Litany, and the first and second prayers at the end of the Commination Service, in the Book of Common Prayer.

PRAYERS FOR THE KING AND QUEENE. Several earlier Primers contained prayers for the sovereign, including Primers of 1494, no title-page, Wynkyn de Worde, Westminster (Hoskins, no. 7, esp. p. 108); 1536, *This prymer of Salisbury use both in english and in latin* . . . London (Hoskins, no. 122, esp. p. 218); 1550, no title-page, London (Hoskins, no. 194, esp. p. 248); 1553, *A Primmer or book of private prayer* . . . William Seres, London (Hoskins, no. 200, esp. p. 296); 1599, *The Primer or Office of the blessed Virgin Mary* . . . Antwerp (Hoskins, no. 267, esp. p. 362); 1564, *Preces privatae* . . .' (Hoskins, no. 247, esp. p. 260). This last is interesting in having the prayers set, as here, in the form of a votive office. Of some interest also are the various versions of the special service on the anniversary of the sovereign's accession. One of these was issued in 1626 for the accession of Charles I, and included Psalms 20, 21, 85, and 98, and as a lesson 1 Tim. 2. 1.

THE PRAYERS. I. II. III. IV. These are from the earlier editions of the Book of Common Prayer.

V. VI. VII. VIII. These prayers are from the Coronation Service, and are based on the *Liber Regalis*. The English version, which apparently formed Cosin's model, occurs in *The Manner of the Coronation of King Charles the First . . .*, ed. Christopher Wordsworth (London: Henry Bradshaw Society, 1892). Thus V. (pp. 27–28): 'O Almighty and everlasting God Creatour of all things King of Kings and Lord of Lords, who didst cause thy faithfull servant Abraham to triumph over his enemies[,] didst give many victories to Moses and Josuah the governours of thy people; didst exalt thy lowly servant David unto ye height of a kingdome, didst enrich Solomon wth the unspeakable gift of wisdom and peace. Give eare, we beseech thee unto our humble praiers, and multiply thy blessings upon this thy servant Charles, whome in lowly devotion we consecrate our King, that he being strengthned wth the faith of Abraham endued with the mildnesse of Moses, armed with ye fortitude of Joshua, exalted wth the humility of David, beautified with the wisdom of Solomon, may please thee in all things, may alwaies walk uprightly in ye way of righteousnesse, may nourish and teach, defend and instruct thy Church and people. . . .'

VI. (p. 29, n. 6): 'God the unspeakeable Author of the world the Creator of mankind the governor of Empyres the establisher of Kingdomes whoe out of the Loynes of thie faithfull freind our Father Abraham, didst chuse a King that should saue all Nations, blesse we beseech thee this our King and his Armye with a rich blessing at the Interrogacōn of all thie Saints[.] Establish him in the Throne of his Kingdome, visit him as thou dydst visit Moyses in the Bush, Josuah in the Battayle, Gedeon in the Feyld, and Samuell in the Temple: besprinkle him with the dew of thie wisedome and giue unto him the blessings of Dauid and Solamon. be thou unto him a Coate Armor against his Enimyes, and an helmet in Aduersitye and protect him allwayes with thie sheyld. . . .'

VII. (pp. 32–33): 'Looke down Almighty God wth thy favourable countenance upon this glorious King, and as thou didst bless Abraham, Isaac, and Jaacob, so vouchafe, we beseech thee by thy power to water him plentifully with ye blessings of thy grace. Give to him of the dew of heaven and of ye fatnesse of ye earth, abundance of corne and wine and oile, and plenty of all fruits, of thy goodnesse long to continue; y^{t} in his time there may be health in our countrey, and peace in our Kingdome, and y^{t} ye glorious dignity of his Royall Court may brightly shine as a most cleare lightning farre and neere in ye eyes of all men. . . .'

VIII. (This follows immediately after the preceding as part of the same prayer): 'Grant Almighty [God] that he may be a most mighty Protectour of his Countrey, a bountifull comforter of ye Churches and holy Societies, ye most valiant of Kings; y^{t} he may triumph over his enemies, and subdue Rebells and Infidels; y^{t} he may be loving and amiable to ye Lords and Nobles, and to all ye faithfull subjects of his Kingdom, y^{t} he may be feared and loved of all men, y^{t} his children may be Kings to rule this Kingdom by succession of all ages. . . .'

The Latin version of these prayers appears in the *Liber Regalis* (printed for the Roxburghe Club, London, 1870): V. 'Omnipotens sempiterne deus' (p. 8); VI. 'Deus ineffabilis auctor mundi . . .' (p. 10); VII. 'Prospice omnipotens deus' (p. 12); VIII. 'Tribue ei omnipotens deus' (p. 12).

PRAYERS FOR THE QUEENE. I. Cf. *The Manner of the Coronation* . . ., p. 58: 'O Alm. & Everlasting G. ye Fountain and Wellspring of all Goodness; who dost not reject ye Frailty of ye Woman, but rather vouchsafest *to* (&) allow, and choose it; and by choosing ye weak things of ye world do'st confound those, y^{t} are strong; who didst somt. cause thy people to triumph over a most cruel Enemy by ye Hand of Judith a Woman: Give Ear, we beseech thee, to our humble praiers, and multiply thy Blessings upon this thy servant M. whom in all humble Devotion we do consecrate our Queen. Defend her *by* (allwaies with) thy mighty right Hand, and wth (ye Buckler of) thy Favour protect her on every side; y^{t} she may be able to overcome and triumph over all her Enemies, both bodily, and ghostly; and y^{t} wth Sarah and Rebecca, Leah, and Rachel, and other blessed and ho^{ble} women she may multiply, and rejoice in ye Fruit of her Womb, to ye Honour of *this* (ye whole) Kingdom, and ye good Government of God's Holy Church, thro X. our Lord; who vouchsafed to be born of a most pure Virgin, that he might visit, and redeem ye World; Who liveth, and reigneth wth thee, O Father in ye Unity of the Holy Spirit throughout all Ages world wth out End. Amen.'

Cf. the Latin version of this prayer in the *Liber Regalis*, 'Omnipotens sempiterne deus' (p. 33).

II. A conflation, with phrases from the second prayer for the sovereign at the Holy Communion, and from Psalms 113, 127, and 128.

III. Cf. the Prayer of Invocation in the Order of Confirmation.

A PRAYER FOR THE PR. PALAT. WITH THE LADY ELIZAB. &c. Cosin has altered or taken account of an earlier alteration to the existing prayer for the Royal family which began with the words, 'Almighty God, which hast promised to be a Father of Thine Elect and of their seed', because at this time the King had no issue. The alteration was carried over into the Scottish Prayer Book of 1637, and into the revision of 1662, by way of *The Durham Book.*

PRAYERS FOR THE FOURE EMBER WEEKES. There appears to be no precedent for an embertide office although the Elizabethan Primer of 1564 has the prayers for the four seasons from the *Precationes Aliquot Novae* of Erasmus.

These two sets of prayers, those common to all the Ember Days and those proper to the seasons, appear to be largely of Cosin's own composition. (This was the unpublished opinion of the late E. Milner-White.) They all follow the same pattern, highly scriptural, ample in expression, and with comparable rhythms; in these respects, and with their occasional echoes of the Prayer Book (e.g. in the prayers 'For consecrating the beginning of every Season unto God' and 'For the ordination of Priests and Deacons'), they are reminiscent of other prayers in the *Devotions* which may be assumed to be Cosin's own. Where he uses models, his typical practice is to enlarge and elaborate them to such an extent that his version is virtually a new prayer.

AMong all the Set-Fasts . . . *Fasting* before hand. Cf. *A Manual of Prayers* (ed. Calice, 1599), following the Calendar: 'Of the Ember dayes [.] / Foure times in the yeare have been also from ancient ages chosen, wherein wee are bound to fast. Upon the wensday, friday, and saturday, perfectly for to obtaine the fruites of the earth, and to give thankes for the same, whereas at those times they are sowed, or begin their growth, or ripen, or are gathered in: partlye to obtaine the grace of the holy Ghost, at such times as holy orders are given: For on the sonday of Ember, the church useth to give them. And it was the custome of the Apostles to fast when they gave holy orders. . . .'

**Leo* de jejun. decimi mensis, Serm. 4. Cf. St. Leo the Great, in J.-P. Migne, ed., *Patrologiae Cursus Completus*, 54 (the first of three volumes of Leo's works), p. 175, § ii: 'De quorum numero est etiam decimi hujus mensis solemne jejunium, quod non ideo negligendum est, quia de observantia veteris legis assumptum est, tamquam hoc de illis sit quae inter discretiones ciborum, inter baptismatum differentias et avium pecudumque hostias esse destiterunt. . . .' The second reference to Leo is to the same series of sermons. Cf. for example, p. 190, § ii: '. . .

quoniam plenum pietatis plenumque justitiae est ut terrenorum fructuum perceptione conclusa agantur Deo gratiae, et sacrificium ei misericordiae cum jejunii immolatione solvatur.'

S. *Hieron.* in *Zach 8.* These references are closely related, for Gratian quotes Jerome in his Distinctio LXXVI, 'Quare in suprascriptis temporibus jejunia lex imperavit' (cf. *Decretum Divi Gratiani . . . Juris Canonici Compendium* . . . [London, 1560], p. 366), and both Gratian and Jerome make reference to Leo. Cf. Jerome's Commentary on the eighth chapter of Zechariah (VI. 252): 'Jejunium quarti, & jejunium quinti, & jejunium septimi, & jejunium decimi . . . domui Juda & Hierusalem in dies festos vertetur & gaudium: . . . In hoc loco nostrorum multi multa dixerunt, & inter se dissonantia. . . . Cogimur igitur ad Hebraeos recurrere, & scientiae veritatem de fonte magis quam de rivulis quaerere. . . .'

*Const. & Canons, *cap.* 31. Cf. *Constitutiones sive Canones Ecclesiastici* (1604). Chapter 31 is titled: 'Jejunia Quatuor Temporum Ministrorum ordinationi decreta.'

THE PRAYERS COMMON TO ALL THE EMBER DAYES.

I. For Gods acceptance of our humiliation. Allusions to Lev. 16. 29–31, and Matt. 5. 16.

II. For consecrating the beginning of every Season unto God. This prayer echoes part of the Collect for Easter Day.

III. For Grace to spend the whole Season aright. Allusions to Heb. 11. 13, 16.

IV. For the fruits of the Earth. This beautiful collect has allusions to Acts 17. 28 and Matt. 5. 45. It is included twice in the Prayer Book of the Church of Ireland (1926), as a prayer 'On the Rogation Days' and in a 'thanksgiving for the Blessings of Harvest', and also in the Scottish Prayer Book of 1929, for use 'On Rogation days'.

VI. For the health of our Bodies. Cf. James 1. 17 for the address of the prayer, and cf. also the third prayer of the Lenten litanies in the Sarum Breviary: 'Deus qui charitatis dona per gratiam Sancti Spiritus tuorum cordibus fidelium infundis: da famulis et famulabus tuis: fratribus et sororibus nostris pro quibus tuam deprecamur clementiam salutem mentis et corporis: ut te tota virtute diligant: et quae tibi placita sunt tota dilectione perficiant' (in F. Procter and C. Wordsworth, eds., *Breviarium ad Usum . . . Sarum* [Cambridge, 1879], II. 254).

VII. For the ordination of Priests and Deacons. This prayer is very typical of Cosin's work, with its Biblical allusions (Acts 20. 28; 1 Tim. 5. 22; 1 Pet. 2. 25) and phrases from the Prayer Book (the Prayer of Oblation and the Prayer for the Church in the Order of Holy Communion). The phrase 'Bishops and Pastors' is intended to denote merely bishops, Cosin maintaining that in antiquity the term 'pastors' was applied only to bishops (cf. Cosin, *Works*, V. 509). This prayer became the first of the two prayers 'In the Ember Weeks' in the 1662 Prayer Book, by way of *The Durham Book*, at which stage and afterwards it underwent slight alteration.

THE PRAYERS PROPER TO THE FOURE SEVERALL EMBER WEEKES. Although the Fasts of the Four Seasons were originally related to the natural seasons, Cosin associates all but the September prayer with the ecclesiastical calendar.

I. In the time of Advent. Cf. the collect in the Sarum Missal for Wednesday in the Advent Ember Week: 'Festina, quaesumus, Domine, ne tardaveris: et auxilium nobis supernae virtutis impende: ut adventus tui consolationibus subleventur, qui in tua pietate confidunt . . .' (*Missale ad Usum . . . Sarum* [Burntisland ed.], p. 30).

II. For the Ember weeke in Lent. This collect, based on John 16. 20 and 22, and with the ending incorporating Rom. 4. 25, may have been suggested to Cosin by a much shorter prayer in the Sarum Breviary, also based on John 16. 20, for the second week in Lent: 'Adesto supplicationibus nostris, omnipotens Deus: et quibus fiduciam sperandae pietatis indulges, consuetae misericordiae tribue benignus effectum' (Proctor and Wordsworth, *op cit.*, I. dcxxxvii).

The conclusion of the Collect for Easter Even in the 1662 Prayer Book, by way of *The Durham Book*, would seem to owe almost as much to this prayer of Cosin's as to the Scottish Liturgy collect of which it is an adaptation: '. . . we may pass to our joyfull resurrection, for his merits, who died, and rose again for us, thy son . . .' (cf. the Scottish Liturgy: '. . . our sins may never bee able to rise in judgement against us, and that for the merit of Iesus Christ that died, was buried and rose again for us').

III. For the Ember weeke after Pentecost. Allusions to Luke 24. 49, Acts 1. 14 and 2. 1–4, Gal. 4. 26.

IV. For the Ember Weeke in September. Like the other prayers for the Ember weeks, this one is filled with scriptural allusions. Here there are phrases from Acts 17. 25, Psalms 65. 4, 11 and 104. 14, 15, 1 Cor. 7. 31, Phil. 3. 20, and Rev. 7. 16.

PRAYERS FOR THE SICKE. Most of the Primers had prayers for the sick and the dying, but not many have them arranged as Cosin does, in the form of offices.

The seven Penitentiall Psalmes. As prescribed in the Sarum Manual, in the 'Ordo ad Visitandum Infirmum'. Cf. *Manuale ad Usum Percelebris Ecclesie Sarisburiensis*, ed. A. Jefferies Collins for the Henry Bradshaw Society, XCI (1960), 97–98.

An humble Protestation of free forgivenesse to others. Cf. *A Manual of Prayers*, p. 132^{v}, where a similar 'protestation' occurs: '. . . desiring moste humblye all and everye one that I have offended, injuried, grieved, or any way angred . . . that they would vouchsafe also to forgyve me'.

After the Creed. Cf. *A Manual of Prayers*, p. 133: the Creed is followed by 'A prayer for the sicke person to saye after his beleefe'.

THE PRAYERS. I. A conflation of the collects for Trinity XI and Septuagesima.

V. Cf. *A Manual of Prayers*, p. 134, the first of several 'Prayers in sicknesse', this one ascribed to Dionysius the Carthusian (1402–71), his 'Dialogion'. Cosin bases his prayer upon the one in *A Manual*, but, as commonly with him, he improves and clarifies the language: 'O Sweet Jesu, I desire nether lyfe, nor deathe, but thy most holy will. Thee O lorde I loke for, be it unto mee according to thy pleasure. Yf thou wilt sweete Jesu, that I dye, receyve my soule. And albeit I come to thee even at the verye eveninge, as one of the laste, yet graunte that with thee, and in thee, I may receyve everlasting rest. Yf thou wilt sweete Jesu that I lyve longer on earthe, I purpose to amende the rest of my lyfe, and offer all into a burnt sacrifice unto thee, for thy honour and glorie, accordinge to thy blessed will: and for the perfoorminge of this I desire the assistance of thy holy grace.'

THE LETANIE. See the litany in the 'Commendatio Anime in Articulo Mortis', and the prayers which follow in the 'Commendatio Animarum', in the Sarum Manual (in the edition noted above, especially pp. 116–18), whence Cosin derives a number of phrases.

God the Father . . . life. *Amen.* Cf. the Sarum Manual: 'Proficiscere anima christiana de hoc mundo: in nomine dei patris omnipotentis qui te creavit. Amen. In nomine iesu christi filii eius qui pro te passus est. Amen. In nomine spiritus sancti qui in te effusus est. Amen. . . . In nomine virginum et fidelium viduarum hodie in pace locus tuus fiat: et habitatio tua in celesti hierusalem. Amen' (pp. 117–18).

PRAYERS AND THANKSGIVINGS FOR SUNDRY PURPOSES. A selection of miscellaneous prayers of this sort was a common feature of the Primer.

A PRAYER . . . CHURCH. The basis of this prayer is the Prayer for the Church in the form which it took in the 1549 Order of Holy Communion. Cosin has reduced the intercessory element and expanded the commemoration of the saints. Several phrases are like some in the Bidding Prayer which Cosin used in his own sermons: '. . . His servants our fathers and brethren . . . humbly beseeching Him that we may continue in their holy communion and religion here . . . and the shining lights of the world, in their several generations before us' (cf. Cosin, *Works*, I. 194, 278).

One phrase from this prayer, 'the holy Catholik Church, the Mother of us all that beare the Name of Christ', has found its way into 'A Prayer and Thanksgiving for the whole Estate of Christ's Catholic Church' in the South African Prayer Book of 1954, in the form, 'Accept, we humbly beseech Thee, our thanksgivings for the Holy Catholic Church, the Mother of us all who bear the name of Christ'.

*Injunct. cap. ult. & Can. 55. Cf. *Injunctions* [of] *Edward VI* (1547), 'The Form of bidding the Common Prayers': '. . . ye shall pray for all them that be departed out of this world in the faith of Christ, that they with us, and we with them at the day of Judgment, may rest both body and soul, with Abraham, Isaac, and Jacob in the Kingdom of Heaven.' And cf. *Constitutiones sive Canones Ecclesiastici* (1604): 'Precationis formula, a Concionatoribus in concionum suarum ingressu imitanda. . . . gratias & laudes Deo reddamus pro illis omnibus, qui in fide Christi ex hac vita excesserunt, humiliter Deo supplicantes, ut per illius gratiam vitam nostram ad pium eorum exemplar dirigamus, ut ita tandem hac mortali vita defuncti, resurgamus cum illis in die Jesu Christi ad coelestem gloriam, & vitam aeternam. . . .'

For our Parents. Cf. *A Manual of Prayers*, p. 113, 'A prayer for our parentes', ascribed to J. Ferus: 'O Almightye and omnipotente God, which haste strictly commaunded us, next unto thee to honour our father and mother, and to pray for their happy and good successe: graunt unto my parentes, and the whole familye, health, & peace: keepe them in the piety and trueth of thy fayth: defend them from all daungers bodily and ghostly: gyve them grace (I humblye beseeche thee) that they offende not thee in any thinge, but that they may alwaye find thee, a loving, gentle, and mercyfull father and God. Amen.' Cf. also the prayer by Erasmus in *Precationes Aliquot Novae*, 'Pro Parentibus', v. 1006, included in the Primer of 1564.

Another for our Parents. A conflation of the opening of the prayer in *A Manual of Prayers* with the prayer 'Of Children' in Thomas Becon's *The Pomaunder of Prayer* (1558) (reprinted by The Parker Society in the Works of Becon and included in the volume called *Prayers and other Pieces*, ed. John Ayre [Cambridge 1844], p. 77): 'Thou hast given a commandment in thy law, O heavenly Father, that children should honour their fathers and mothers: I most humbly beseech thee therefore to breathe thy Holy Spirit into my breast, that I may reverence and honour my father and mother, not only with outward gestures of my body, but also with the unfeigned affection of the heart; love them, obey them, pray for them, help them, and do for them, both in word and deed, whatsoever lieth in my power; that thou, seeing mine unfeigned hearty good-will toward my parents, mayest become my loving heavenly Father, and number me among those thy children whom thou hast appointed from everlasting heirs of thy glorious kingdom, through thy well-beloved Son Jesus Christ our Lord. Amen.' This prayer, and the next, had occurred slightly earlier, in a Primer of 1553 (Hoskins, no. 200).

For our children. Cf. the prayer 'Of Fathers and Mothers' in Becon, op. cit., p. 77: 'The fruit of the womb and the multitude of children is thy gift and blessing, O Lord, given to this end, that they may live to thy glory and the commodity of their neighbour. Forasmuch therefore as thou of thy goodness hast given me children, I beseech thee, give me also grace to train them up even from their cradles in thy nurture and doctrine, in thy holy laws and blessed ordinances, that from their very young age they may know thee, believe in thee, fear and love thee, and diligently walk in thy commandments, unto the praise of thy glorious name. Amen.'

A Prayer ... with Child. This and the next two prayers are based upon a similar set of three prayers in a Primer of 1560, *A Primer or Book of private prayer, needful to be used of all faithful christians* (Hoskins, no. 243, p. 300). Thus: [1] 'Prayer for a woman to say travailing of child. O almighty and merciful father, which of thy bountiful goodness hast fructified my womb . . .'; [2] 'A woman with child's prayer. Father of mercy, and God of comfort and all consolation . . .'; [3] 'Prayer for a woman to say when she is delivered. O my Lord God, I thank thee with all my heart. . . .'

A Prayer ... Birth. Besides the many scriptural allusions, 1 Chron. 29. 13, Pss. 20. 9–10, 90. 12, and 139. 13, Jn. 18. 37 and Heb. 9. 14, there are phrases from the Sanctus, and the General Confession in Morning and Evening Prayer.

A Prayer ... Baptisme. This prayer, too, has many scriptural allusions, Jn. 3. 3 and 5, Rom. 6. 3 and Jas. 1. 27, and phrases from the Order of Holy Baptism, the Holy Communion, and the Catechism.

A PRAYER WHEREWITH S. AUGUSTINE BEGAN HIS DEVOTIONS. This is based closely on the translation of St. Augustine's *Confessions* by Sir Tobie Matthew, published in 1620.

INDEX

AN INDEX TO COSIN'S SOURCES AND THE COMMENTARY

(The Bible and the Book of Common Prayer as sources are not included in the Index. Page references to the Commentary are in italics.)

INDEX TO SOURCES AND COMMENTARY

INDEX TO SOURCES AND COMMENTARY

PRINTED IN GREAT BRITAIN
AT THE UNIVERSITY PRESS, OXFORD
BY VIVIAN RIDLER
PRINTER TO THE UNIVERSITY